TOWARD A FEMINIST ETHICS OF NONVIOLENCE

# Toward a Feminist Ethics of Nonviolence

Adriana Cavarero, with Judith Butler, Bonnie Honig, and Other Voices

TIMOTHY J. HUZAR AND
CLARE WOODFORD, EDITORS

Fordham University Press
NEW YORK    2021

Copyright © 2021 Fordham University Press

All rights reserved. No part of this publication may be reproduced, stored in a retrieval system, or transmitted in any form or by any means—electronic, mechanical, photocopy, recording, or any other—except for brief quotations in printed reviews, without the prior permission of the publisher.

Fordham University Press has no responsibility for the persistence or accuracy of URLs for external or third-party Internet websites referred to in this publication and does not guarantee that any content on such websites is, or will remain, accurate or appropriate.

Fordham University Press also publishes its books in a variety of electronic formats. Some content that appears in print may not be available in electronic books.

Visit us online at www.fordhampress.com.

Library of Congress Cataloging-in-Publication Data available online at https://catalog.loc.gov.

Printed in the United States of America

23 22 21    5 4 3 2 1

First edition

Contents

Prelude      1
    *Timothy J. Huzar*

Introduction: Adriana Cavarero, Feminisms, and an Ethics
of Nonviolence      7
    *Timothy J. Huzar and Clare Woodford*

Scenes of Inclination      33
    *Adriana Cavarero*

Leaning Out, Caught in the Fall: Interdependency and Ethics
in Cavarero      46
    *Judith Butler*

How to Do Things with Inclination: Antigones, with Cavarero      63
    *Bonnie Honig*

SCHERZO

Thinking Materialistically with Locke, Lonzi, and Cavarero      93
    *Olivia Guaraldo*

ÉTUDES

Cavarero, Kant, and the Arcs of Friendship      109
    *Christine Battersby*

Bad Inclinations: Cavarero, Queer Theories, and the Drive      121
    *Lorenzo Bernini*

| | |
|---|---|
| Querying Cavarero's Rectitude<br>*Mark Devenney* | 131 |
| From Horrorism to the Gray Zone<br>*Simona Forti* | 141 |
| Violence, Vulnerability, Ontology: Insurrectionary Humanism in Cavarero and Butler<br>*Timothy J. Huzar* | 151 |
| Queer Madonnas: In Love and Friendship<br>*Clare Woodford* | 161 |
| Coda<br>*Adriana Cavarero* | 177 |
| Bibliography | 187 |
| List of Contributors | 199 |
| Index | 203 |

Toward a Feminist Ethics of Nonviolence

# Prelude

TIMOTHY J. HUZAR

I met Adriana Cavarero halfway up a mountain in Sicily. People from across Europe had convened to talk about life, politics, and contingency; Cavarero, as a political philosopher and the foremost Italian feminist scholar writing today, was among a number of keynote speakers asked to contribute their thoughts.[1] As a student of the relationship between violence and politics I was aware of Cavarero's *Horrorism: Naming Contemporary Violence*; however, I hadn't encountered the rest of her oeuvre, and the book, in isolation, had been swept up in a large number of texts I was reading in the early stages of my Ph.D.[2] Cavarero's talk was in Italian, and having no Italian, I was left with the sonority of her voice and her embodied communication; Cavarero at times sitting behind her desk, at times standing and leaning in to the audience, her paper discarded as her oration carried her into the room, focusing in on the interventions from those who contributed their thoughts, provocations, and disagreements. In between the talks people would gather in the courtyard to smoke and drink coffee or beer, sheltering under the shade of a grafted citrus tree from the relentless midsummer Sicilian sun. I spoke to Gianmaria Colpani and other students of Cavarero's about my thesis, and they introduced me to some of the key themes that can be found across her work: not only the extrapolation and exploration of horrorist violence, but a prolonged engagement with vocality, feminist materiality, narration, and, above all, Hannah Arendt's category of uniqueness.[3] It became clear that there was a glaring gap in my research, perhaps accounted for by the sway of the biopolitical tradition in Italian political philosophy that Cavarero sits in proximity to, yet apart from. Toward the end of the first evening

Cavarero and I spoke briefly, but it wasn't until the second evening, when enough time had passed for people to get to know one another and to relax some of the unspoken proprieties that lie just below the surface of the social world of academia, that a sense of *who* Adriana Cavarero was became more apparent.

One of the many themes that can be found in Cavarero's work is an insistence on a respect for the palpable truthfulness of the everyday: that in people's everyday experiences something of the world is revealed to them, just as they continuously reveal themselves to the world. This means that despite her classical training and her sophisticated and extensive engagements with some of the major debates in twentieth-century continental philosophy, Cavarero's work insists that meaning is not to be sought in the rarified conceptual worlds of great thinkers, but is present in the ordinary world for anyone to see or hear if they only knew how to see or hear it. Her work gives us the tools to make these sensory adjustments: each of her books functions something like an eyeglass or a hearing aid that we can use to help learn what it is to see meaning in the everyday and unlearn the compulsive turning to those tropes dear to the Western tradition that are now wearing thin.

During the evening of the second day of the summer school, Cavarero demonstrated that her skill at manifesting the meaning present in the everyday was not restricted to her academic work. As the sun set and people drank and smoked, Cavarero suggested that song might be a good tonic for the heady metaphysics that were given form in the reasoned dialogue of that day's talks and discussions.[4] With the help of Adriana's enthusiasm, as well as the limoncello and grappa that began to flow at the bar, people stood or sat in the now star-lit courtyard, voices raised in song reverberating around the centuries-old stone walls. Some of these songs were known by all, and so the soloist quickly became a member of the chorus, while others began as solo and were slowly joined by other people as they either learned the patterns, remembered the words, or clapped to the rhythms. Other songs were known only to the singer and so stayed as a singular voice. Yet even here, this was a singularity destined for the ear of another, or in this case many others; and the sociality that was convoked in this space—or what Cavarero would now call the *pluriphony*—was palpable to all those present.[5] Cavarero, for her part, performed an operatic duet from Mozart's *Don Giovanni*—"Là ci darem la mano"—embodying both masculine and feminine parts and, in the process, providing further evidence for Lorenzo Bernini's intimation in this collection that her reticence regarding Judith Butler's notion of gender performativity is itself something of a performance.[6]

In the months after the conference I read all of Cavarero's work, and her thought profoundly shifted the direction of my thesis. As well as being inspired by her thematic foci, I found validation in her inter- and transdisciplinarity: it was clear that for Cavarero, responding to the major questions of twentieth-century continental philosophy required answers that did not discriminate when it came to the form or content from which they took their resources. As well as some of the major theoretical debates of the twentieth century, Cavarero also engages classical Greek texts, contemporary literature, European visual arts, and contemporary feminist politics. Each of these bodies of thought helps her articulate a philosophy that is anti-metaphysical, mounting a relentless critique of the presumptively masculine subject of the Western tradition; she demonstrates the absurdity of this figure, juxtaposing him to the singular lives of those who live in the plurality of the world. However, Cavarero is not content with critique alone. More important for her is the articulation of other forms of life—other ways of being or modes of existence—that are systematically overlooked by the gaze of the Western philosophical tradition. For Cavarero, while it is necessary to develop a critique of this tradition, including the subject fabricated by this tradition, the politics of this intervention falls short if this subject's deconstruction becomes the telos of this work.[7] For Cavarero, then, it is necessary to name the forms of life that she sees as existing despite this presumptively masculine subject, a naming that derives from the lived experience of those whose existence does not conform to his morphology or onto-epistemology. This means her interventions are necessarily identitarian but are also left productively open, encouraging others to pick up her concepts and make use of them, causing trouble in the archives of the canon of Western thought and articulating a different tradition, hidden in plain sight.

Over the next year I had the opportunity to present work to Cavarero and her colleagues in Verona, and her colleagues and students presented work at Brighton where I was studying. At various conferences I attended, Cavarero's name was frequently mentioned by people presenting work from a variety of disciplines. It seemed strange that, given her extensive and diverse influence, an event dedicated to her thought hadn't happened, at least in the English-speaking world. A group of us, including her colleagues Olivia Guaraldo and Lorenzo Bernini and Mark Devenney and Clare Woodford at Brighton, proposed organizing an international conference on Cavarero's work, to be titled, "Giving Life to Politics." The event would coincide with the English-language publication of Cavarero's *Inclinations: A Critique of Rectitude*, as well as marking Adriana's seventieth birthday.[8] Judith Butler and Bonnie Honig—both long-term interlocutors of Adriana's—were invited as keynotes, and both readily accepted. The event brought together academics from across the world; there were so many compelling responses to the call for papers that the event was extended to three days. Some of those who attended had been reading Adriana since the start of her academic life; others, like me, had only recently discovered her thought. Some were long-term friends with countless stories of their time with Adriana, some not dissimilar to the story of her orchestration of the singing in Sicily where I first met her; other people were meeting Adriana for the first time. Despite a sweltering early-summer heat wave, the event was relaxed and friendly, absent of the jostling of egos that typically mark academic conferences. Like all conferences, people debated the finer points of Cavarero's work, and while these conversations were important, what was also significant was the presence of generative conversations that occurred in between sessions, or just before a session started, or in a pub at the end of the day, or over food during dinner. Here new friendships were formed, inchoate but nonetheless important points could be expressed, support could be offered, and celebration could flourish. These ways of being can be found in any academic conference, but it is no coincidence that a conference on Cavarero's work fostered this furtive, generative, and celebratory "co-appearing," as she might say.[9] Her work authorizes us to build new worlds; to take risks in the hope that a new sense of what it is to be—which has been right under our noses the whole time—might be made apparent. Cavarero gives us a taste of freedom that stems from her work's generosity, free from a proprietorial control over its arguments, playful yet studiously diligent in its engagement with the thought of others. Adriana's work is seemingly effortless in generating something akin to Hannah Arendt's "public happiness," and this quality is carried over into the life she leads, demonstrated by the remarkable community of people who gathered to engage with her work, to renew old friendships, and to forge new ones.[10]

I most recently saw Adriana in Verona, where I presented a paper and spoke to her about how this edited collection was progressing. As ever, she was supportive and encouraging, expressing her happiness and gratefulness at how the project was developing, humbly asking for feedback on her contributions and taking seriously the few substantive comments I had. As we walked back into town from the university, she bought me a gelato, and I asked about her politicization as a young person. Her earliest memories of being politically engaged involved the internal migration of southern Italians to the Northern industrial city of Turin during her teenage years in the 1960s and her activism resisting the racism that confronted them. Since then she has been involved in a number of political projects, most notably in Italian feminist movements and research groups in Padua and Rome and Diotima at the University of Verona; these were a major contributor to the development of Italian sexual difference theory, with its emphasis on an embodied, materialist approach to understanding sex/gender.[11] As Olivia Guaraldo notes in this volume, these political experiences have profoundly influenced Cavarero's work: they contributed to shaping an original combination of materiality and conceptuality; a theoretical concreteness always engaged in naming philosophically embodied singularities and their irrepressible vitality.[12] It is not by chance that Cavarero's current thought brings together two new conceptual devices to intervene in contemporary politics: first, the concept of pluriphony, which is neither the unpleasant noise of cacophony nor the pleasant noise of harmony, and is a way of articulating the vocalic sonority of a plurality of people; and second, the concept of surging democracy, which describes the pluralizing interaction present at the inaugural moments of political movements. In this way, Cavarero continues to furnish an "imaginary of hope," which is a form of care for the world and for the singular, plural lives who both inhabit this world and constitute it, refusing their superfluity and manifesting an alternative in their everyday, spectacular sociality.[13]

Notes

1. Life, Politics, Contingency Summer School, University of Palermo, Erice, Italy, June 8–12, 2015.

2. Adriana Cavarero, *Horrorism: Naming Contemporary Violence*, trans. William McCuaig (New York: Columbia University Press, 2011).

3. Hannah Arendt, *The Human Condition* (Chicago and London: University of Chicago Press, 1998), 176.

4. See Cavarero and Elisabetta Bertolino, "Beyond Ontology and Sexual Difference: An Interview with the Italian Feminist Philosopher Adriana Cavarero," *differences: A Journal of Feminist Cultural Studies* 19, no. 1 (2017): 161, https://doi.org/10.1215/10407391-2007-019; and Ryan Dohoney, "An Antidote to Metaphysics: Adriana Cavarero's Vocal Philosophy," *Women and Music: A Journal of Gender and Culture* 15 (2011): 70–85, https://doi.org/10.1353/wam.2011.0002.

5. See Cavarero, *For More than One Voice: Toward a Philosophy of Vocal Expression*, trans. Paul A. Kottman (Stanford, Calif.: Stanford University Press, 2005), 7; and Cavarero, Konstantinos Thomaidis, and Ilaria Pinna, "Towards a Hopeful Plurality of Democracy: An Interview on Vocal Ontology with Adriana Cavarero," *Journal of Interdisciplinary Voice Studies* 3, no. 1 (2018): 84, https://doi.org/10.1386/jivs.3.1.81_1.

6. Lorenzo Bernini, "Bad Inclinations: Cavarero, Queer Theories and the Drive," in this volume.

7. Cavarero, Thomaidis, and Pinna, "Towards a Hopeful Plurality of Democracy," 88.

8. Cavarero, *Inclinations: A Critique of Rectitude*, trans. Amanda Minervini and Adam Sitze (Stanford, Calif.: Stanford University Press, 2016).

9. Cavarero, *Relating Narratives: Storytelling and Selfhood*, trans. Paul A. Kottman (London and New York: Routledge, 2000), 89–90.

10. On public happiness, see Arendt, *On Revolution* (London: Faber & Faber, 2016), 123–24. See also Olivia Guaraldo, "Public Happiness: Revisiting an Arendtian Hypothesis," *Philosophy Today* 62, no. 2 (Spring 2018): 397–418, https://doi.org/10.5840/philtoday201866218.

11. For more on this history, see Dohoney, "Antidote to Metaphysics," 71.

12. Guaraldo, "Thinking Materialistically with Locke, Lonzi and Cavarero," in this volume.

13. Cavarero, Thomaidis, and Pinna, "Towards a Hopeful Plurality of Democracy," 88. For more on superfluity, see Arendt, *The Origins of Totalitarianism* (London: Penguin, 2017), 599. For more on refusal, see Tina Marie Campt, "Black Visuality and the Practice of Refusal," *Women & Performance: A Journal of Feminist Theory* 29, no. 1 (2019): 79–87, https://doi.org/10.1080/0740770X.2019.1573625; and Bonnie Honig, "How To Do Things with Inclination: Antigones, with Cavarero," in this volume.

# Introduction

*Adriana Cavarero, Feminisms, and an Ethics of Nonviolence*

TIMOTHY J. HUZAR AND CLARE WOODFORD

> The painting of the mother and child is held up as an example to be strategically exploited in order to make inclination a good point of departure, a point from which we might rethink the ontology of the vulnerable and constitutive relationality in the terms of a postural geometry that, far from displacing the human on the straight axis, displaces it according to a multiplicity of contextual, contingent and intermittent, and at times even random, directions. The maternal inclination, in as much as it is a posture linked to the scene of birth, can become the fundamental schematism, the founding gesture of a new postural geometry.
> —ADRIANA CAVARERO, *INCLINATION: A CRITIQUE OF RECTITUDE*

Adriana Cavarero's work is at the center of a feminist rethinking of relationality. It seeks to overcome the traditional blindness of philosophy and political thought to the real conditions of enfleshed bodies that relate to one another in love, in hate, and in the spectrum of relations that lie between. This is not to imply that prior to Cavarero philosophy or politics did not concern the body. Rather, it has typically subordinated the body and, in a particular way, the bodies of women. Although Cavarero's work forms but one part of a much wider feminist endeavor, this volume celebrates in critical spirit her extraordinary contribution to philosophical and political debate over four decades. It demonstrates how her wide-ranging and critical interventions have helped reinvigorate a stagnant political scene, asserting against persistent claims that There Is No Alternative that there are *many* alternatives lived by people across the world in spite of, and even in defiance of, the marginalization and exclusion to which they are subjected.

The exchange that follows stems from a conference in the summer of 2017 at the University of Brighton. Although inspired by Cavarero's recent work on an ethical maternal posture of inclination,[1] the responses by

Judith Butler, Bonnie Honig, and seven other interlocutors situate Cavarero's argument in her more longstanding themes of nonviolence and uniqueness, which not only offer a critique but also an alternative to the masculine symbolic of philosophy. This introduction endeavors to introduce Cavarero's work, as well as to chart the journey of an increasingly productive dialogue between Cavarero and other traditions within feminism, bringing together what were initially perceived to be radically divergent positions. It also seeks to capture the collaborative but provocative spirit of the inspirational scholarly friendship between Butler, Honig, and Cavarero as they contest the boundaries of their common project for a pluralistic, heterogeneous, but urgent feminist ethics of nonviolence.

It is first worth noting two features of this volume, both of which seek to challenge the traditional boundaries of political philosophy. First, some of its interventions, following Cavarero's example, draw on images and objects, beginning and ending with Leonardo Da Vinci's painting of *Madonna and Child with Saint Anne*, but passing through sixth-century icons of the Madonna Theotokos; two further portraits by Leonardo Da Vinci (*St. John the Baptist* and an image of St. John later painted over with an image of Bacchus); two Renaissance Madonnas (Raphael's *Sistine Madonna* and Bellini's *Alzano* Madonna); as well as Caravaggio's *Death of the Virgin*; an inscribed goblet belonging to Immanuel Kant; Marie Stillman's *Antigone Giving Burial Rites to her Brother Polynices*; and Sigmund Freud's image of the vulture in the folds of the women's dresses in Leonardo's Madonna. Each informs discussion of different aspects of human relations, in particular those of motherhood, sorority, friendship, and love. The use of these images emphasizes the aesthetic qualities of our affective relations, overflowing theoretical debates.

Second, in tribute to Cavarero's theorization of pluriphony for philosophy,[2] this collection stages its conversation between critical but friendly voices in the style of a musical arrangement. As Timothy Huzar notes in the preface, Cavarero's pluriphony is neither cacophony nor harmony, but the plurality of singular voices. The interventions are presented as a medley, each of which forms a part of the wider ensemble. The themes laid out by Cavarero in the opening essay are problematized by Butler and Honig, yet defended by Guaraldo's *Scherzo*, emphasizing the novelty of Cavarero's ethics of inclination and the importance of her methodology. This is followed by six short études that reflect on inclination and nonviolence. These respond not only to Cavarero but also to Butler, Honig, and to one another. The interwoven and multilayered argument that emerges seeks to combine—without failing to acknowledge the differences between—

the work of Cavarero, Butler, and Honig; to acknowledge Honig's debts to Cavarero and to acknowledge Cavarero's influence on Butler, which may come as a surprise to Anglo-American audiences; and to posit fruitful directions for future research that brings feminists of different stripes together to think a nonviolent future, in the context of an increasingly belligerent international political scene.

## Inclination in the Work of Adriana Cavarero

We begin our brief introduction to Cavarero's work with the guiding image of Leonardo's Madonna, central to Cavarero's account of a postural ethics of nonviolence. The painting is an unusual portrayal of three figures from the Christian Holy Family. Rather than the child Jesus with his mother, Mary, or also with his father, Joseph, it shows Jesus and Mary with Mary's mother, Anne: two mothers, two children, Anne with her daughter, Mary, sitting on her lap while Mary's child, Jesus, plays alongside. It inspired Cavarero because, in its time, it was a subversive image of motherhood despite its apparent orthodoxy today. What may seem an innocent decision to place Jesus at Mary's side contravened the dominant convention that required the child Jesus to be seated on Mary's lap, held in her arms but with his back to her, facing the viewer. Mother and child were not meant to look at one another. The same convention dictated that all figures should be structured vertically. Instead, Leonardo portrays all three figures inclined and twisted around each other. In Cavarero's words the painting

> breaks with this system of symmetrical verticality, presenting a mother who is face to face with her child; a child whose head is twisted back to face the one who visibly tilts and stretches out to support him; and an Anne who observes them both with a smile. The asymmetry of this portrait, modulated as it is by inclination, translates nicely into the movement of a relationality that reflects the everyday experience of the maternal rather than the monumentality of the sacred.[3]

It subverts the authoritative conventions of its time and in doing so emphasizes maternity and the dependence of the child—here representing for Cavarero the vulnerable more widely—on the care that the mother provides.

It may seem strange to readers from an Anglo-American background that Cavarero chose a religious image at all, for even this once subversive image appears today as orthodox, traditional, and stereotyped. But Cavarero is not using the image in a religious context. Nor does she repeat traditional tropes of motherhood as passive or subordinated. Rather, she seeks to "strategically exploit" the imagery of motherhood to think differently about the everyday postures of our lives. The painting is her "point of departure," an inspirational provocation that upends the everyday privileging of the "upright" and the "straight" in morality and philosophy as unnatural, artificial, and strange. As we read in the beginning epigraph, she is not simply replacing the archetypal straight man of philosophical and moral thought, but instead complicates the archetype, displacing it in "a multiplicity . . . of directions."

Despite distancing herself from the religious significance of this image, Cavarero still mobilizes the religious element of this painting in two ways. First, the love characteristic of an ethic of inclination is the "enigmatic" love of Leonardo's Madonna.[4] The sense of mystery that this evokes is romantic, poetic, but, given its context, can never be totally separated from the spiritual or the religious. It draws on a particular Christian formulation of an ethical relationship of care for the other. Second, the use of this image shows maternity as more human than convention dictated, and yet still sacred. It holds a place in our symbolic imaginary, so much so that Cavarero uses it, as cited in the epigraph, to beget a "fundamental schematism" founding a new order.

A feminist ethics inspired by a religious image representing maternity may seem incongruous today. However, discussion of religious iconography is not irrelevant to the world of the twenty-first century. The appropriation of cultural images and the imaginary of the maternal are a ripe political battleground, given that years of feminist struggle are at risk of being undone by a vicious backlash that blames feminism for many, if not all, of the world's ills.[5] While this battle over the appropriation of religious imagery may resonate in some countries or communities more strongly than in others, the logic it utilizes is that of political contestation. Cavarero recognizes dominant social imaginaries as sites of struggle.

In this light it is helpful to dwell for a moment on the wider context and key debates that shape the terrain on which the dialogue of this book intervenes. Italian feminism has long struggled over the imaginary of motherhood in Italian life. Cavarero strikes at the heart of a certain hypocrisy in Italian politics, but one that is also identifiable beyond Italy's borders, as noted by Janice Richardson in 1998:

> Given the ubiquity of portrayals of the Christian mother and son in Italy [Cavarero] describes Italian feminists' particular desire to resymbolise motherhood and birth. In so doing she theorises a link between the "sickly sweet" sentimentality popularly associated with

portrayals of motherhood and the blindness of metaphysics to the (flesh and blood) mother.[6]

In the face of those who abuse religion and motherhood in the interests of misogyny, patriarchy, and inequality, Cavarero's heterodox reading restores importance to the oft-subordinated role of motherhood. It reinclines the maternal and the religious toward another ethic. It reanimates a tradition that valorizes natality and maternity, from Arendt to Irigaray, as a political resource for thinking relationality, inclination, and vulnerability.

A reader may think the image chosen by Cavarero is still too stereotypical: that it reinforces rather than troubles the sexual stereotype of women as caring and maternal. In response, note that her methodology of stealing from within the very tradition that oppresses developed out of her engagement with Italian feminist movements both within and outside of the academy. In tracing the trajectory of Cavarero's project and placing it in the context of Italian feminism, we may better come to understand the stereotyping at play here.

## Cavarero and Feminism

Known for its strident stance on sexual difference, female separatism, and militancy, Italian feminism can seem confusing and at times even contradictory to an Anglo-American audience. Similarly to the sexual difference theory emerging in Anglo-American feminism in the 1970s and '80s, Italian feminists mobilized sexual difference to intervene in major philosophical debates and sought to use it as a tool to free women from their entrapment within these debates, enabling the construction of an alternative symbolic order apart from phallogocentrism.

References to sexual difference today typically evoke the essentialism/constructivism feminist debates of the '70s and '80s, which emerged from a prior debate between "liberal" and "difference" feminism. In schematic terms, liberal feminists argued that women were formally equal to men and should have the same rights as men. In contrast, difference feminists, including feminist women of color, emphasized that women are different from men and should not have to be the same to warrant equal status. For many feminists, this then triggered discussion regarding the status of this difference—were women different in essence or just through social construction? In contrast, Italian feminism could be understood as sidestepping this debate by instead seeking to develop a position that refused either pole of the essentialist/constructivist binary.[7]

Indeed, *il pensiero della differenza sessuale* (sexual difference theory)[8] was shaped less by the opposition to liberal feminism that influenced the development of feminism in the U.S. and rather more by its response to the traditional split between conservativism and communism in 1970s Italian politics as well as a new post-Marxist leftism still imbued with misogyny. Invitations for women to join with men politically, despite purportedly being on equal terms, ended up dominated by male perspectives.[9] As a result, the target of sexual difference theory was not primarily liberal equality feminism, as was the case for American sexual difference feminism, but *any* notion of politics based on a notion of equality as sameness. This was because equality as sameness reinforced the same old gender hierarchies. As a consequence, Italian feminists were particularly attuned to the problem of male bias presented as a supposed neutrality. To be able to oppose this, and inspired by the work of Luce Irigaray, Italian feminism had to assert that there was something that was not man, that was typically referred to as "woman." This something, inasmuch as it was not man, could be understood, in Gisela Bock and Susan James's words, as "a primary, originary female difference [which] has, in all areas of social life, been homologized or assimilated to a male perspective which hides behind a mask of gender neutrality in order to subordinate women."[10] This was an understanding of sexual difference that was neither based on the claim that there is a female essence that we can know nor simply repeating the sexist and patriarchal imaginary of women as different and lesser. Instead, it provided an assertion of female difference as different in a positive sense, in a way that did not need men to create the conditions for women's existence or self-understanding.

The argument for sexual difference asserted that the sexed female body is not only something that is perceived to operate within and to significantly affect our contemporary world, but is an irremediable aspect of existence. This is why Cavarero stresses that sexual difference is "given." Whether we like it or not, our bodies are sexed: to exist as an embodied being is to exist as a sexed being, even if the meaning and significance of this "sexedness" is affected by normative conceptions of sex/gender. Cavarero expresses this through her primary distinction, borrowed from Hannah Arendt, between *who* we are and *what* we are.[11] Our sexedness is integral to who we are—to our embodied uniqueness—whereas the meaning and significance of this sexedness describes what we are; what we could otherwise call our "identity." But in either case, what is crucial for both Italian sexual difference theory and Cavarero is that our sexedness is a necessary part of our existence. There is no neutral terrain that we can inhabit free of our sexedness, and neither is our sexedness merely a discursive inscription on the otherwise inert matter of our bodies.

Cavarero acknowledges that it may appear as if both sexes find themselves in the same quandary. If we pose sexual difference as secondary and nonessential, then it would seem that women and men alike find themselves already spoken, defined, and controlled in the social sphere. Yet, like many other feminist thinkers, Cavarero emphasizes that any idea of a neutral, non-sexed identity is actually already a space taken by Man. The neutral image of the human is always already male. If women are to appear, they can be neither male nor neutral; women find themselves obscured by a presumed neutrality that also operates at the level of their sexedness. Those designated women are subordinate to either Man or to the so-called neutral being. Consequently, Italian difference feminism asserts that to resist the fact that the space of neutrality is already taken by Man, women have to find a way to appear as women but to refuse to do so in the way that has always been demanded of them—as a subordinate. For sexual difference feminists, it is only by asserting something called sexual difference that, in Cavarero's words, we open up "the possibility of the woman to speak herself, think herself, and represent herself as a subject in the proper sense of the word."[12] Thus because woman as a nonessential being risked overlooking the exploitation of women, sexual difference theorists preferred to risk the essentialism that will always accompany their assertions of difference. However, it is worth acknowledging that sexual difference theory does not need to assert difference as an essence in any ontological sense. It can simply provide a focus on who women are at any point in history,[13] understood predominantly as the experience not of a concrete essence of what it is to be a woman but just what it is to be that which is separate, that which is not man. As Fanny Söderbäck notes, "The crucial point . . . is that all individuals are sexed, not that there are or should be only two sexes."[14] Thus, difference feminism seeks to acknowledge our inability to escape the body, even though difference is not intended here as a ground.[15]

Indeed, although Cavarero's work, especially her early work, has often appeared to take an essentialist position, she clarified in a 2008 interview with Elisabetta Bertolino that where she has treated the body as an essence, this was done so strategically.[16] This may appear as a change of approach but is less surprising when we realize that even in her earlier work Cavarero was uneasy with the limitations of an abstract understanding of "woman." This was signaled by her concern that any position of strong or positive sexual difference that seeks to define what woman is may lead to the opposing problem of mirroring the subjection of woman that is affected by man.[17] As Diana Fuss suggested in her assessment of Spivak's "strategic essentialism," such a strategic approach could be seen as a "'risk' worth taking," since although strategic essentialism can be dangerous "in the hands of a hegemonic group," it can, notwithstanding, be a powerful tool for subalterns to subvert and displace current power relations.[18]

Despite her unease with essentialism, and particularly pertinent for the dialogue in this volume, Cavarero's sexual difference theory did initially establish itself in opposition to both liberal and what she referred to as "postmodern" philosophy, specifically represented by the work of Judith Butler.[19] Cavarero's concern was that both liberal and postmodern feminists unwittingly used the metaphor "woman" from a male perspective and thus ended up only responding to problems generated by the male subject of philosophy.[20] As Richardson explains, for Cavarero both liberal feminism and postmodern feminism stressed "the priority of language over the 'fact' of the sexed body."[21] Cavarero therefore argued that despite their apparent differences, the postmodern "attempt to fragment the subject was 'simply the other side of the coin to the [liberal] emphasis on the "one."'"[22] For Cavarero, postmodern feminism did not escape the sexing of its multiple or fragmented subject as male. While recognizing the problems of women's subordination, it underplayed the force of sexual difference. It recognized the complexity of female oppression but denied recourse to address this from the position of actual women. Consequently, Cavarero's intervention between liberal (or in Cavarero's words "metaphysical")[23] and "postmodern" feminism was to insist that neither accounted for the singularity of each woman; that her embodied, sexed, lived experience—*who* she was, or her uniqueness—was rendered "superfluous" (for liberal feminists) or "a kind of trick" (for "postmodern" feminism).[24]

Furthermore, while much poststructuralist feminism owes a particular debt to Freudian psychoanalysis, many Italian feminists, Cavarero included, reject this tradition, despite having been influenced by Irigaray. For Anglo-American readers this may be seen to contribute to Cavarero's over-idealization of the maternal and failure to acknowledge the ambivalence and antagonism in the mother-child relationship.[25] On this reading Cavarero overlooks the possibility of disavowal or refusal in characterizing the apparent opposition between inclination and rectitude. Indeed, these concerns are at the crux of Honig's intervention, which reads Cavarero's feminism alongside Freud to emphasize the more sinister side of maternal care.

Yet, could we read sexual difference theory as complementary to the "postmodern" project of undermining the binary between construction and essentialism?[26] Indeed, both approaches begin by denying that there is something that "women really are."[27] Further, as Bock and James argue, sexual difference theory opposes the threefold assumptions upon which the essentialism debate rests. First, "the over-neat distinction between biology and culture that underpins the Anglo-American division between sex and gender and incorporates a vision of women's bodies as separable from culture"; second, that we could avoid essentialism by assuming that women are fundamentally different from men, which is no less essentialist than assuming that women are fundamentally the same; and third, that we cannot know of "any essence of woman which is independent of their past and present conditions."[28] This could be seen to demonstrate that the theory of sexual difference shares with so-called postmodern feminism a refusal of sameness and a refusal of neutrality.

Although sexual difference theory insists on the difference that is women's experience, which is always taken to be different from men's, the refusal to engage in a debate about what women are reveals that this focus on bodily difference was not intended as an attempt to tie a body to its biology. It conversely sought to "address the problem of how to avoid fixity, and the danger of tying women to their essential natures, rooted in biology or the psyche, while still insisting on the salience of the sexed body to subjectivity."[29] Hence Italian sexual difference theory came to be characterized by the significance of feminist materiality as a beginning point to account for the privileging of a presumptively masculine figure at the heart of the philosophical imaginary of the Western tradition. This led many Italian feminists to emphasize on the one hand the necessity of separatist movements to create the conditions from which an alternative symbolic order could be constructed and, on the other, the focus on the imagery of the maternal as a key battleground for establishing this alternative symbolic.

With regard to the relationship between Cavarero's feminism and the work of Judith Butler, it is true that Butler's work was challenged by many sexual difference theorists, including Cavarero. However, the objections were largely premised on a misreading of Butler's theory of performativity as assuming that sexual identity could be chosen at will. Butler's argument that gender is constructed did not imply voluntarism. Social construction is constitutive of the whole realm of subjectivity, not just one individual experience. Thus, gender cannot be dispensed with at will, since our very social existence as meaningful beings requires us to operate, at least to some degree, within the confines of gender norms.

Responding to the exclusions within both feminism and lesbian and gay politics of the '70s and '80s, Butler's motivation was to understand why, while we seem to need gender identity, it will always exclude. As such, she wanted to avoid mobilizing around a new theorization of identity, however radical, and instead sought to loosen the way that gender identity affects us. She argued that the potential for resistance and change does not lie in a refusal of identity, nor an alternative identity, but instead in the renegotiation and subversion of norms. Drawing on J. L. Austin's speech act theory, as well as the work of Jacques Derrida, Butler argued that gender is produced by repetition. She acknowledged that perfect repetition is never possible, since our gender identities are always to some extent a parody of an idealized norm. Yet it is precisely because of the impossibility of perfect repetition that Butler finds a space in which gender norms can be challenged. By repeating norms in a "wrong" manner, it may be possible to loosen the strictures of what counts as either male or female and the constraints that gender identity imposes on our lives. This is not to dissolve sexual difference or to multiply sexual difference in a way that completely dissolves woman as a subject position; rather, it could help de-binarize sex/gender and decenter its restrictive and controlling social function. Would it be too much of a stretch to argue that in this way Butler's work could be seen to develop the project of sexual difference theory even further, as she opens up the idea of that which is not man, beyond what is usually referred to as woman?

Reservations about Butler's work do remain for theorists of sexual difference, particularly regarding whether it indirectly diluted feminist struggle and prioritized sexuality as the dominant mode of relationality, thus displacing care or dependency.[30] However, Butler's position among Italian feminists was considerably enhanced by Cavarero, who engaged with Butler's argument as early as 1996, when she wrote the Preface to the Italian edition of *Bodies That Matter*. Furthermore, Butler's work on vulnerability and precarity, developed in part in conversation with Cavarero (see Bernini's étude, later in this volume), addressed many of these initial concerns and helped to emphasize that both were circling the same issues from different perspectives: how to resist liberal individualism and avoid androcentrism without prioritizing certain sexual identifications over others.

Honig's relation to these two thinkers charts a rather different trajectory. Like Butler's work on performativity, Honig's reading of Arendt was also inspired by the performative in Austin. While Butler's extension of the theory of performativity to sex/gender inspired Honig's radical reading of political action in Arendt,[31] rather than simply apply Butler's theory Honig has developed a unique feminist theory of her own, navigating the tension between her poststructuralist approach and her longstanding sympathy for Cavarero's sexual difference project. Indeed, Honig's "agonistic sorority"[32] operates in the very space between—in fact, the space opened up by—this "postmodern"/sexual difference debate.

For Honig, recognition of the complex dilemmas we encounter in political theory are exemplified by, though not limited to, debates around sex and gender. Her interest is in the way that any such agonistic struggle "exposes the remainders of the system"[33] by revealing how systems of knowledge or power minoritize those who do not fit their parameters. Instead of opting to resolve disagreement, Honig seeks to radicalize it,[34] holding disagreement open and exploring it—itself a political gesture that refuses the closure so often sought by political theory. With respect to the feminist debate that concerns us here, Honig emphasizes that each position has opened something up in its agonistic rival that may elevate or extend those who confront it, and open new unimagined possibilities for worldbuilding.[35]

By tracing the development of Cavarero's feminism in this section we have seen how her perceived initial distance from Butler has lessened over time, and that Honig's agonistic feminism provides us with a way to productively map their differences. We will see in the next section that Honig's more direct engagement with agonism leads to her effort to take an alternative path to Cavarero's heterotopian feminism. This also generates Honig's distinctive critique of the politics of nonviolence that has come to unite Cavarero and Butler's recent work.

## Key Themes in Cavarero's Thought

As noted, Cavarero has made an extraordinary contribution to political and philosophical debate over the last four decades. Pertinent to this volume is her method of theft; her critique of the role of the body in the philosophical tradition; her reappropriation of the body as unique, narratable, and vulnerable; and her consequent ethics of nonviolence concerned with inclined relationality and care.

Throughout her work, Cavarero steals and adapts familiar images, tropes, or stories of women, refiguring them to emphasize their central role in the myths and theories in which they fleetingly appear.[36] We have seen how in *Inclinations* she takes an orthodox image of the Madonna and child to undermine our ordinary relations of independence and uprightness. In *In Spite of Plato*—which reread the texts by Plato, Parmenides, and Homer, founding fathers of political philosophy—Cavarero subverted the masculinist themes of death and struggle by focusing on four female figures—Demeter, Penelope, Diotima, and a maidservant from Thrace—usually overlooked due to their marginal positions in the texts. This simultaneously revealed their constitutive exclusion from the Western tradition and created a space for them to be something more than a "functional subspecies" of humanity.[37] This method enables her to subvert patriarchy by reappropriating and renarrating the figures of the philosophical tradition.

In rethinking the philosophical tradition Cavarero identified a paradox at its heart. On the one hand, beginning with Aristotle, politics is premised on a conception of the human as disembodied: human to the extent that he is in possession of logos, his body is an unhelpful distraction from the task of expressing what, within the political community, is useful and harmful, what is just and unjust. On the other hand, the Western political tradition continuously articulates its principles, theories, and treatises with recourse to the metaphor of the body. This body, however, is not female but male. Nonetheless, the presence of a body as the guiding metaphor of the Western political tradition maintains an excess that the putatively disembodied accounts of politics found in this tradition are unable to fully master.[38]

In considering what it might mean for political thought to take the body, and in particular the female body, seriously, Cavarero borrows Arendt's category of uniqueness, famously articulated in *The Human Condition*.[39] For Cavarero, Western metaphysics has overlooked *who* people are, instead focusing on *what* people are. Who a person is—one's uniqueness—is not a quality proper to a person, but emerges between people and is expressed by their singular, embodied form as much as, if not more than, their reasoned speech. For Cavarero, one always needs another to give one a sense of who one is; one's uniqueness is not something that can be discerned on one's own. Who a person is can be made apparent through the storying of one's life by another. The figuration of selfhood only becomes apparent when narrated by another, often in hindsight. If Western metaphysics has focused almost exclusively on what people are, rather than who they are, then this distinction can be mapped onto the previously noted androcentrism of this tradition: its implicit, or often explicit, assumption that Man, far from being universal, is the morphological and onto-epistemological sine qua non of being. By presenting an abstract figure—Man, or the human—and analyzing what he is, this tradition fuses masculinity with this search for what it is to exist, abstracted from the everyday lived experience of particular people.

As noted, for Cavarero, this androcentrism means that women face a double exclusion: first, like many people, women are forced to reckon with a tradition that refuses to engage who they are in favor of what they are; and second, this *what*, which is presented to women in the figure of the universal Man, is masculine.⁴⁰ However, for Cavarero, one consequence of this double exclusion is that women, having been historically alienated from a universal conception of what it is to be, have instead sought forms of expression that, rather than drawing on the abstraction inherent in philosophy, have instead engaged the resources of storytelling to focus on the particularity of their embodied singularity.⁴¹ Men, by contrast, seeing themselves (or what they think of as themselves) reflected back in this universal figure of Man, have little impetus to search for other forms of expression outside the tradition of Western metaphysics. Cavarero's response to this double exclusion is a philosophy of narration (or narration in opposition to philosophy) that focuses not on death but on birth. This brings into focus the figure of the mother (in both a literal sense and as any person responding to the primary ethical choice of either care or abandonment) as the primary person who reveals who the newborn infant is.

Furthermore, Cavarero identified the voice as expressive of a person's uniqueness, understanding the significance of this voice not in the semantic meaning that it conveys, but in the voice understood as an embodied phenomenon that communicates a person's uniqueness prior to any transmission of speech. Cavarero engaged here in a deconstruction of the Western tradition as "voice" has been understood in some of its most famous texts, demonstrating how the voice as an embodied phenomenon has been assigned to women, understood as feminine, whereas speech is the privilege of men and masculinity. This can be seen, for Cavarero, in one of the foundational texts of the Western political tradition: Aristotle's *Politics*, in which he identifies logos, or reasoned speech, as the defining capacity of the properly political animal that is Man.⁴² For Cavarero, Aristotle, as well as the entire Western tradition, has obscured the fact that logos was, for the Greeks, both *phone* and *semantike*; it is the latter that has come to dominate accounts of speech, signifying the reason that is communicated in speech, while a person's voice is at best understood as a mere vehicle for the expression of reason, at worst a quality that is dangerous, seductive, and properly feminine.⁴³ Cavarero traces this misogynistic history, identifying the ways women are consigned to the vocalic, but further, mining these counter-histories to demonstrate the absurdity of a masculine political tradition that believes it can do away with embodiment. The stereotype that Cavarero identifies is thus stolen from the masculine tradition and mobilized as a means of bringing to an end this tradition, opening a way of understanding vocality and embodiment as something more than the other of the disembodied, reasoning, autonomous Man.

Cavarero mobilized her account of uniqueness to make sense of a contemporary form of violence that she names as "horrorism." Cavarero's analysis emerged from the inadequacy of the notion of terrorism to name a violence that, rather than making one flee in terror, fixes one in place in the horror of its enactment.[44] For Cavarero, horrorism describes a violence that targets the uniqueness of a typically helpless person as it is expressed through her body. She describes this as an "ontological crime," as it targets a quality—uniqueness—that is essential to what it is to be a human being, even as this essential quality does not reside within a person but emerges in relation to another.[45] Horrorist violence might include, for Cavarero, suicide bombing, whereby the embodied singularity of victim and perpetrator is collapsed in the extremity of the explosion; torture, where one is rendered helpless in the face of the infliction of extreme pain by a seemingly absolute power; and Auschwitz, where the figure of the *Muselmann* was the end result of an experimental, systematic destruction of humanness.

As well as developing a conceptualization of violence, Cavarero also developed an account of vulnerability as central to the human condition, engaging in a dialogue with Butler who was also theorizing vulnerability in her *Precarious Life: The Powers of Mourning and Violence*, and later *Frames of War: When Is Life Grievable?* Both thinkers assert that vulnerability could provide the starting point for a powerful conception of ethics. By accepting our vulnerability rather than trying to hide or overcome it—as philosophy has traditionally sought to do—we might be able to build a more caring society in which we are all more attentive to the vulnerability of others.[46] While there is much overlap in Cavarero and Butler's conceptions of vulnerability, in Cavarero one finds an emphasis on the dual meaning of vulnerability as something that both exposes us to violence (highlighted by the etymology of the Latin term *vulnus* as wound) as well as exposing us to care, affection, and caress (in the etymology of *vel* as bare, exposed skin).[47] This dual focus is important, as it signals the way that throughout Cavarero's work she is not content to fall into the biopolitical trap of only focusing on the violence enacted on "bare life,"[48] seeing this as a reiteration of a masculine trope central to metaphysics that can only understand humanness as a being-toward-death. Instead, for Cavarero, an important part of her feminist project is the articulation of forms of life that emphasize pleasure and happiness as being central to human existence, where life is to be lived and in its living gives human life meaning—what she describes in the "Coda" of this volume as an "imaginary of hope." Indeed, it is this that makes the ethical stakes of the extreme violence she confronts in *Horrorism* all the more stark.

Honig has raised concern over the possibility that Butler's and Cavarero's work on vulnerability reflects a certain "mortalist humanism." It is worth noting for those not familiar with political theory that there has long been suspicion of humanism as grounded on universal claims that can only ever include some and exclude others. As a consequence it may have seemed surprising to see these thinkers appear to turn back to questions concerning something Honig referred to as "humanness" and to increasingly refer to the human in their work, emphasizing that politics occurs in the very signification of what, or rather who, counts as human. As Timothy Huzar notes in this volume, it is clear that both Cavarero and Butler are not humanists in the traditional sense: they are not trying to define the human, but engaged in projects that work at the borders of what is deemed to be human, to question and problematize the notion of humanness at work and draw attention to the violence that such a notion effects. Yet more than just problematize the way that humanness functions for political thought, they both develop an ethics based, in Honig's words, on "the ontological fact of mortality" that operates as a challenge to the traditional philosophical understanding that it is the capacity to reason that distinguishes the human from the nonhuman.[49] In contrast, mortalist humanism, for Honig, makes central the capacity for "vulnerability and suffering."[50] Indeed, it is from here that Cavarero's and Butler's emphasis on nonviolence stems, since they mobilize this fact of vulnerability to assert a value for life and compassion that emerges from our equal capacity to suffer—and, particularly for Cavarero, to be cared for.

However, for Honig the specification of nonviolence as an ethics risks undermining this project, since any assertion of our shared mortalism and vulnerability could never guarantee the type of ethical response that is hoped for and risks disavowing its inherent violence.[51] In contrast, Honig calls for an agonistic humanism that is not founded on our shared vulnerability, but that "sees in mortality, suffering, sound and vulnerability resources for some form of enacted universality."[52] Since these are "no less various in their significations than are the diverse languages that unite and divide us,"[53] the appeal to ethics may attempt to circumvent the violence of political struggle; a violence that may be necessary in order to convince or persuade the witnesses of suffering that it is suffering that they are witnessing and that they should respond compassionately. Thus, for Honig, Cavarero's ethics cannot avoid the risk of violence, and more worryingly, violence may even be necessary to defend the type of pacifism that both Butler and Cavarero articulate.

Indeed, Butler's recent work *The Force of Nonviolence* suggests that vulnerability needs to be part of a wider constellation of "vulnerability, rage, persistence and resistance."[54] In this way, vulnerability is less ontological and appears more like Honig's "resources for some form of enacted universality." This is a resource that can inspire resistance through a movement for nonviolence that is, for Butler, a particular form of refusal.[55] This is a refusal that is an engagement in struggle even if it refuses the violence that is expected and indeed demanded of it. For Butler, such a refusal of violence forms part of a wider politics of equality, a thread that links up what may otherwise appear to be separate movements. Relationality is at the heart of any politics of equality, but for Butler, rather than celebrate any particular form of relation, including care, it is important, if our solidarity is to succeed, to acknowledge the ambivalence of our relations with one another, the limits of our abilities to care, the value of our rage, and our ability to sometimes restrain our inclinations to lean toward or away, as she suggests in her contribution to this volume.

In the account we have provided here, we have endeavored to chart the criss-crossing paths of interaction and inspiration among these three thinkers, underscoring the productive tensions among their different yet complementary struggles. Read in this way, we can see that their work is engaged on different fronts. First, while Honig's focus is always on the political tools that we and others can use to act upon the world, Butler and Cavarero here enact politics within the discipline of philosophy, their ethics posing a challenge to traditional ethics: "an insurrection at the level of ontology."[56] Second, perhaps both Cavarero and Butler are positing their ethics not necessarily as an achievable way of life but as a polemical challenge to our current way of living, demonstrating what is lacking in the space between our way of living and the vision they defend. In this sense, while Honig's essay emphasizes the risks involved in fighting for political alternatives, and Butler's asks if—and how—we might be able to avoid those risks while still engaged in the struggle, Cavarero offers a parallel vision of a world without those risks. In this sense, perhaps it is Cavarero who offers us the most hope, by daring to dream the wildest dreams.

Indeed, while Cavarero does invoke an ethics, this is not a traditional ethics in the form of a search for principles. Rather than something to be "deduced,"[57] it is given a priori. It arises from the "*altruistic* ontology of the human existent as finite,"[58] something akin to a Levinasian ethics of an encounter with the other. It is in support of this ethic that she mobilizes the stereotypical maternal scene to both highlight its initial deployment and to undermine the binary that gives rise to the stereotype in the first place.[59] Despite concerns raised here, and in the interventions that follow, Cavarero does try to avoid fetishizing inclination; instead, her intention is to break the stereotype away from this tradition and use its resources to think a "new relational ontology of the vulnerable."[60] Bringing the various strands of her thought together, this relational ontology of the vulnerable insists that life cannot be disentangled from our relations to others; that embodiment is a crucial component of this relation; and finally that, rather than characterize life as a selfish existence turned toward death, an altruistic ethics can be discerned in the natal scene, where a mother is confronted with an irrefutable, primary ethical choice of either care or abandonment.[61] Despite Honig's realism and Butler's caution, for Cavarero (and emphasized by Huzar later in this volume), this ethical relation and the rearticulation of existence that is coterminous with it are intended to contribute to an "imaginary of hope": a postural geometry that indicates, in its collision with our current ways of being, not only that another mode of existence is possible, but that it has been lived together by people throughout history, despite being overlooked by philosophy's dominant narrative (or, perhaps, *because of* this overlooking).[62] By reading Cavarero's work as a staging of this collision between alternative imaginaries and one's current way of being, it becomes clear that although not a self-proclaimed agonist, she is not necessarily circumventing political struggle, but dramatically counterposing one image of the world with another, performatively remaking it through the stories that she tells. It is true that her vision may appear to celebrate what has until now been a subordinate role of caring, but perhaps this need not be the case anymore. By insisting that we place inclined ethical relations center stage, Cavarero wishes to us this consciously naïve imaginary to disrupt and subvert—even if only by a little—the "pathetic blunder" that is our all-too-common conception of the world as comprised of apparently independent, self-sufficient beings.

## Summary of Contributions

The essays that follow engage with different aspects of Cavarero's project. Cavarero's opening essay presents her ethic of inclination as responding to a postural geometric imaginary in the philosophical tradition that is irrefutably gendered. Opening with a reflection on the character of Irina in Italo Calvino's *If on a Winter's Night, a Traveller*, she draws out the inclined, sinuous, curving shapes of the female and contrasts them to the straight, upright, correct, and erect male figure. Linking this rectitude back to ancient Greek etymology, she traces its progress through the work of Plato and Kant, finishing with Proudhon, where the moralizing of philosophy's gendered posture is explicit. Here, women are the embodiment of vice, physically weak, and always inclined in their two roles, sex and childbirth. The male subject is he who directs his own life, while the woman lives for and through others.

Yet it is from this devalued imagery of the female body as maternal that Cavarero begins her subversion of the philosophical tradition. Following Arendt's valorization of the natal scene, Cavarero emphasizes the distinctive role of the inclined mother as caregiver as a central symbol of human interdependency rather than a weak, supporting role. This image of inclined motherhood forms the basis of Cavarero's ethic of inclination—an altruistic ethic that upends the "imagined wholeness" of the dominant liberal model of the independent, self-sufficient, male individual.

Although Butler's *Leaning Out, Caught in the Fall: Interdependency and Ethics in Cavarero* opens with shared points of agreement between herself and Cavarero, Butler then seeks to emphasize the importance of ambivalence in our affective ties, including the maternal ties that Cavarero celebrates. Butler begins with the observation that all upright bodies presuppose support that comes from inclination, including not only the inclined bodies of those looking after us when we are young or old, inclining over us to care, stabilizing us as we learn to walk, but also those who support us throughout our lives. Despite our adult claims and aspirations to "stand on our own two feet . . . no one stands on her own." We are instead always dependent on the care and support of others. Further, Butler draws attention to the material, technical, and infrastructural support that exceeds caring relationships, such as the maternal and familial as emphasized by Cavarero, but also the sororal and friendly, as emphasized by Honig, Battersby, and Woodford, in this volume. Butler is indicating to us the necessity of welfare systems, healthcare access, social support systems, all of which are precarious and often under threat. Butler expresses her own gratitude to Cavarero, upon whom she admits that her own thinking relies more than can be easily acknowledged in a single chapter. She indicates, for example, her agreement with Cavarero's argument regarding uniqueness, her critique of individualism, her Levinasian approach to ethics, and her critique of the masculinity of the "I." However, Butler wishes to complicate Cavarero's reading of inclination to emphasize that both the inclined and the erect figure "are *not* radically distinct and never fully oppositional"; instead we all move through inclination and uprightness throughout our lives. Crucially, Butler indicates that Cavarero's stereotypical reading risks enacting the very move that she seeks to avoid: it could imply a denial of the dependency of the male subject; a denial of inclination in philosophy. Instead Butler seeks to reveal this dependency. Butler shows how Kant's description of the vertigo that philosophy experiences in the encounter with the sublime reveals the inclination that is already at the heart of philosophy (an argument further extended by Christine Battersby's research on Kant's friendships in her contribution to this volume). This leads Butler to ask whether we need to be cautious of Cavarero's analogies between geometry and bodily posture and geometry and morality. Butler argues that when considering the relationship between ethics, politics, and nonviolence it may be necessary to distinguish a predisposition, a disposition, an inclination, and a bodily movement or posture. We may be inclined to "lean" a certain way, but may restrain ourselves, perhaps for ethical reasons. Indeed, if we consider the ethical commandment "Thou shalt not kill," Butler notes that such a clash of inclinations could be the decisive moment in resisting violent action. If we wish to further Cavarero's project to establish a feminist ethics of nonviolence, then for Butler it is to this ambivalence at the heart of inclination that we must turn.

Indeed, it is precisely this ambivalence that runs through Honig's "How to Do Things with Inclination: *Antigones*, with Cavarero." In this essay Honig turns inclination toward sorority, agonism, and heterotopia on behalf of a more egalitarian and contestatory politics. Noting that care relationships are often rather more ambivalent than Cavarero seems to acknowledge, Honig urges us to recognize the agonism in inclination that she suggests could form part of a politics of refusal. Any such agonistic inclination would have to confront the violence that Cavarero disallows. In the female protagonists of Sophocles's *Antigone* and Euripides's *The Bacchae*, Honig identifies figures of inclination characterized by agonistic sorority instead of Cavarero's maternity. Turning to Freud—so often disavowed or ignored by Cavarero and many Italian feminists—Honig recalls his argument that there is the figure of a vulture hidden in the folds of the painting Cavarero uses to inspire her theory of inclined maternity: Leonardo's *The Virgin and Child with Saint Anne*. This draws attention to the darker side of maternal care (albeit also, as Honig points out, to Freud's misogyny). Honig questions whether Cavarero's ethics of inclination might be too separatist, failing to act against the order of rectitude, and crucially overlooking the epistemicide that any act of separation comprises. This confronts Cavarero's feminist ethics of nonviolence with the inescapability of violence for politics. Honig is not seeking to promote violence. Rather, she heralds a politics of refusal that—in spite of and in full acknowledgment of the ever-present threat of violence—insists on a "return to the city" to continue the struggle against dominatory power.

These essays are then followed by a short *Scherzo* by Olivia Guaraldo, who defends Cavarero's approach to rethinking the relationality of the sexual encounter. Reading Locke alongside Carla Lonzi and Cavarero, she argues that, surprisingly, there is continuity between Locke and Lonzi in that both read the sexual encounter as conflictual. This, however, is for different reasons. Locke's aim is to domesticate the sexual, while Lonzi's is to exaggerate it to resist sexual domination. Since for Locke, the sexual act is what founds the order of property, Guaraldo shows how redistribution of property is dependent on a rethinking of our sexual relations. A step toward this is found in Guaraldo's reading of Cavarero's theorization of sexual relations as beyond conflict. She therefore argues that the uniqueness found in Cavarero's understanding of our relationality offers a more hopeful imaginary; a pleasurable, erotic, and empowering experience such that it need not comprise appropriation (Locke), control, or domestication (Lonzi).

We then move through the collection of études that respond to Cavarero's provocative text in multiple ways. Simona Forti's "From Horrorism to the Inclination of the Gray Zone" explores a disjunction between Cavarero's work on horror and violence and her relational ethics of inclination. She begins with Cavarero's argument that our human existence makes us dependent, opening us simultaneously to care or wounding. She then turns to Cavarero's argument that horrorist violence is that which takes on an ontological dimension by striking at the heart of that which makes us unique. Yet, reading Cavarero alongside Primo Levi, Forti emphasizes the limitations of Cavarero's reading of violence as comprised of victim and perpetrator, suggesting, in a counterpoint to Honig, that an ethic of nonviolence needs to appreciate the deeper complexity of power relations. This complicates the ethic of inclination, emphasizing alongside Honig and Devenney that horror, and indeed violence, can emerge from inclination. As such, this postural ethics, which valorizes inclination over rectitude, may form part of a wider problematic radicalization of evil, prevalent in much post-holocaust ethical thought.

In a development of Butler's turn to Kant, Christine Battersby draws on new research concerning Kant's social life to consider whether Cavarero's relational ontology can help us reorient the grounding principles of political and ethical theory toward vulnerability. The urgency of such a task is exacerbated today by the violences of power inequality and dependency, from what is taken to be the private lives of individuals right through the arena of international governance. Drawing on the history of a recently discovered champagne glass dedicated to Kant and his circle of friends, Battersby provides an account of this circle, and particularly Kant's friendship with Joseph Green, an English merchant, to argue that Kant did value inclination, albeit not in the maternal form. Instead, his close circle of friends exemplifies another mode of relationality, one that unlike maternity or sorority is free of kinship ties. In reflecting on the importance of friendship for Kant, Battersby seeks to defend Kant, although differently to Butler's defense in this volume. Complimenting Butler, Battersby finds a Kant inclined in friendship, against Cavarero's "caricature." Perhaps Kant was not quite as upright after all, and maybe inclination can be found in friendship as well as maternity.

Lorenzo Bernini's contribution, "Bad Inclinations: Cavarero, Queer Theories, and the Drive," celebrates Cavarero's contribution to philosophy and elaborates on the dialogue between Cavarero and Butler's work. It then, however, identifies an alternative queer theory that more strongly challenges Cavarero's ethics of inclination, in particular because of Bernini's use of the Freudian concept of drive. Rather than coinciding with sexual instinct, drive is a perversion of it and is often associated with homosexual sex as a way to exclude and subordinate homosexuality. Instead of responding, as Butler does, by seeking to struggle for recognition for sexual minorities, Bernini emphasizes Edelman's argument that minorities should remain "antisocial"—outside of the spheres of signification and intelligibility, and also outside of the prioritization of the child and relationships of maternity and kinship. Complementing Butler's and Honig's emphases on ambivalence, Bernini recognizes the ambivalence of the figure of the child for our social lives, questioning the value of reproduction and virility for not only sexual relationships but care relationships, too. Bernini argues that by recognizing the interconnections of care and sex or even sex without care, we may be able to offer an alternative theorization of vulnerability for nonviolence, which, still in inclination, but without the mother and child relation at its center, radically exposes the self to the other.

In "Querying Cavarero's Rectitude," Mark Devenney begins by agreeing with Cavarero's contention that inclination can subvert the order of masculinity and rectitude. Similarly to Butler, Devenney emphasizes the dependence of the upright "I" on the support of others. Yet he is concerned that Cavarero's argument undermines itself and ends up itself enacting a violence—a form of propriety concerning the correct way to read philosophy—on the texts she reads. Submitting Cavarero's text to an improper reading,[63] Devenney suggests, in agreement with Honig, Butler, and Bernini, that there is more ambivalence in the mother-child relationship than Cavarero indicates. For Devenney this means that it cannot provide the basis for any ethics, since the very founding of an ethics introduces new hierarchies and order to the proper, however attractive they may seem to their designer. Devenney argues that in asserting an ontology of inclination, Cavarero enacts a new rectitude or rightness: inclination is now that which is correct. This move undoes inclination's subversive power. Along with Honig and Forti, Devenney sees a violence in this forcing that cannot be acknowledged by Cavarero. Rather than assert a separatist heterotopian schematism, Devenney suggests that a project of nonviolence must instead engage in hegemonic struggle in the here and now, but that this must be a struggle that is not founded on a prescribed ethics.

In "Violence, Vulnerability, Ontology: Insurrectionary Humanism in Cavarero and Butler," Timothy Huzar is more sympathetic to Cavarero's position, seeing a deep complementarity between Cavarero and Judith Butler. He argues that both enact what Jacques Rancière would call a "poetics of politics" by staging an understanding of vulnerability that is not so much ontologically grounded but made urgent by particular histories of violence associated with normative conceptions of humanness. As a consequence, disentangling the ethical, ontological, and political stakes of their interventions becomes a difficult, if not impossible, task. By overlooking the scenes of violence that make urgent their account of vulnerability, Huzar argues that it becomes too easy to dismiss their interventions as merely ethical, or as another ontology of the human. Instead, the insurrectionary humanism of their accounts of vulnerability reveals the imbrication of the ethical, the ontological, and the political.

Finally, Clare Woodford's étude "Queer Madonnas in Love and Friendship" mobilizes alternative Madonna iconography against Leonardo's inclined Madonna to ask whether the rectitude of an upright Madonna and the inclination of subordinated bodies might complicate Cavarero's ethic of inclination. Woodford unearths a queer kinship in the orthodox Catholic narrative of the Virgin Mary to question maternity as a familial and caring relation. Echoing Honig's, Devenney's, and Forti's concerns, she highlights the veiled violence in the maternal relation. Exploring a theme introduced by Battersby's étude, Woodford considers the importance of non-kinship relationality in the form of friendship. She notes the intertwining of rectitude and inclination in any friendship—the interplay of eros and filia that can dwell in any caring relation (as also discussed by Bernini) and that emerges in points of agreement and disagreement (and may threaten any friendship, exceeding, in such cases, Honig's agonism). Unpicking the assumed necessary links between maternity and inclination, Woodford instead asks whether a provocative friendship that consents to dissent reveals the struggle at the heart of any care relation. This account of dissenting friendship, both inclined and upright, could offer a more promising relationality for a politics, rather than an ethics, of dissent and nonviolence.

In the Coda, Cavarero responds to the pluriphonic "surging democracy" that emerges in the exchanges herein. With exemplary graciousness, she acknowledges that she may have neglected Kant a little in her reading, but in the main stands by her methodology of theft and her provocative reading style with "bad intentions" to read a text against itself. Against concerns that she has overplayed the analogies between morality and geometry, overemphasized maternity and the altruistic side of care, and repeated a certain naïve imaginary of motherhood, she emphasizes the urgency of this purposefully naïve vision. This is not in ignorance of its limitations; instead, she asserts that these limitations cannot stand in our way of hoping—and therefore working—for a better future. Cavarero acknowledges a certain strategic utopianism. Inspired by the feminist movements of the sixties, her work sounds a note of discord in contemporary philosophy recalling us to "the generative power of interaction" that can be mobilized by any such "imaginary of hope." By using the everyday exceptionalilty of Leonardo's mother and child image, Cavarero has communicated to us the possibility of a world where altruism is not naïve or far-fetched, where caring for others is not deemed to be an exception, and where exclusion is opposed rather than accepted. The power of this vision resides in its simplicity. It generated the palpable dynamism and sense of community at the conference that inspired this volume. Its ripples continue to inspire and provoke across the globe today, bringing diverse scholars together engaged in a shared project: a feminist ethics of nonviolence, in pursuit of a better world.

## Final Thanks

Sincere appreciation is owed to the Centre for Applied Philosophy, Politics and Ethics at the University of Brighton for hosting the initial meeting that inspired this volume. As a result, we extend a massive thanks to all participants, particularly those not published here as authors but whose interventions still ring throughout these engagements. Thanks also to Mark Devenney for the immense work in coordinating the conference and to Ian Sinclair for his fabulous organizational skills. None of this would have been possible without Tim Huzar and German Primera for instigating the whole affair, including Tim's initial matchmaking between CAPPE at the University of Brighton and two research centers in Verona: the Hannah Arendt Centre (with Olivia Guaraldo) and PoliTesse (with Lorenzo Bernini), each of which collaborated with and supported the publication of this volume. Thanks to Bonnie Honig for reading and commenting on the entire draft. Thanks also, of course, to all of our contributors for their timely editing and responses, to Margaret Ferguson for her comments and enthusiasm, to Karen Bouchard and Matthew Martin, who went well beyond the call of duty, along with other librarians at Brown University to help with sourcing images, and to Tom Lay, Eric Newman, and Aldene Fredenburg at Fordham University Press for their endless patience and encouragement. Finally, this work is dedicated to Adriana Cavarero, whose exemplary generosity, care, and spirit of collegiality continue to provoke, support, and inspire our intellectual endeavors.

Notes

We are indebted to Mark Devenney, Joanna Kellond and Bonnie Honig for their incisive and generous comments on earlier versions of this introduction. We take full responsibility for any remaining errors.

1. See Adriana Cavarero, "Scenes of Inclination," in this volume, and Cavarero, *Inclinations: A Critique of Rectitude*, trans. Amanda Minervini and Adam Sitze (Stanford, Calif.: Stanford University Press, 2016).

2. Cavarero, Konstantinos Thomaidis, and Ilaria Pinna, "Towards a Hopeful Plurality of Democracy: An Interview on Vocal Ontology with Adriana Cavarero," *Journal of Interdisciplinary Voice Studies* 3, no. 1 (2018): 84, https://doi.org/10.1386/jivs.3.1.81_1.

3. Cavarero, *Inclinations*, 99.

4. Ibid., 174.

5. See, for example, the rise of religious and political opposition to what is called "gender ideology"; Judith Butler, "Judith Butler: The Backlash against 'Gender Ideology' Must Stop," *New Statesman*, January 21, 2019, https://www.newstatesman.com/2019/01/judith-butler-backlash-against-gender-ideology-must-stop.

6. Janice Richardson, "'Beyond Equality and Difference': Sexual Difference in the work of Adriana Cavarero," *Feminist Legal Studies* 6, no. 1 (1998): 108.

7. In sidestepping the "liberal"/"difference" debate, it could be argued that Italian feminism also sidestepped the question of race and racialization raised by black feminist scholars as a crucial rejoinder to this very debate.

8. See "translators' note" in Cavarero, *In Spite of Plato*, xx.

9. Gisela Bock and Susan James, "Introduction," in *"Beyond Equality and Difference": Citizenship, Feminist Politics, Female Subjectivity*, ed. Gisela Bock and Susan James (Abingdon: Routledge, 1992), 5.

10. Ibid., 6.

11. See, for example, Cavarero, *Relating Narratives: Storytelling and Selfhood*, trans. Paul A. Kottman (London and New York: Routledge, 2000), 20, 50; Hannah Arendt, *The Human Condition* (Chicago and London: University of Chicago Press, 1998), 178–79.

12. Cavarero, "Towards a Theory of Sexual Difference," in *The Lonely Mirror: Italian Perspectives on Feminist Theory*, ed. Sandra Kemp and Paola Bono (London: Routledge, 1993), 196.

13. Ibid., 203.

14. Fanny Söderbäck, "Natality or Birth? Arendt and Cavarero on the Human Condition of Being Born," *Hypatia* 23, no. 2 (2018): 278.

15. Diane Elam, *Feminism and Deconstruction: Ms en abime* (London: Routledge, 1994), 174.

16. This could be taken to imply that Cavarero's work was in conversation with Gayatri Spivak's strategic essentialist position developed (although later disavowed) in the 1980s. However, at the time it was developed, Spivak's work was situated in the very school of thought that, during the 1980s, Cavarero sought to resist: poststructuralist theory.

17. Cavarero, "Diotima," in *Italian Feminist Thought: A Reader*, ed. Paola Bono and Sandra Kemp (Oxford and Cambridge, Mass.: Blackwell, 1991), 183.

18. Diana Fuss, *Essentially Speaking: Feminism, Nature, Difference* (New York and London: Routledge, 1989), 32.

19. See Richardson, "'Beyond Equality and Difference,'" 115 and nn. 4 and 43, where she cites an unpublished essay by Cavarero: Cavarero, *Rethinking Oedipus: Stealing a Patriarchal Text*, paper at the U.K. Society of Women and Philosophy Conference, 1996.

20. Again, see Richardson, "'Beyond Equality and Difference,'" 115 and nn. 4 and 43, citing Cavarero, *Rethinking Oedipus*; Richardson, "'Beyond Equality and Difference,'" 116; Alison Jardine, *Configurations of Women and Modernity* (Ithaca, N.Y.: Cornell University Press, 1985); Susan Feldman, "Reclaiming Sexual Difference: What Queer Theory Can't Tell Us about Sexuality," *Journal of Bisexuality* 9, no. 3–4 (2009): 259–78, 260, 116.

21. Richardson, "'Beyond Equality and Difference,'" 116.

22. Ibid.

23. Adriana Cavarero, "*Who* Engenders Politics?," in *Italian Feminist Theory and Practice: Equality and Sexual Difference*, ed. Graziella Parati and Rebecca West (London: Associated University Presses, 2002), 88.

24. Richardson, "'Beyond Equality and Difference,'" 94 95.

25. Thanks to an anonymous reviewer for this point.

26. Feldman, "Reclaiming Sexual Difference," 275n6.

27. Bock and James, "Introduction," 6.

28. Ibid., 6.

29. Gill Jagger, "Beyond Essentialism and Construction: Subjectivity, Corporeality and Sexual Difference," *Women Review Philosophy: Special Issue of Women's Philosophy Review*, ed. M. Griffiths and M. Whitford (1996): 141.

30. Richardson, "'Beyond Equality and Difference,'" 116.

31. Honig, *Political Theory and the Displacement of Politics* (Ithaca, N.Y.: Cornell University Press, 1993), 123, 209–10; and Janell Watson, "Feminism as Agonistic Sorority: An Interview with Bonnie Honig," Minnesota Review, New Series, no. 81 (2013): 102–25, 111–12.

32. Watson, "Feminism as Agonistic Sorority, 102–25.

33. Honig, *Political Theory and the Displacement of Politics*, 208

34. Ibid.

35. Watson, *Feminism as Agonistic Sorority*, 106.

36. Cavarero, *In Spite of Plato: A Feminist Rewriting of Ancient Philosophy*, trans. Serena Anderlini-D'Onofrio and Áine O'Healy (Cambridge: Polity, 1995), 4–9.

37. Ibid., 3.

38. Cavarero, *Stately Bodies: Literature, Philosophy, and the Question of Gender*, trans. de Lucca and Deanna Shemek (Ann Arbor: University of Michigan Press, 2002), xi.

39. Arendt, *Human Condition*, 176.

40. Cavarero, *Relating Narratives: Storytelling and Selfhood*, trans. Paul A. Kottman (London and New York: Routledge, 2000), 49.

41. Ibid., 58.

42. Aristotle, *The Politics*, 60.

43. Cavarero, *For More Than One Voice: Toward a Philosophy of Vocal Expression*, trans. Paul A. Kottman (Stanford, Calif.: Stanford University Press, 2005), 33–41.

44. Cavarero, *Horrorism: Naming Contemporary Violence*, trans. William McCuaig (New York: Columbia University Press, 2011), 4–9.

45. Ibid., *Horrorism*, 29.

46. Butler, *Giving an Account of Oneself: A Critique of Ethical Violence* (New York: Fordham University Press, 2005) 100.

47. Ibid., *Horrorism*, 20–24.

48. Giorgio Agamben, *Homo Sacer: Sovereign Power and Bare Life*, trans. Daniel Heller-Roazen (Stanford, Calif.: Stanford University Press, 1998).

49. Honig, "Antigone's Two Laws: Greek Tragedy and the Politics of Humanism," *New Literary History* 41, no. 1 (Winter 2010): 1–33.

50. Ibid., 1.

51. Ibid., 3.

52. Ibid., 1.

53. Ibid., 4.

54. Butler, *The Force of Nonviolence: An Ethico-Political Bind* (Brooklyn: Verso, 2020), 192.

55. Ibid., 202.

56. See also Butler, *Precarious Life: The Powers of Mourning and Violence* (London, Verso, 2006), 33.

57. Cavarero, *Relating Narratives*, 87.

58. Ibid. Here *"altruistic"* is in italics in the original to emphasize its double meaning as a moral disposition as well as a more literal meaning denoting a more general orientation toward the other—"other-ism."

59. Cavarero, *Inclinations*.

60. Ibid., 129.

61. Ibid., 97–106.

62. Cavarero, Thomaidis, and Pinna, "Towards a Hopeful Plurality of Democracy," 88.

63. Mark Devenney, *Towards an Improper Politics* (Manchester: Manchester University Press, 2020).

# Scenes of Inclination

ADRIANA CAVARERO

Among the many characters of Italo Calvino's novel *If on a Winter's Night, a Traveller*, we meet Irina, a woman with limbs "supple and restless, in a slow dance where it is not so much the rhythm that counts but the knotting and loosening of serpentine lines."[1] This image of the weaving serpent-like figure is not accidental. It appears often in the text, revealing the text's poetry. The knotting and loosening of the lines of narrative that connect and intersect without ever concluding, without ever combining into a single thread, allude explicitly to the original structure of this part-experimental novel constructed by Calvino as a series of incipit interruptions that arrest the reader but infinitely defer her toward other twists and turns. Nonetheless, in the pages in question, Calvino deals specifically with Irina's defining characteristics. The thread of his story (which alludes to the erotic relationship between Irina and two men) emphasizes the contrast between the moving tangle of shapes representing the female figure and the rigidity of the straight line attributable to the male characters, the two lovers that Irina attracts and dominates.

Irina is a militant, part of a growing "secret revolution that would transform the powers of bodies and sexes."[2] In the midst of revolutions that were sweeping through cities one winter, she is portrayed by Calvino to represent the tangle and flexibility of the serpent for reasons that the author is quick to render explicit. Indeed, one of her lovers explains, "The first article of faith of the cult that Irina had established [was] that we abandon the standard idea of verticality, of the straight line, the surviving ill-concealed male pride that had remained with us even when we accepted our condition as slaves to a woman who allowed no jealousies between us, no supremacies of any kind."³ Unfortunately, the reader is not told if the revolution of bodies and sexes in which Irina believes succeeded. It gets entangled with other lines of narrative, and the account is soon interrupted after this sincere admission of the conceit of vertical masculinity. Even in this brief treatment, though, the framework is clear, as well as extremely intriguing. In his sketch of sexual difference, Calvino introduces an intriguing postural geometry: man is represented as straight, while woman is gripped in a vortex of folds. As well as giving Irina the honor of providing a feminine principle for the narrative tangle in which the text takes pleasure, Calvino also assigns her the perhaps more original task of denouncing vertical masculinity and the misplaced pride that exhausts it; that is, she is given the task of loudly heralding a critique of rectitude. Rectitude is in fact the essential virtue of man: "rect" inasmuch as he is erect.

That the erect stance is characteristic of the human species is a point of fact, indeed, an indisputable fact, that positions the human animal in a space perceived to be oriented vertically. The vertical posture, coinciding with the line of gravity, produces a perception of space that makes the body "the absolute centre of direction: over, under, in front, behind and so on."⁴ In the mere fact of man's stance and upright walk there is already therefore an intrinsic geometry, a certain immediate and natural geometric configuration, organized according to dimensions, lines, places, topologies that define him in relation to the absolute direction of the vertical body. This is the case, naturally, for men and women, but, curiously, in the symbolic tradition, it comes to apply in a special way only to men. This is suggested by Calvino in the aforementioned pages and confirmed by Simone de Beauvoir in *The Second Sex* when she notes that

> a man is in his right by virtue of being a man, it is the woman who is in the wrong. In fact, just as for the ancients there was an absolute vertical that defined the oblique, there is an absolute human type that is masculine.⁵

This sentence, which names right and wrong, is, among other things, valuable for noting an evident but usually overlooked detail. In Latin *rectum* corresponds to the Greek *orthos*, denoting "correct," "right," from which originates a wide-reaching and complex semantic chain, from which, among other things, come the various words that in modern languages denote the functioning and force of law: *diritto, derecio, droit, right, Recht*. The same happens to the term that designates the virtue of upright man: Italian *rettitudine*; Spanish *rectitud*; French *rectitude*; English *righteousness*; German *Rechtschaffenheit*. In language, as in the symbolic, there is a vertical order, a geometry of vertically oriented sense, where the upright man and the "right" align themselves on the same perpendicular line. One could recount the story of this erection of the subject—evidently virile—in many ways.[6] For brevity, drawing on the imaginary of philosophy, it will be sufficient for our purposes here to probe two eminent philosophers, representing two diverse epochs but both of them crucial: Plato and Kant.

The myth of the cave that is at the center of Plato's *Republic* is perhaps one of the most noted passages in the history of philosophy. Imagine an underground cave, says Socrates, where men sit, from childhood "necks and legs fettered, able to see only in front of them, because their bonds prevent them from turning their heads," observing a sequence of shadows on the opposite wall (514a).[7] Theirs is an uncomfortable position, bent double, ignoble and base. Unable to turn their heads, they are prisoners of a complex mechanism of visual illusions. One of them, however, Socrates continues, frees himself from his shackles and, abandoning the humiliating posture that forced him to the ground, gets up. He stands at last. The first conquest of the freed captive is the erect stance. He appears literally as *Homo Erectus* in Plato's myth. Then he turns, discovers the trick of the shadows produced by strange puppet masters, masters of illusion, and runs toward the mouth of the cave. The road is steep, and the man grows tired. After all, this is the first time he has ever walked. His eyes in particular have suffered from the journey out of darkness into the light that penetrates far enough into the cave to dazzle him. His sight gradually adapts; as he leaves the entrance, he lowers his eyes. The liberated captive sees first the images of things reflected in the mirrored pools of water in the natural landscape that surrounds him; then, raising his eyes, he sees the things themselves. At last, raising his eyes further, erect in his whole body and with face upturned, he looks directly at the sun. His goal is achieved. We are at the culmination of the account. Stood firm, under the perfectly perpendicular shadow-free rays of midday, the philosopher at last turns his eyes to the sun and, recognizing it as the source and beginning of all that is visible, contemplates it without being blinded. The protagonist of our adventure has now become a philosopher, rather, *the* Platonic philosopher that contemplates the idea of the Good of which the sun is a metaphor.

In the development of the story, the erect stance conquered in the cave was only a proposition, a sort of premonition. Only when he had reached his goal, contemplating the Good, straightening himself along the axis of truth, does the new man—that is, the philosopher—become truly erect. Satisfied with his vertical posture, he would like to remain there forever "and refuse to go down again to the prisoners in the cave and share their labours and honours, whether they are of less worth or greater" (519d). But the story does not finish here. There is more. The philosopher, Socrates adds, turns and goes back down into the belly of the cave. Therein, with stinging eyes no longer accustomed to the cavemen's strange circus, he exhorts the prisoners as to the falsity of their visions and, unfortunately, frees them from their chains. They kill him. His return ends unhappily. The myth's conclusion is enigmatic: it would have been better for the philosopher if he had remained in the world above and not returned below. Better to remain forever erect on the noetic axis of truth. Light as a metaphor for truth, destined to grand fortunes not only in the ambit of philosophy, finds here one of its more celebrated expressions. Derrida calls this "the platonic heliotrope"—that is, the structural and functional element of the very construction of metaphysics.[8] The geometric system is clear: offspring and image of the Good, the sun, that is outside and on high, illuminates everything, vertically providing a system, and within it, the posture of the subject. Even if, for the *philosophus erectus* of the platonic myth, this perfect and definitive posture is realized through the glance directed at the sun, Socrates does not fail to note that "to him it would be easier to observe the celestial bodies and the heavens, at night, by the light of the stars and the moon, rather than, by day, the sun and the solar light" (516a–b). The passage is short and seems even to suggest that nocturnal contemplation of the starry sky is a useful passage for preparing one's eyes for the sight of the sun. Not forgetting, after all, that the formative education of the philosopher, illustrated in the *Republic*, also prescribed the study of astronomy. The culmination of this education was not, however, the observation of the firmaments, but the contemplation of the sun-Good, which—evoking a relation of transcendence that the interpreters never cease to interrogate—is symptomatically placed by Plato *epekeina tes ousias*, above and beyond being (509b).

Although the myth of the cave has a clear political meaning, it is by now accepted opinion that it describes the complete process the philosopher goes through—or, if you prefer, the man of whom the philosopher is now the archetype—to reach knowledge of the truth. In the vast critical literature on this theme, the position of Heidegger stands out significantly, particularly his *The Platonic Doctrine of Truth*, which, published in the early 1940s, was dedicated to a rereading of the myth. Heidegger's thesis is that the essential comprehension of truth (the Greek name of which *aletheia* or, better, *a-letheia*, Heidegger translates as "non-latency" and "un-veiling") undergoes a transformation with Plato. According to Heidegger, in the account of the cave *aletheia* loses its originary significance of "unveiling" and becomes instead *orthotes,* correctness, accuracy of the glance with respect to things. That is, it becomes epistemological rectitude as the essential foundation of the ethic of rectitude.

Curiously, the term *orthotes* is nowhere to be found in the text on the myth of the cave, and Plato rarely uses it elsewhere. There is, however, here and in many other places in the Platonic dialogues, the adjective *orthos* and its adverbial form, translatable as "right" and "straight" and of frequent use in Ancient Greek. Banal in everyday language, the word notoriously gives rise to the conceptual line, nothing short of sensational, that we have touched upon. From *orthos* originates the authoritative philosophical thread—notwithstanding theological, ethical, and juridical—that sharing with the Greek *orthos logos* and passing through the Latin *recta ratio,* or "right reason," supplies the technical vocabulary of that which (and not for nothing) we call *right, Recht, droit, derecho* or indicate as rectitude or moral righteousness. To this, one should add that already in Ancient Greek, as in modern languages, "right" tends to be synonymous with "just" and "correct."

Moreover, Greek etymological dictionaries teach that *orthos* and its lexical family are often used to indicate something straight that lifts itself up vertically, including in the obscene sense of "erection" as a "rightening" of the penis.[9] The same can be said of *euthus* with respect to the "ithyphallic." There is an element of virility in straightness and in rectitude. Maybe it is not by chance that the expression "righteous man" is common in the Italian language, while there is no female equivalent, and if there were, it would sound wrong. A virtuous woman, in Italian, is instead denoted by the term "honest."

The figure of the righteous-erect man, as a model of virtue, traverses the entire history of philosophy, assumes various forms, and in Kant found one of its most ardent supporters. Even Kant praises the rectitude of the subject and does so in a particularly original way. By this point in modernity the essential characteristic of the subject is autonomy: the righteous man, erect and correct, is the rational individual that rules over himself and finds within himself his moral law, which is, moreover, universal. Rectitude, with Kant, coincides perfectly with a verticality that, rather than rising up toward the truth or the Good or God, establishes and supports itself, in perfect equilibrium, balanced firmly on its proper axis. There is a famous phrase of Kant's in the closing pages of the *Critique of Practical Reason* that synthesizes this verticalized structure:

> Two things fill the mind with ever new and increasing admiration and reverence, the more frequently and persistently one's meditation

deals with them: *the starry sky above me and the moral law within me.*[10]

To elaborate, the spectacle of the starry sky above reveals to the individual that he is a simple point in the universe, an insignificant part of the sensible world. The moral law, the ethical imperative

> elevates infinitely my worth as that of an *intelligence* by my personality, in which the moral law reveals to me a life independent of animality and even of the entire world of sense.[11]

Each of the two worlds has its own verticality. The first, the physical world, on the axis that rises from the Earth to the sky, symptomatically conforms with the characteristics of the human's erect posture. The second coincides, however, with the autonomy of a free and rational being that, releasing himself from the world, flies off. Regarding the first verticality, it is worth underlining, with respect to Plato, that the referent of the *philosophus erectus* is no longer the sun but the nocturnal firmament. In this image, every transcendence of the principle or, if you prefer, every placing over there and above being, or in Kantian terms, every figurative evocation of heteronomy, is symptomatically avoided in order to best highlight the autonomy of the subject. Not forgetting that every modern doctrine on the free and autonomous individual, possessor of rights, which is at base the foundation of the modern democratic model, finds one of its most decisive sources in the philosophy of Kant. His description of civil society as functioning according to the individualist ontology is one example: "But once enclosed within a precinct like that of civil union," writes Kant, egotistical "inclinations have the most beneficial effect. In the same way, trees in a forest, by seeking to deprive each other of air and sunlight, compel each other to find these by upward growth, so that they grow beautiful and straight,—whereas those that put out branches at will, in freedom and in isolation from others grow stunted, bent and twisted."[12]

Foucault notes correctly that the Kantian era is one of straightening and rectifying: from pedagogy to military discipline, passing through medicine, orthopedics, and gymnastics, we find a series of technologies aimed at producing a postural rectitude, whether on the physical plane or that of ethics, politics, and society. The subject of these "rightening" verticalizations is decisively virile. And the aim of this straightening is to avoid, correct, and dominate the inclination that leads man to deviate from his vertical axis, poking his head out, twisting himself, distorting himself, overreaching himself, unbalancing himself. In terms of bodily posture, we find here the opposition between straight and crooked, and in terms of ethical juridical "posture," that of right and wrong. Founded on the vertical axis that functions as the norm, the geometric imaginary is common to both fields. Crucially, according to this imaginary, both "straight" and "right" find their antonyms in terms indicating either what is inclined and drooping or what is twisted (*tortuoso*) and wrong.[13]

On the topic of norms and normalization, it is perhaps worth remembering that wrong (*torto*) and twisted (*tortuoso*) come from the Latin *torquere*, a word that is also at the origin of the English word "queer." Of course, in the Anglophone world, *queer* has become a derogatory label for homosexuals as opposed to *straight*, which instead denotes the heterosexual and therefore "correct," normal orientation. The growing popularity, also in the academic sphere, of *queer studies*, dedicated to valorizing the field of queer sexuality and subjectivity, challenges precisely this normative and normalizing valorization of "straight." The challenge is strategically significant. Holding itself in balance on the straight line that serves as an axis and a norm, the vertical subject fears in fact every force that undermines its rectitude. And in the philosophical field, it fears above all the inclinations that unbalance the posture of the self.

This is keenly noted by Hannah Arendt in her essay "Some Question on Moral Philosophy": "Every inclination turns outwards, it leans out of the self."[14] When I incline myself, she adds, I cannot incline myself in isolation but must incline "towards that which is outside of me, objects or people."[15] Arendt's words have the benefit not only of reminding us that the significance of the word "inclination" refers again to a geometric imaginary, but also reiterate yet again that in the theatre of philosophy, at the center of the scene there is a self in a straight and vertical position. Not by chance, words such as "rectitude" and "uprightness" are invoked since the Middle Ages frequently in the dictionary of morality to "rectify" inclinations. Beginning with Plato, inclination is, for philosophy, a perpetual source of apprehension that is renewed in every era and that in modernity, with the arrival of the free and autonomous self celebrated by Kant, assumes a particular weight. The push of inclination tears the self away from its internal center of gravity and, making it lean outward "on objects and people," undermines its stability. Rather than a moral problem, in the modern conception of the self, what is at stake is the issue of a structural equilibrium and therefore, in the final analysis, an ontological question. An inclined ego leaned outward is no longer right—that is, it leans with respect to the vertical axis on which it stands and that renders it an autonomous and independent subject because it balances on itself. This explains why philosophers are obsessed with controlling and disciplining, to the extreme, to eliminate the inclinations. Kant, not by chance, uses the term "inclination" (*Neigung*) as a general category to denote desires, affections, and passions.

This is based, however, on an old story, already present in Plato and then inherited by all philosophical stories. Perilous for the stability of upright man, the inclination is synonymous with passion in general and the most dangerous and destabilizing passion in particular, which is, by near unanimous consent, that of the erotic. The philosophers, together with the moralists, fear in particular the impetuous and difficult to dominate inclinations that dwell in the turbulent realm of eros, where lust and other carnal pleasures intertwine. The common theme here, which allegedly stands out the most prominently, is the female propensity for lasciviousness. Contrary to that suggested by Calvino, in the postural geometry of the sexes, the feminine figure would not therefore consist of a tangle of serpentine lines but would rather cleave to the inclined line that slides toward lust. According to some, if observed from this angle, in the geometric imaginary relative to the virility of rectitude, inclination enters the scene as eminently female. Toward the middle of the nineteenth century Pierre Proudhon, a philosopher noted for his innovative and revolutionary ideas, wrote on this topic:

> To speak of sensual relations, it is a law of nature among all the animals that the female, lured by the reproductive instinct, and employing many means, seeks out the male. Woman does not escape this law. She has naturally more of a penchant for lasciviousness than man; first because her ego is weaker, and liberty and intelligence struggle less in her against her inclinations of animality, then because love is the great, especially singular occupation of her life, and in love, the ideal implies always the physical.[16]

Although this obviously stems from a mind imbued with misogyny, it contains intriguing elements.

Indulging a widely accepted theory, Proudhon sustains that love, with all its pathologies and excesses, is rooted substantially in the natural and animal phenomenon of sexual inclination, understood not as an orientation toward a determined sex but toward an instinct to have sex. He suggests, moreover, actually affirms, that such an instinct is subordinated in the woman, as in the female of other species, to the instinct of procreation and that therefore, in the final analysis, the erotic inclination and the maternal inclination spring, in her, from a selfsame instinctive core, as imperious and indomitable as nature. Obviously, if she were like the male of the human species, a free and rational being, capable of cultivating the virtue of rectitude, the woman would also be able to oppose herself to this domination, but, since nature has given her a weak ego, "liberty and intelligence struggle less in her against her inclinations of animality."[17]

The most interesting aspect of Proudhon's text is that not only do women become identified with the oblique line of inclination as counterposed to the virile verticality of rectitude, but, he argues, there is an explicit link in women between erotic inclination and maternal inclination. The woman is inclined to the destabilizing eros of lust because she wants to give birth to, and care for, children. That is to say, "by nature" the woman inclines twice, in two intertwined and overlapping ways: first she inclines toward a lover that impregnates her, and then she inclines toward the children to whom she gives birth. In philosophical terms, instinctually leaning toward inclination, the woman is never for herself, but always for the other, the lover or the children that attract her; they make her lean out of herself, and they impose on her as natural—typical and stereotypical—an inclined posture.

It is worth reiterating that there is obviously a stereotype, a sexist and misogynistic prejudice to all this. But it enables us to see clearly the two models of subjectivity, related to two geometries, two postural ethics. There is, according to a schematic mode, a vertical masculine subject, characterized by and for himself, and an inclined feminine subject, characterized by and for others. The iconography of maternal inclination never tires of portraying myriad versions, more or less stylized and edulcorated of a mama leaning lovingly over her child. Is this not, after all, proper, the archetypal image of care "for the other"?

The stereotypes—one could call them "frames of meaning" or, according to a certain feminist lexicon, "culturally constructed sexual identities"—are notoriously difficult to dismantle. The stereotype of maternal inclination, particularly if the self-sacrificing role is emphasized, is peculiarly so. All in all, between the aspects that recommend the maternal ethical paradigm as an alternative to that of virile rectitude, there is one, often obscured, feature that merits special attention. It is drawn from the scene of birth, and especially the ontological framework this scene presents to the philosophical tradition, which is usually distracted from the theatre of beginnings by its preoccupation with death. It is of course found in the work of Hannah Arendt, who, in speaking of natality as the fundamental condition of human existence, makes it coincide with "the naked fact of our original physical appearance."[18] Arendt emphasizes moreover that the human being is in the world, indeed, appears there, as being, in the initial stage, in the crucial inaugural moment of her appearance (which lasts, after all, for each of us, as long as our existence) constitutively exposed to the other. Furthermore, it is—in spite of Arendt's reticence on the topic—in the first place, exposed to the mother. As the stereotype of maternal inclination confirms, in the scene of birth, a mother and infant are necessary. Embodying the other in relation to the newborn over whom she leans, the mother not only confirms the relational character and anti-verticalism of the scene, but predisposes it to an altruistic ethic, requiring us to understand it in terms of dependency. It is worth noting that to advance a critique of rectitude, the principle problem is how to force the ego, proudly encapsulated in its verticality, to renounce its pretense of autonomy and independence. The newborn— the infant, the child—becomes in this way an ideal figure: for if put in confrontation with the primary roots of his existence, the natal condition, the transparent and self-referential subject of modernity falters and reveals its vanity. It is not by chance that this is traditionally the subject of ethics. Closed in its narcissism, on the moral level, and before that, the ontological level, the self of philosophical tradition neither exposes itself nor sticks out: it aims rather to render itself immune to the other mediating a gesture of self-foundation that pretends to not need the inclination of others. Denying this immunitary definition of the self,[19] the newborn, however, not only exposes himself totally and irremediably, but exhibits a congenital vulnerability as his constitution and condition. Already indebted to the other by his coming into the world and his ongoing existence there, through his vulnerability, he belongs to a scene in which he depends on her who, inclining herself and therefore leaning outside of herself, leans over him. Even more so when the self-sacrificing posture of the mother is emphasized, this figure keeps in check the vertical system in general and the verticalized subject in particular.

    Plato and Kant, as the major authors that drive the tangled path of Western philosophy toward the reinforcement of the verticalizing system, are paradigmatic of this point of view. As paradigmatic is the insistence, above all in modernity, on a self-sufficient and selfish model against which, in more recent times, after the fragmenting feat of the postmodern, emerges a model that is instead relational and altruistic. Distilled from the stereotypical framework that carries through the centuries, presented as a form of geometry perhaps not immediately naturalistic, but nonetheless realistic, maternal inclination helps precisely to explore this second model. As argued in *Inclinations,* Leonardo Da Vinci's painting of the mother and child (Virgin and Child with Saint Anne) offers an example to be strategically exploited in order to make inclination a good point of departure, a point from which we might rethink the ontology of

FIGURE 1. Leonardo Da Vinci, *The Virgin and Child with Saint Anne* (1503–19), on Poplar Wood, Louvre, Paris. Source: Wikimedia Commons.

the vulnerable and its constitutive relationality in the terms of a postural geometry that, far from placing the human on the straight axis, displaces it according to a multiplicity of contextual, contingent, intermittent, and at times even random directions. The maternal inclination, inasmuch as it is a posture linked to the scene of birth, can become the fundamental schematism, the founding gesture of a new postural geometry in which the subject not only leans on the other, but where mother and child are evidently in a relation of structural asymmetry. That does not mean, of course, that all the asymmetric relations indicated by this new geometry are simply recasting the radical unbalancing relation between mother and child, nor that all the postural variants are simple copies, more or less faithful to the inclined posture. Instead it signifies that in this relational ontology of the vulnerable as it is understood geometrically, the centrality of the vertical posture, so valued by the sovereign individual and by his dreams of autonomy, appears very unlikely. Schemes based on verticality and symmetry result here as an anomaly, and the idea of "a subject that shores itself up, seeks to reconstitute its imagined wholeness, but only at the price of denying its own vulnerability, its dependency, its exposure,"[20] results in a pathetic blunder.

## Notes

This essay was translated from the Italian by Clare Woodford, with sincere thanks to Olivia Guaraldo and Adriana Cavarero.

1. Italo Calvino, *If on a Winter's Night a Traveller*, trans. William Weaver (London: Vintage, 1998), 172–73.
2. Ibid., 171–72.
3. Ibid., 173.
4. Cf. Arnold Gehlen, *L'uomo: La sua natura e il suo posto nel mondo* (Milan-Udine: Mimesis, 2010), 318.
5. Simone de Beauvoir, *The Second Sex*, trans. Constance Borde and Sheila Maldvany-Chavallier (New York: Vintage and Random House, 2011), 25.
6. Developed more fully in Adriana Cavarero, *Inclinations: A Critique of Rectitude*, trans. Amanda Minervini and Adam Sitze (Stanford, Calif.: Stanford University Press, 2016).
7. All quotes taken from Plato, "Republic," in *Plato Complete Works*, ed. John M. Cooper, rev. ed. G. M. G. Grube, rev. trans. C. D. C. Reeve (Indianapolis and Cambridge: Hackett, 1997).
8. Jacques Derrida, "White Mythology: Metaphor in the Text of Philosophy," in *Margins of Philosophy*, trans. Alan Bass (Brighton: Harvester, 1982), 250–72.
9. See the entry for "voice," *orthos*, in Pierre Chantraine, *Dictionnaire étymologique de la langue greque: Histoire des mots* (Paris: Klinkseieck, 1984).
10. Immanuel Kant, *Critique of Practical Reason*, trans. Werner S. Pluhar (Indianapolis: Hackett, 2002), 203. Italics added.

11. Ibid., 203. Italics in original.

12. Kant, *Idea for a Universal History with a Cosmopolitan Purpose*, in *Political Writings*, trans. H. B. Nisbet (Cambridge: Cambridge University Press, 1970), 46.

13. Translator's note—*tortuoso* could also be translated as "crooked" or "winding," but "twisted" renders a moral implication too—of perversion.

14. Hannah Arendt, "Some Questions of Moral Philosophy," in *Responsibility and Judgment*, ed. Jerome Kohn (New York: Schocken, 2003), 81.

15. Ibid.

16. Pierre-Joseph Proudhon, Selections from "Pornocracy, or Women in Modern Times," *Cultural Critique* 100, nos. 44–64 (2018): 47.

17. Ibid.

18. Arendt, *The Human Condition* (Chicago: University of Chicago Press, 1998), 176.

19. For further reflection on this topic, see Roberto Esposito, *Immunitas: The Protection and Negation of Life*, trans. Z. Hanafi (Cambridge: Polity, 2011).

20. Judith Butler, *Precarious Life: The Power of Mourning and Violence* (New York and London: Verso, 2004), 41.

# Leaning Out, Caught in the Fall

*Interdependency and Ethics in Cavarero*

JUDITH BUTLER

Adriana Cavarero's postural ethics values inclination understood as what deviates from the straight and narrow path of philosophy and from its masculinist norms.[1] For Cavarero, geometrical models are important not only for understanding the masculinist presumptions that go along with the *Homo Erectus* that conventionally informs moral philosophy, but also the feminist or feminine deviation conventionally disparaged as unruly inclination in need of mastery and containment. For Cavarero, inclination is inclination toward another, a posture of desire and love and an implicit relation of care, characterized by a responsiveness to those who are dependent. In a way, the insistent verticality of the masculine norm, conflated with a moral norm, requires the inclined body it disparages. The body that leans or strains outside itself, offering or seeking support, always somewhat unbalanced, is presupposed by the upright body. For how did that upright body rise up and stand as it does? It was not born into the world a standing person, which means that the upright body is formed in dependency. In the beginning, no one stands. But the point can be more broadly generalized: even now, for those who can stand, or who sometimes stand (and not all of us can), no one stands on her own. We talk that way, for sure: "It is time for you to stand on your own!" or "Finally, I am out from under some form of dependency and can stand on my own two feet." The exhilaration of that self-standing is not to be underestimated. It is the "jubilant" moment in Lacan's mirror-stage. But I want to add to this formulation: all bodies from the start require support to stand on their own, if they are able to stand at all, and they never outgrow that requirement.

We may think that it is possible to distinguish between groups of people who require support to stand and those who do not, but disability studies has taught us to reflect upon the forms of support that everyone requires getting and staying vertical in a world. Of course, not everyone can stand, and all of us potentially can become a person who cannot stand. There are, of course, some who are too young to stand and some who are too old, and there are those who require technical supports to stand or to move. It should be of concern to all of us when supports for standing or moving are not always in place; when, for instance, public spaces are not accessible. But the more general point here is that for those who stand or for those who establish forms of uprightness without precisely standing, as many people in wheelchairs do, this is the result of an established domain of infrastructural support provided by public or private means, including machines and devices, chairs, crutches, and curb stops, technology in broader and narrower senses, platforms, pathways, sidewalks, elevators, lifts, roads, and floors. So this leads to a general point about the available figures we have for expressing self-sufficiency, for whether able-bodied or not, no one actually stands on their own. Standing can only figure self-sufficiency by eliding the infrastructural conditions of its very possibility. This means as well that the sort of standing that humans do is conditioned and formed by objects and material conditions that are constituent moments of standing upright as a human.

I would add here that this is a largely unpursued point implied by Lacan's well-known discussion of the mirror-stage, where the *"stade"* in *stade du miroir* draws on the notion of the theatrical stage or platform, operating as a minor proscenium. Feminist critics have rightly pointed out that it is probably a mother who stands behind the infant, propping him, and not, as Lacan claims, a *trotte-bébé*.[2] As important as that criticism has been for pointing out the elision of the maternal, it would be wrong to assume that a technical support simply substitutes for the mother, as has been widely argued, effacing her acts of care. After all, maternal care also requires technical and material supports, platforms, and ambulatory devices. And the infant, not yet able to stand or move on her own, is supported by humans whose genders span a spectrum and by technical instruments belonging to the infrastructure that lets the various postures of autonomy assume form and become part of the very form assumed. But parents of whatever gender are not simply supports, since they have to be supported to do the supporting they do. So even as a parent intervenes to stop a child from falling, someone has to intervene to stop the parents from falling as well. In other words, no human can be simply identified as support without in some sense requiring support as well.

If standing proves to be possible, it happens for no one without a practice that is repeated in time, an iterable negotiation of gravity and space. So though we speak about standing as a state, it is the body's form of rectilinear equilibrium achieved again and again through time, and never once and for all—that is a precarious bodily form. Falling is part of the practice of standing both as experience and potential, and learning how to fall—rather, learning that one sometimes *can* learn how to fall—usually comes late, if it comes at all; the primary absence of motor control never quite loses its grip on the human, no matter how adult and self-standing that creature may seem; losing balance and hoping that someone or something catches one in the fall is part of the constitutive anxiety of subject-formation, the potentially perilous incline at the heart of every upright figure. The upright figure, no matter how self-standing it claims to be, is implicitly in the process of warding off an infrastructural disaster, even when its proprioceptive orientation is working well. If it wishes to appear as radically self-standing, it can do this only by standing on something that permits or enables the very posture. Posture always indexes that dependency, that problem of the fall, that potential situation of no one or nothing checking the fall.

Cavarero wagers that we might find "two postural paradigms" that correlate to two distinct forms of subjectivity, two ways of negotiating autonomy, the first of which is individualistic and the second relational. And in some ways these two postural paradigms correlate with masculinist and feminist perspectives, respectively. I agree in the most enthusiastic way with her brilliant and precise efforts to expand upon the notion of a relational ontology in relation to Levinas and to the problem of care and to make more incisive and compelling existing criticisms of individualism. Frankly, there is no one upon whom I rely philosophically in the way that I rely on her. I am leaning on her all the time—no adequate number of footnotes can capture this form of reliance. I know no one whose work has such a mix of erudition, imagination, and precision and who makes these arguments as well as she does. Cavarero does not have to make the argument about the uniqueness of the person to me, since I know already the uniqueness of Cavarero. So let me mention three points on which I utterly concur:

1. The doctrine of individualism consistently elides and defers the understanding of our ethical relation to another. The claim that is made on me by others precedes the formation of the differentiated "I."

What Cavarero calls the "accusative me" is primary.³ I am called upon, and only then do I waken to the other, the other's life and so, at the same time, to the interdiction against taking that life. I will return to the profound politics of nonviolence that we find here toward the end of this essay.

2. Ethics is articulated through interdiction and prohibition, but the relation to the other, in a Levinasian vein, is not simply a matter of checking desire or aggression. One is born into a relation that is precontractual; it is involuntary, passionate, and susceptible and bound up from the start in what might be understood as a covenant, a form of ecstatic belonging that precedes any egological stance and whose ethical import has to be recovered and animated within an ethical and political culture that assumes the primacy of the ego. The prohibition against killing must be understood as a broader argument against violence. The problem of violence cannot be adequately posed or answered from within an egological framework. On this, there is profound agreement between us.

3. The first-person "I" has a relation to masculinity that is deftly exposed by Virginia Woolf and Cavarero's incisive reading.⁴ The first-person masculine tends to be bent on its own self-centering; it is, as it were, inclined toward itself and what we might call its rectitude. When women become figured as the repository for all inclination and inclination is deemed unruly and unmasterable, then the self-inclination that forms the reflexive structure of the "I" is elided, and that elision forms the basis of the idea of the subject as above all inclination. And when this particular allocation of inclination proceeds, we also find that women are never identified with forms of thinking, since forms of thought and embodied forms are meshed in the masculinist geometrical imaginary. If women do think, they are muddled, or they are figured as monstrous or masculine (or monstrously masculine), or beneath their reason it is assumed that they are driven by irrational passions and unbridled metonymy.

Perhaps my departure from Cavarero is already evident in the brief sketch with which I began this essay. I want to ask whether the inclining figure shadows forth in the upright figure such that the two are *not* radically distinct and never fully oppositional. It is not just that the upright figure can fall, and has surely fallen, started out on the ground, and that the inclining and caring figure seeks to catch the fall, but she sometimes finds herself falling as well. In fact, both figures of embodiment are confronted with problems of gravity and balance that require infrastructural support (if not public services). Further, to be upright at all means to have emerged from an inclination of some kind, a leaning out, a losing of balance, risking potentially disastrous encounter with unwilled gravity that can break a body, especially when no one or nothing is there to catch or hold the body, or when infrastructure, the provision of support, turns out to do the very damage from which one needs protection and repair.

So let us consider that for Cavarero, inclination is related to geometry, to the incline, but also to the body, to the differential allocation of rectilinearity and inclination to the masculine and feminine, respectively. But there is another dimension—namely, the relation of inclination to ethical relationality. Cavarero turns to Hannah Arendt's "Some Questions of Moral Philosophy" to illuminate the importance of inclination to moral dispositions. She cites Arendt: "Every inclination turns outward, it leans out of the self in the direction of whatever may affect me from the outside."[5] Here as elsewhere, Arendt offers Cavarero a chance to elaborate on the geometrical imaginary, one that is starkly counterposed to the image of the moral man who "conforms to a vertical axis." Over and against the free and autonomous moral man given to us in the philosophy of Kant, Cavarero, with Arendt, offers an alternative geometrical imaginary, where, as she puts it, "the thrust of inclination knocks the I from its internal center of gravity and, by making it lean to the outside, 'whether to objects or to people,' undermines its stability."[6] The moral *dispositif* figured by inclination destabilizes structural equilibrium. "An inclined I," she writes, "leaning toward the outside is no longer straight."[7] And when one falls in love, not only is there a felt sense that one's balance has come under attack, but one's center of gravity has moved over to the other: one is leaning, stretching, straining toward an other in such a way that gravity no longer holds. It is not that I am here and leaning over there. I become this leaning over there and no longer know how to find or keep my balance and frankly do not care. As Cavarero puts it, "In the case of 'falling in love' and other sweeping passions, inclination is not only a powerful force that pushes the self outside itself, but also an oblique plane on which the self slides without bannisters." "Inclination," she writes, "bends and dispossesses the 'I.'"[8]

There is something queer in this most compelling set of arguments, for the upright posture is from the start formed by a history of inclining and leaning out, enabling or disabling care, faltering and falling, a history that does not precisely come to an end, even for the most self-standing of the able-bodied among us. When uprightness serves as the geometrical imaginary for masculinist individualism, it does so precisely by forgetting or projecting that history of dependency, exposure, inclination, and falling. If and when it is projected outside, in another figure, then it is perhaps our task as readers to track the mechanism of that externalization and disavowal and to accept as a methodology that difference. After all, the difference is wrought through disavowal, and if we accept that difference as a point of departure, we cover over and continue that disavowal. So perhaps we might seek those traces of undoing in the figure of uprightness itself. Does it somewhere admit to its own impossibility, to the inclination that potentially floods its rectilinearity?

In her chapter entitled, "Kant and the Newborn," Cavarero seems to find in Kant's moral philosophy the exemplary modern instance of the ontology underwriting the "free, rational, and autonomous self," emphasizing the ways in which he disparages "*Neigung*" or inclination (also translated as "propensity").[9] She notes the way in which the life of the philosopher is distinguished both from the maternal act of caring and the infant in need of care. So one question I have is whether Kant turns out to be upright as he claims to be and whether this effort to externalize and disavow this sphere of dependency and passionate inclination comes back to haunt his position in a rather queer way.

Since Cavarero has launched us into a critique of rectitude, which includes a critique of straightness, I am wondering if I might then follow up on the queer aspect of her remarkable readings and suggest some directions based on this incisive and consequential book. She cites Lorenzo Bernini, who points out that "heterosexuality is traditionally associated with moral rectitude."[10] Many good jokes and some serious theory could follow, tracking the relation between, say, rectum and rectitude, both of which call upon some notion of what is right and straight. Can there be a bodily posture of rectitude without the rectum? If the upright posture requires—or implies—the rectum, then a certain form of inclination is presupposed by a form of rectitude built upon its denial. In other words, precisely what is required for rectitude is denied.

As is known, the term "queer" is now used in many ways. I am old enough, however, to remember that in English and in the United States, across several class contexts, it was a paralyzing insult, a stigma that did not simply hurt one's feelings at the time of being addressed, but constituted one as unaddressable, perhaps more of a stain than a stigma. As a young person, if you were called by that name, you became someone no one would talk to; it was an address that stopped all further address: you are someone who cannot be addressed; an interpellation that has to enact what it prohibits to take effect. The worst kinds of slurring are still addresses to someone, perhaps part social display (I am the one who has the power to confer stigmatization on this person, a speech act performed for others, present or imagined, but also an effort to exercise the power of interpellation: "You are what I say you are; my speech defines you"). At least in my neighborhood, not being regarded or interpellated as straight could get you beat up or ostracized, so straightness seemed to promise a protection from violence; that is, if you could walk that walk, or pass in some way, you would be left alone from that kind of harassment. Of course, interpellations of this kind missed their mark, and that missing is a queer feature of any act that seeks to constitute a subject in that way (a strange sort of subject-formation that has the social negation of the subject as its aim). It was odd to think that one could say "yes" to queer or to subject it to a chain of significations that exceeded and confounded the initial interpellation. Queer's resignification as a term of subversive pride occurred within social movements mainly organized to fight untreated HIV, emerging from and countering the confused shame of sexuality and fatal illness in the 1980s, but also to draw attention to the images and narratives that seemed to imply erasure or fatality. In *Epistemology of the Closet*, Eve Kosofsky Sedgwick also insisted that the oblique angle, the non-straight narrative trajectory, could be found right at the center of the most exemplary models of straightness. The straight line of heterosexual narrative could not stay straight; the swerve, the oblique angle, were both part of the very life of straightness and the potential for the undoing of its compulsory or normative character.

Kant, of course, is a strange example, since he is not only unmarried, as Cavarero reminds us, but widely regarded as a sexless creature whose main physical activity in life seemed to be that *peripatesis* around Königsberg. He seemed for the most part to walk without assistance, and yet in that city, an imperial center, there were streets and paths, and there was a state who quite explicitly sought to protect his vocation and his citizenship. He was free to walk in public, and he belonged to the public sphere in which he walked. If Kant's moral philosophy is the exemplary instance of modern rectitude, then we should look closely to see whether the emphatic verticality he is said to embody is really so straight after all.

There are two occasions that come to my mind when Kant writes about the loss of gravity and the problem of vertigo, both of which unsettle the upright posture. The first appears in his discussion of the sublime in the Third Critique. The second is from his book *The Conflict of the Faculties*, where he reflects upon the perilous consequences of walking and philosophizing at the same time. It seems that for Kant, the sublime is precisely that which inclines the mind toward the limits of its concepts. Kant writes that "the mind feels itself moved in the representation of the divine in nature, while in aesthetical judgments about the beautiful it is in restful contemplation."[11] He continues, "This movement may (especially in its beginnings) be compared with a vibration (*eine Erschütterung*), i.e. to a quickly alternating attraction toward, and repulsion from (*Abstossen und Anziehen*), the same object."[12] What is most overwhelming or passionate (*Das Uberschwengliche*) for the imagination, that toward which it is driven in the conception of the intuition, is "an abyss, in which it fears to lose itself."[13] It makes sense that the imagination might fall into such an abyss, since it is a sensuous way of knowing, and the sublime opens onto an infinity that exceeds and destroys sense itself. It cannot be that a body is simply wandering about that abyss intact; the abyss marks the limit of all bodily wandering, figuring the unknowable beyond. And it cannot be that the body falls into the abyss, but only that the body meets its limit there, and the abyss is precisely the unfathomable. For Kant, as is known, this feeling of the inadequacy of what imagination can offer to satisfy reason's demands is linked with a feeling of respect, of pain, of humility, but it is also said to be "a moral feeling."[14] Whatever that nonmathematical magnitude is that is called infinite is that for which no image or figure can suffice. This is one reason that the commandment Kant most favors, the one he calls "most sublime," is the one that communicates the interdiction against making "to thyself any graven image, nor the likeness of anything which is in heaven, or in the earth or under the earth."[15] No graven image of the most powerful, that which exceeds intuition, concept, and image. I point this out only to show that there is surely an inclination, something that drives the imagination toward this limit, and before which failure and pain are encountered, the occasion for humility. So whatever emerges in these discussions is not an all-powerful "I"; not the masculine form of the first person, but its wreckage in the face of a power it cannot fathom. Indeed, in the next section, Kant writes, it would appear that no feeling of the sublimity resides in our own nature, for sublimity is rather a form of "subjection (*Unterwerfung*), abasement (*Niedergeschlangenheit*), and a feeling of complete powerlessness, is a fitting state of mind in the presence of such an object"; the sublime that, of course, does not, strictly speaking, conform to the necessary conditions of an object. In Kant's word, it is the "abyss that threatens to overwhelm everything."[16]

Perhaps something similar is at work in the final section of *The Conflict of the Faculties*, published in 1798, six years before his death at the age of seventy-four.[17] There Kant writes on the distinction between the faculty of philosophy and the faculty of medicine in the form of a letter to a Professor Hufeland, who has written a treatise on the art of prolonging life. Kant's writing here is insistently autobiographical, preoccupied with various medical problems of his own, taking up gout, insomnia, and sporadic spasms that interrupt his reading and afflict his vision. For the most part he argues that firm moral resolution can alleviate physical suffering, and Cavarero's view is confirmed that for him neither women nor children are really capable of that virile form of self-determination. In one section entitled, "On Pathological Feelings That Come from Thinking at Unsuitable Times," he remarks that thinking is a scholar's food and that sometimes it is necessary to resolve "to go on a diet with regard to thinking."[18] For instance, according to Kant, one should not eat and think, since the double task will result in hypochondria. The other instance he provides is walking: if one thinks and walks at the same time, it can bring on vertigo (or *Schwindel*). The man who thinks philosophically while walking will become drained of energy. But why is he at risk of vertigo? Thinking seems to interrupt or weaken the mechanical operation of the feet. One has the sense of falling, or of losing orientation in space and time. One has, as it were, lifted oneself out of the parameters of space and time by thinking, started to move outside the body upon which one is relying for the walk itself. Oddly, one cannot easily stay upright and moving while one is thinking, which suggests that the thinking I works in another direction from the walking body.

Of course, in the case of the sublime, the power of the thinking I is made more powerful as it moves toward the thought of the nonmathematical sublime, that magnitude for which there is neither number nor image. The abyss that threatens self-loss—exerting its own push and pull—marks the limit of what the embodied thinker can know, but also the capacity of the embodied thinker to steady himself. The simultaneous action of walking and thinking indicates the need to depart from the mechanics of the body in order to begin philosophical thinking. In both cases, the possibility of a fall seems to be there alongside the act of thinking. A man can entertain himself with thoughts (engaging in a kind of imaginary variation of ideas), but he cannot think, since thinking pulls in another direction from where the feet are going. He loses balance, becomes dizzy, and cannot advance in any direction.

Kant here concedes the possibility of the undoing of the rectilinear subject. He cannot stand up straight all the time and must guard against the possibility of losing his balance and orientation. He comes up against the constraints of the body all the time, working with and against them. Toward the end of his letter, he remarks on the various involuntary processes that afflict his body and interrupt his thinking, and in the final note he remarks on the growing problem of losing his sight: "A certain brightness suddenly spreads over the page, confusing and mixing up all the letters until they are completely illegible."[19] At such a moment, his reliance on an able body for reading and writing is called into question, and though he tries in the face of the medical profession to assert the healing powers of moral self-determination, he becomes increasingly preoccupied with a body that is losing its sight, its upright posture, and whose coordinated movements are not to be assumed. He reflects on his own living and aging body, wondering at what point it no longer makes sense to live, calling himself "this candidate for death" who is tolerated among the living only because of the animal functions that one still performs.[20]

I do not mean to defend Kant against the many criticisms of his moral theory and his presumptions of moral autonomy, but rather to show that he is not quite the exemplar of individual moral autonomy for whom the vertical and able body is taken for granted. Further, he is hardly above inclination, especially at those moments in which he is pushed and pulled in relation to the sublime and its threatening void. He is, in fact, almost falling, time and again, into a bottomless void, a figure for radical groundlessness. As much as he proffers a morality based on radical autonomy, he also offers, at least in the Third Critique, a way of thinking about the *sensus communis* that could also be understood as non-egological, the basis of an impersonal and shared sense of judgment—a judgment produced in the course of its communicability—the one that Arendt herself found most important for trying to think about morality under dictatorship. This form of judgment seems tenuously connected with moral autonomy, understood as the prerogative of a distinct and arelational "I." It would be interesting to know how Cavarero accounts for Arendt's turn to Kant for her own moral reflections; not so much the categorical imperative, but the Third Critique, to think about forms of judgment that have to be made under historical conditions that are in no way presupposed by existing legal convention. But I will leave that question open. Here are some others, and then finally I will return to the topic that con cerns us perhaps most urgently, the argument for nonviolence outside of egological terms.

To do that, however, we have to return to moral philosophy, and it is here that the notion of inclination proves central. As much as moral philosophy emerges in part from an inclination that departs from the model of rectitude, I am wondering whether geometry and morality are also presumed to relate to one another. Indeed, I find myself wondering whether there might not be a Pythagorean presupposition in Cavarero's *Inclinations*. Can the spatial character of geometry account for the temporal dimension of inclination? What happens when inclination takes narrative form, or when it occurs within the breaks and departures from narrative coherence? Are bodily inclinations like the incline of a geometrical plane? At what point, if any, does the parallel between somatics and geometry break down?

Contemporary moral philosophy, informed partially by psychoanalysis, surely asks us to distinguish between what our inclinations might be and what acts we perform. A subject might have an inclination to undertake an act, but the body may not express that inclination. So it is one thing for a subject to have an inclination or to be disposed in a certain way and quite another for a body to manifest that inclination by bending or leaning. It is also possible to bend or lean without having an inclination to do so, especially if one is forced to bow or is involuntarily pushed against a barrier. Inclination can be closer to a predisposition than to a disposition, distinct from an embodied posture or movement, although, yes, sometimes an inclination that is felt is also embodied in a lean or a stretch or a reach. It is only in the last of these cases that it makes sense to understand morality as following from inclination.

So perhaps it serves us to distinguish among a predisposition, a disposition, an inclination, and a bodily movement or posture. Indeed, it becomes important to make such distinctions and not presume their immediate overlap when, for instance, we are inclined to move or act in a certain way but also restrain ourselves from giving bodily form to that inclination. That seems most emphatically to be the case in relation to inclinations of destructiveness that translate into physical acts of destruction. Ethically considered, the gap between the inclination and the embodied action remains an important one, for we may find ourselves wishing to destroy others or ourselves and constraining ourselves from doing so, at which point the inclination remains unacted and, thus, morally neutralized. If there were no difference between an inclination to act and the act that embodies the inclination, then we would have no choice but to act on inclinations, even those that are most destructive. But the fact is, we have a choice, even if it is a hard one, even if it does not feel like a choice, and the moral task is to engage in a process of working-through rather than acting out.[21]

Cavarero directs our attention time and again to the relation of care that is figured between mother and child, counter-posing this figure to the erect, self-sufficient, and thinking man, the consummately uncaring figure. Rectitude implies the loss of care; care implies inclination and the defeat of rectitude. She is careful not to assume that all women are mothers, or that they are all by nature *caring*; nor does she indict men for all being figures of rectitude. She is dealing with generalizations that do not always fit the instance. So it makes no sense to find examples of uncaring mothers and caring fathers, since all that is surely possible without the dominant norms becoming fully dislodged from their place. The larger problem seems to be the hegemonic rule of egology and the assumption that the self is arelational and that its drive toward self-preservation licenses the violence it unleashes in the name of defending or continuing its own life. Does violence emerge precisely when the ego takes precedence over the relational? If by ego, we mean not only an egocentric position, but a desire to preserve and enhance the self, considered as the ontological basis of politics, then perhaps the moral status of self-preservation has to be subject to a critical reconsideration. I have always thought that self-preservation is overrated as a moral ideal. Cavarero goes further, arguing explicitly for both a version of altruism and of pacifism. I cannot do justice to the fine turns of her argument in the closing chapter of *Inclinations*, but they involve a rich discussion that (a) counters Hobbes with Levinas and then (b) qualifies Levinas with Arendt.[22]

There she writes of Levinas, "In the 'face-to face' encounter ... there is no longer an I characterized by the *conatus essendi*, a selfish and possessive I, but an I, a *me*, that already has been dispossessed by the 'thou shalt not kill' that is expressed by the face of the other; which precisely constitutes me through this 'thou.'"[23] Are we to assume, with Hobbes, that violence follows from the ontology of the possessive and selfish "I" and that it is then prohibited through a binding insight into a primary dispossession in and through ethical relationality?[24] Cavarero's position in *Inclinations* condenses part of her contribution to the coauthored volume *Thou Shalt Not Kill: A Political and Theological Dialogue*, recently published by Fordham University Press.[25] And we should not underestimate the contribution that egologically based politics make to violence, but what about the contributions of group psychology that tends to dissolve the ego into group formations, including fascist and nationalist ones? Speaking of Freud, what about the death drive, which seeks to destroy the individual life as fiercely as the life of the other? Indeed, something of that drive may well be at work in the Kantian sublime, showing how the figure of the erect, masculine, and independent individual is wrecked from within precisely by inclinations, or drives, that run counter to self-preservation and set us on a circuitous or quick route toward death. In other words, what if we include among those inclinations most morally salient those tendencies or propensities that ward off destruction and self-destruction alike? What difference would that make to the oppositional framework that pins Hobbes against Levinas? For Hobbes, it is unrestrained self-preservation that leads to violence; but for Freud, self-preservation cannot account for those forms of violence that yield no pleasure and know no end, repetitive, deteriorating, and potentially fatal to both the ego and the world.

So if we are to take seriously the commandment not to kill, we would have to take account of those forms of destructiveness that take aim both at individuation and the social bond. Cavarero is surely right that we cannot understand what it would be to obey that commandment, or live within its terms, without a sense of the relational ontology that the commandment articulates. The commandment links this life with another life that it is obligated not to kill, the preservation of which is obligatory. It not only prohibits murderous action but articulates a relation that must be preserved. Moreover, the interdiction establishes that relation as prior to the ego. Can it establish that relation as prior to the death drive? Or does the prospect of that form of destructiveness imply an ongoing struggle and an ethical imperative to work through such inclinations so that they do not emerge as acts? If the commandment articulates a covenant, which is more primary and nonvolitional than any contract, could it be understood as a form of ethical community (borrowing from Hegel) or relational ontology that is always negotiating the destructive powers of egology and the death drive? If we accept that destructiveness is among the inclinations that can and do assume bodily form, what challenge does that possibility pose to the commandment not to kill? We may be tempted to think that restraining destructive inclinations requires a consolidation of the "I," strengthening the ego, or subjecting the ego to the superego, but following Cavarero leads to another perspective, one that Freud could not fathom in the 1930s as he registered the rise of European fascism. It was perhaps in the communities of resistance that one could see most clearly how leaning, reaching out, and affirming invariable dependency could lead to a form of community that sought to establish the conditions of survival against a violent onslaught.

For Cavarero, the priority of the ethical relation cannot be adequately captured by the discourse on dependency, and I see why she makes this claim. The susceptibility to the ethical claim made upon me is not the same as the dependency or vulnerability I may feel as an infant in relation to those who offer, or fail to offer, what sustains me. And yet, interpreting the covenant as interdependency allows us to understand that to take another life is at once to attack the life that is mine, and in several senses. First, the other life is bound up with my own, since lives are defined from the start by their interdependency. From the start, they do not steady themselves: they lean into a body, a structure, that facilitates the way to uprightness. What I "am" is this dependency on a "you," he, and they, which means that specific to my singular ontology is this social tie of dependency on other living beings (one could rethink Levi-Strauss's influential discussion of the kinship defining power of pronouns along these lines). So the I may burrow inside the self to find what defines it essentially only to find that it is defined essentially by the social relations in which it is constituted and that articulate interdependency.

This is another way of qualifying Levinas through a return to natality, one that borrows more from Freud than Arendt: for if none of us ever fully outgrows dependency, then we can dispute the scheme according to which we are dependent only in childhood and then assume independence in adulthood. As anyone familiar with psychotherapy can tell you, childhood stays with us, and dependency is never fully surmounted. That dependency is not restricted by socially dyadic forms but extends to systems of food distribution, the politics of housing, ecological politics, and global health care. Further, I may calculate that my life is separate from the other life by virtue of the bounded character of my body, its finitude, and its singularity. But the body is, as Cavarero has argued, always exposed and so defined from the start by its susceptibility and vulnerability. I am exposed to an obligation, but am I not exposed as a living creature, one whose life is bound up with dependency? The boundaries of the body are exposed to a world in such a way that they do not mark off my singular and separate existence; what I call that "singularity" is in fact sustained by various social relations and infrastructural conditions, by the environment, shelter, food, by modes by which life itself is coproduced with agents both human and technical. So there is no sustaining of singularity outside the context of constitutive sociality and ecology. And by listing sociality and ecology in that way, I do not mean to separate them absolutely as separate spheres, since the social is embedded in the ecological at the same time that the ecological is defined by the social. So when we speak about my life or your life, we are already, with the term "life," naming a connection that can be variably sustained or ruptured, which means that the "I" is, prior to its individuated state, even prior to the possibility of self-reference, a living creature, which means that its ties to creaturely life and to living processes precede and condition its individuation and continue to sustain and limit the claims of individuation itself.

So if we turn to the question of nonviolence, how would such a framework change our way of thinking and acting? We agree that it will not be only a question of a vigilant ego (or superego) imposing restraints on itself but a radical rethinking of the vigilant ego and its superegoic accompaniment in light of a version of ethical life conceived as ethical relationality: whether or not that ethical relationality is a living interdependency is a question we have yet to pursue.

According to Cavarero, the absolute prohibition against violence in Levinas implies an opposition to all forms of war and empire. Significantly, no already existing "I" receives this commandment. The summons inaugurates the "I" into a primary relation to the commandment, such that whatever the "I" might be is understood only in terms of that binding ethical relation. The task is not to love one's neighbor as one loves oneself if that means that self-love becomes the model for loving the other. For Levinas, the commandment implies a departure from all narcissism or the destitution of the subject. But if aggression does not only emerge from a drive for survival, but can take form precisely as an attack on survival—of the ego and the other—how then do we rethink pacifism? This was the substance of Freud's rejoinder to Einstein, since the death drive and human destructiveness more generally now take aim at the conditions of survival, offering up a fatal destitution of the subject of precisely the kind that Levinas rightly rejects.[26]

I propose to conclude with this suggestion: the postulation of a primary interdependency prior to the process of individuation would seem to coincide with this notion of an "I" that is from the start outside itself in its constitutive social relations. It is living, but that life does not yet belong to the life of the ego. It is bound up with others, sometimes intolerably so, and aggression is there, if we accept Melanie Klein, at the outset. This is clearly different from what Levinas means by a primary ethical relation, and Cavarero is right to caution us against the conflation of the one with the other. And yet, the ethical obligation not to kill seems to follow from both perspectives. Am I bound to you from dependency? Or I am bound to you by a summons into covenant predicated upon and articulated through the commandment not to kill? Do these overlap? What follows if we affirm that those bonds of interdependency are not only primary but ambivalent ones, that aggression can emerge in the midst of intolerable forms of dependency, and that the death drive can operate in a way that seeks not only to break relational bonds but the claims of the ego as well? This threat to life emerges with the onset of life, so a living politics might obligate us not only to affirm interdependency but to struggle with—and work through—the aggression that emerges from the fact that we do not stand on our own and never have. Or the maternal aggression that emerges as she gazes down at that infant, threatening or even extinguishing the life of the child.

We have yet to fathom the implications of such forms of destruction to the task of politics, but perhaps it will make a difference to remember that Dr. Martin Luther King Jr. argued in his famous "Letter from Birmingham Jail" that interdependency serves as the condition of nonviolence. "It really boils down to this: that all life is interrelated. We are all caught in an inescapable network of mutuality, tied into a single garment of destiny. Whatever affects one directly, affects all indirectly. We are made to live together because of the interrelated structure of reality. Did you ever stop to think that you can't leave for your job in the morning without being dependent on most of the world? You get up in the morning and go to the bathroom and reach over for the sponge, and that's handed to you by a Pacific islander. You reach for a bar of soap, and that's given to you at the hands of a Frenchman. And then you go into the kitchen to drink your coffee for the morning, and that's poured into your cup by a South American. And maybe you want tea: that's poured into your cup by a Chinese. Or maybe you're desirous of having cocoa for breakfast, and that's poured into your cup by a West African. And then you reach over for your toast, and that's given to you at the hands of an English-speaking farmer, not to mention the baker. And before you finish eating breakfast in the morning, you've depended on more than half of the world. This is the way our universe is structured, this is its interrelated quality. We aren't going to have peace on earth until we recognize this basic fact of the interrelated structure of all reality."[27]

Of course, Dr. King's description relies on a certain version of the global division of labor, and we might question how the division of labor comes to inform his concept of interdependency. Is he assuming, for instance, a capitalist mode of production? That still leaves the more worrisome problem—namely, that people can make this very recognition of interdependency and rail against it, seeking the dissolution of global interdependency in favor of renewed nationalism or explicit racism. The obligations of cohabitation follow from the fact that we produce the conditions of/for each other's life. We cannot want our own lives without wanting other lives to live, nor can we destroy the one without destroying the other. The form that concerted action must take is one that can recognize and work through the aggression in and against interdependency, the ambivalence that informs and imperils all social bonds, including those that sanction our ethical conduct. The task is to find those public ways of continuing to work through those forms of ambivalence. The task would not be to resolve them into false harmonies, but to engage the struggle without which it is not possible to honor the obligations of cohabitation among those who sometimes wish each other dead. Luckily, that destructive inclination does not always take form as an action but can be the part of our shared condition on which we can work, with which we are obligated to struggle, guided by inclination toward a different future—leaning out, working through, catching the fall and being caught in time.

## Notes

1. See Adriana Cavarero, "Scenes of Inclination," in this volume, and Cavarero, *Inclinations: A Critique of Rectitude*, trans. Amanda Minervini and Adam Sitze (Stanford, Calif.: Stanford University Press, 2016).
2. Jane Gallop, *Reading Lacan* (Ithaca, N.Y.: Cornell University Press, 1985), 85.
3. Cavarero, *Inclinations*, 155.
4. Cavarero, *Inclinations*, 35–44.
5. Hannah Arendt, "Some Questions of Moral Philosophy," in *Responsibility and Judgment*, ed. Jerome Kohn (New York: Schocken, 2003), 6.
6. Cavarero, *Inclinations*, 6. My slightly altered translation of Arendt.
7. Ibid., 6.
8. Ibid., 7.
9. Ibid., 25, 27.
10. Lorenzo Bernini, *Queer Apocalypses* (Berlin: Springer-Verlag, 2017), 3.
11. Immanuel Kant, *Critique of Judgment*, trans. J. H. Bernard (London: MacMillan, 1951).
12. Ibid.
13. Ibid. (G156, E97).
14. Ibid. (106).
15. Ibid. (29).
16. Ibid. (E111).
17. Kant, *The Conflict of the Faculties*, trans. Mary J. Gregor (1979; Lincoln and London: University of Nebraska Press, 1992).
18. Ibid., 199.
19. Ibid., 211.
20. Ibid., 209.
21. Sigmund Freud, "Recollection, Repetition, and Working Through," in *The Complete Psychological Words of Sigmund Freud*, standard ed. (London: Hogarth, 1974), 12:147–56.
22. Cavarero, *Inclinations*, 133–75. Whole dissertations could, and should, emerge from the final chapter and the coda of this remarkable text.
23. Ibid., 163.
24. Emmanuel Levinas, "The Face," in *Ethics and Infinity*, trans. Richard A. Cohen (Pittsburgh: Duquesne University Press), 87.
25. Cavarero and Angelo Scola, *Thou Shalt Not Kill: A Political and Theological Dialogue*, trans. Margaret Adams Groesbeck and Adam Sitze (New York: Fordham University Press, 2015).
26. "Why War? An Exchange of Letters Between Freud and Einstein," accessed August 7, 2019, https://www.transcend.org/tms/wp-content/uploads/2017/06/Why-War-Freud.pdf.
27. Martin Luther King, "Letter from Birmingham Jail," Martin Luther King, Jr. Research and Education Institute, Stanford University, https://kinginstitute.stanford.edu/king-papers/documents/letter-birmingham-jail.

# How to Do Things with Inclination

## Antigones, with Cavarero

BONNIE HONIG

> All true radicalism has to begin in the body.
> —SAMUEL DELANEY, "RADICALISM BEGINS IN THE BODY"

As developed by Adriana Cavarero, "inclination" is the posture of maternity, altruism, heterotopia. This postural perspective is enormously useful for theorizing ethics and politics. But, I argue here, inclination should be turned to sorority, agonism, and heterotopia on behalf of a more egalitarian and contestatory politics of inclination.

Indeed, this essay builds on Cavarero's account to propose an "agonistic inclination." The reasoning for the move is generated by looking at "how to do things with inclination" (in the spirit of J. L. Austin).[1] Through inclination-centered readings of Greek tragedy and myth, I suggest that inclination is part of a politics of refusal that may, therefore, encounter or engage in violence, which Cavarero disallows. In the examples that follow, I confront Cavarero's aspiration to a feminist ethics of nonviolence with what I take to be the inescapable violence of politics. This is not to promote or favor violence but to chart its workings and prepare to meet it.

I begin by briefly summarizing the argument of Cavarero's book. I then test it out in relation to the *Bacchae*, the *Antigone*, and the myth of Oedipus's encounter with the Sphinx.[2] Most of these Cavarero has treated elsewhere, but not in *Inclinations: A Critique of Rectitude*, the book that is the focus here. And the perspective of inclination makes them new again. I illustrate the usefulness of the concept or perspective of inclination for these texts and materials, noting the bacchants' inclined enjoyment of heterotopia on Cithaeron in Euripides's *Bacchae*; Antigone's altruism toward and her loving agons with her sister, Ismene; Oedipus's encounter with the Sphinx, whose real lesson, in my view, is the precarity of erectness;

and, crucially, one of Cavarero's own examples in *Inclinations*: Leonardo's *Madonna*, which I read as a *Bacchae* image, finding the Greek that shadows the Christian. The resonance of that rich Renaissance image with the ancient *Bacchae*, I argue, turns the *Madonna* from a scene of pacifist maternity to one of sororal agonism (a point explored in a complementary way in this volume's "Queer Madonnas," by Clare Woodford).[3] That resonance opens up still further interpretative approaches to Leonardo's painting than Cavarero provides and demands that we take maternal ambivalence (and the filicide that is sometimes its dramatic expression) seriously as an aspect of—and not alternative to—the care that Cavarero wants to promote for her ethics. Care, that is to say, may be more agonistic, even more violent, than Cavarero allows.[4]

Finally, I will assess the attractions and limitations of heterotopia, specifically Cavarero's idea that inclination can ground a heterotopian ethics or politics *apart from* rectitude, independent of the dominant verticalist regime or episteme of ethics and politics. Setting inclination apart is Cavarero's acknowledgment of its vulnerability to its rival and expresses her longtime commitment to this condition of feminist flourishing. However, the risk of separatism is that it insulates inclination from the agonism it needs to empower it against rectitude and to secure room for alternatives where hegemony wants to deny them.

## Postures of Refusal

One great merit of Cavarero's critique of rectitude is that it calls philosophical and political attention to posture, as such. Cavarero contrasts the erect or vertical posture of patriarchy to the inclined posture or inclination of maternity, claiming each one represents a distinct normative ontology.

Although the vertical is often associated with *refusal*—think of the iconic raised revolutionary fist, for example—Cavarero associates the *vertical* with what she wants to *refuse*: philosophy and its masculinist ideal of autonomy. She turns to inclination to underwrite an alternative, perhaps even a subversive, ethics of altruism. And she identifies that altruism specifically with maternity.[5] Inclination is the posture of altruism and maternity, the gesture of care.

Cavarero argues that Plato, Kant, and others in philosophy's canon figure philosophical wisdom in verticalist terms, treating honorifically terms like rigor, affiliated with *standing* at attention, being upright, and not bent over. In Plato's cave, in the *Republic*, the first to escape bewitchment by the shadows and to perceive the true Ideas in their stead is the first to stand up straight and tall. In Kant, the starry night sky is contemplated by the erect moral subject (although see in this volume the chapters by Butler and Battersby for a more relational depiction of Kant as himself inclined).[6] In philosophy, art, and literature, generally, Cavarero argues, *inclination* is gendered feminine and is deprivileged by the upright ethos of erectness, which connotes rectitude, responsibility, and rightness. Care, specifically maternal care, is Cavarero's preferred response to rectitude, her refusal of the hegemony of Philosophy's upright ethos.

We may compare Cavarero's caring bodies of inclination to Deleuze and Guattari's *body without organs*, the BwO, which is, in effect, Deleuze and Guattari's own critique of *verticality*. Their aim is to open the body to pleasures that are prohibited to it by its current organization as a body with organs (an erect body with an inside and an outside, whose outside protects the inside, whose inside is never inhabited; sometimes this body is called Oedipal). Their project is arguably radically inclinational. For them, the refusal of rectitude must go all the way down, even to refusing our habituation to thinking of our bodies as having insides and outsides. Deleuze and Guattari suggest trying to "walk on your head, sing with your sinuses, see through your skin, breathe with your belly."[7] To do all this is to render the Oedipal body inoperative, to open up to new pleasures, new becomings, new postures, or (as Jacques Rancière would say) new partitions of the sensible.[8] In Deleuze and Guattari, the BwO's inclination acts as a kind of inoperativity with the potentially radical power, not just to offer an alternative to verticalism, but to undo it entirely.[9]

Giorgio Agamben's version of inoperativity also features an inoperative body, but his iconic Christian version—the "Glorious Body," which is the body of Jesus postmortem—becomes an aesthetic object for contemplation rather than an organism of appetites and desires, something quite different from the BwO.[10] Agamben sees in the Christian Glorious Body an instance of what he looks for everywhere: a refusal of use by way of an aestheticized ethics. Since we now live in societies in thrall to use—profit, efficiency, productivity—Agamben believes the refusal of use must reach for things cloaked in aesthetic or sacred concepts, like glory and beauty, where they have been kept safe from instrumentalization. We may see the Glorious Body as Agamben's reworking of Deleuze and Guattari's Dionysian figure of re-sorted and non-instrumental pleasures. But his Glorious Body turns their body without organs into a body without *functioning* organs. And the nonpurposive purpose of the Glorious Body is not to experience new pleasures but to exhibit the perfection of God's creation. In their disused state, the organs' perfection can be apprehended.[11]

Cavarero turns by contrast to the living Jesus, the natal child at play in the company of mother(s). Where Cavarero's inclination valuably intensifies our sense of embodiment, inoperativity as Agamben thinks of it is, curiously, both attentive to the body and quite unbothered by it: unencumbered by the body's needs, demands, and pleasures.

Thus Cavarero does not opt for *inoperativity*. She reaches, rather, for *inclination* because her feminist project aims to *decenter* the vertical, not neutralize or transcend it, exactly. Her aim is to intensify the body, not abandon it, to sexuate the subject, not distill it into desubjectified sensations or objectify it for aesthetic contemplation. She seeks not to undo normativity on behalf of something that is not-yet, but, rather, to reorient normativity toward worldly care and altruism.[12] In this, she works in Hannah Arendt's tradition of world-care, even if *Inclinations* moves from Arendt's famous focus on natality (Arendt cites the glad tidings—"a child has been born to us") to maternity (though Arendt's "to us" might position us all as mothers, too).

Inoperativity may seem more agonistic than Cavarero's inclination because inoperativity does not seek to add to the existing array of postures in the ethicopolitical mix, but rather to neutralize the governing terms of ethics and politics. This way of putting it, however, begs the question of inclination's relationship to change and conflict. What happens when we add to the governing terms, geometries, or choreographies of ethics and politics a new (or previously denigrated) posture like inclination? Postural alterations or interruptions, introduced by Cavarero, might ultimately have neutralizing effects, generate heterotopian rehearsals, or produce agonistic conflicts. Cavarero says she is proposing "an imaginary *completely apart* from geometric verticalism." She locates inclination in some sort of heterotopia.[13] But this does not mean conflict is successfully avoided. After all, even outside the city on Cithaeron, as we shall see, Euripides's inclining bacchants are intruded upon: they attack the intruders to protect themselves from the male gaze.

The painting Cavarero takes to exemplify her ideal, a depiction of the Madonna with her own mother and child, situates the trio out on an isolated, even unworldly, plateau: a heterotopia. In the painting, known as "*The Virgin and Child with Saint Anne*" or "*St. Anne with Two Others*," the mothers incline, each to her own child, Anne to Mary and Mary to Jesus, though possibly perhaps to the lamb. Here is one of Cavarero's key claims about the painting: "Right at the heart of the self-sacrificing stereotype [that is, the patriarchal view of maternity], right there where patriarchalism seems once again to triumph," we find in the women's "enigmatic smiles," "the imaginary resources for pacifism," there, "in the face of the mother inclined over her child."¹⁴ Cavarero's point is this: The posture of inclination, though mistakable for subservience, is not that. Recall Hegel's claim that the lamenting Antigone is the *eternal irony of the community*. Antigone seems only to lament, but she brings down a king. Similarly, for Cavarero, we might say, Leonardo's Madonna is the *eternal irony of the community*: enigmatically caring, but not subservient, and possibly possessed of some radical powers.¹⁵ Could she, too, bring down a king?

We have seen how Cavarero's inclination is a refusal of rectitude in Philosophy, exposing rectitude as Philosophy's unthought corporealization. But her embrace of inclination is also, in a way, a refusal of the iconography of refusal as such. And this is one of many reasons it is interesting to think with her. As noted earlier, refusal is often depicted, figured, or performed in hard, verticalist terms that mirror or mime what it opposes, as for example in Cocteau's iconic rendering of Antigone and Creon or in Sara Ahmed's example of the Grimm Brothers's story "The Willful Child," featuring a girl with a willful arm, unbending, even after death.¹⁶ In the horrible Grimm Brothers fable, the mother is brought to the graveyard with a rod to beat the girl's arm, postmortem, until it is finally withdrawn, underground—not exactly the sort of mother envisioned by Cavarero. Such stiff-armed refusal sometimes wins, sometimes loses, but always risks reproducing that which it opposes: in the Grimm Brothers's story, the girl's stiff arm *mirrors* the rigid rod she opposes to extend her existential battle postmortem.

Cavarero offers another way. She invites us both to see inclination as refusal and to stage our refusals inclinationally—not vertically—in order to escape dead-end oppositionality while also rejecting the abstentions, aestheticisms, and transcendences of inoperativity. I take up her invitations here while arguing that they lead us not to maternity but sorority and not to pacifism but to agonism.

## An Inclination Reading of the *Bacchae*

Inclination, Cavarero notes, is etymologically connected to the Greek *klinē*, which means "bed" or "couch."¹⁷ In Euripides's *Bacchae*, such inclination is precisely what is at stake. Women scandalously enjoy daytime *klinē*, but their audacity is not granted the status of refusal, though the women do refuse the king's orders and the city's norms, as well. Thebes' king, Pentheus, orders the women back to their looms and their household responsibilities, but the women refuse to return to work and insist on their right to incline. Their abolitionism is evident in the collapse of the walls of the prison to which Pentheus seeks to confine the women. The women then escape from the city to a heterotopia on Cithaeron, where they worship and incline in ways that Pentheus can only (wrongly) imagine. Later, the women will return to the city hoping to transform it with their new skills and powers.

Pentheus himself feels the call of inclination, and, lured by Dionysus, the king hides to spy on the women outside the city. He does not want to wonder what they are up to; he wants to see for himself, and, in a ruse that will ultimately be his undoing, Dionysus helps Pentheus, disguises him, and puts him onto a treetop, promising a great view. This very verticality is an offense against Dionysus's women worshippers, as is the king's illicit watching of mysteries he wants only to see and not experience or suffer.

Three of the women below him are sisters. One, Agave, is his mother, and two are Pentheus's aunts, Ino and Autonoe. They and the other bacchants join forces and all together force Pentheus's tree into an incline: they pluck Pentheus from the top, dethroning and then dismembering him.

His body parts are flung far and wide by the women, who do not seem to hear his cries and certainly do not respond to them. Are these Cavarero's women of inclination? They could be. They are mostly pacifist, but they are also capable of violence. Twice in response to male intrusions into their gynocentric space, the women attack. First, the bacchants slaughter animals with their bare hands to frighten off intrusive shepherds, then the women kill and dismember the king, again with no weapons, a point of contrast to the city's male warriors in which Agave will later take pride. Read as a political parable of inclination, the *Bacchae* teaches that agonism and even violent self-defense may be needed to protect heterotopian experiments in living that should expect to be greeted with intolerance by defenders of the status quo. The world, which some try to leave behind in order to rehearse another in its place, sometimes chases after its fugitives to pull them back and restore what it posits as the only way. To respond defensively, even violently, risks mimicking what we oppose. To not take that risk, however, is to court others, like reabsorption or exile. The bacchants get the worst of both options. They commit the violence and do not win. They return to the city expecting glory and are met with disbelief. After a failed effort at reabsorption by the city, they are sent into exile. The sister-leaders leave the city again in the end, this time (perhaps) holding hands.

When the bacchants gather themselves together against the king on Cithaeron, they reach for the symbols of erectitude (the tree and the monarch) and topple them. In other words, they commit the violent regicide that Cavarero never *names* as the true aim or power of inclination. If it goes unnamed, that is because Cavarero imagines inclination in unagonistic terms—as an (often demeaned) alternative to rectitude, not as a direct contestatory rival to it. This protects her pacifism but leaves vulnerable the heterotopia that is a condition of pacifism's existence.

Cavarero wants her heterotopia to decenter the regnant verticality of Philosophy and make room for inclination, too. In that sense she seems to be a pluralizer or a pluralist, as Carol Gilligan also claimed to be, against Lawrence Kohlberg, when she made clear there is more than one way to reason morally. This seemed to leave Kohlberg's ethics a place, or perhaps it just put him in his place. But even such pluralization, whether Gilligan's or Cavarero's, is not innocent. If we follow their lead, then a kind of regicide will have taken place in the field, in the discipline of Philosophy. Perhaps we might call it an *epistemicide*.

## An Inclination Reading of *Antigone and the Sphinx*

Sophocles's *Antigone* features a different king of Thebes, Creon, also brought down by women on the incline. The sisters in this play, Antigone and Ismene, surely lean in when they whisper to each other in the night. This is certainly how many stage directors over the years have imagined them, posturally, as Antigone invites her sister to conspire with her against Creon.

Cavarero's inclination invites us to note that posture is actually a theme throughout Sophocles's play. When Antigone stands accused before Creon, he says, "You, with your eyes looking down."[18] Why doesn't she stand up straight, eyes forward? Perhaps she is too inclinational for him. Indeed, for Creon, citizenship is all *about* posture: the good man, he says later, when he argues with his son, Haemon, is "a loyal, unflinching comrade at your side. Staunch in the storm of spears—he'll stand his ground."[19] To step out of line—to bend or break—is to break the military geometry of the time, the phalanx formation, and the result, Creon says, is "anarchy."[20]

Creon's son, Haemon, calls attention to this geometric verticalism, and he warns his father to not be too "rigid" when dealing with Antigone's resistance. Haemon tells his father to be *willing* to "bend"; even the arboreal inclines, Haemon reminds his father, citing trees in a storm: "Bend or break," he says, before pleading, "Oh give way" (795–805). Is it a more relational autonomy he seeks? Perhaps so. But, to Creon, these supplications mean only one thing: Haemon—"is fighting on her side, the woman's side." For Creon, to argue for inclination is to side with the women in these tragedies, with those who, like the women in the *Bacchae*, are famously able to bend trees to their will.[21]

What Creon recognizes here, though like so much else he doesn't know it, is that resistance to his model of vertical citizenship comes not just from Antigone's famous violation of his edict (she buries her brother Polynices, even though Creon has forbidden it) but also from the posture or axis of inclination that we may take as a figure for the conspiracy that I have elsewhere argued blossoms between the sisters, Antigone and Ismene, in this play, hiding in plain sight.

The clash between the vertical and the inclinational is personified in Sophocles's tragedy by Creon and Antigone, who inclines over her brother Polynices to bury him and toward her sister Ismene to conspire with her against Creon. But the clash is also prefigured in the origin story of Oedipus, invoked if not retold in Sophocles's prequel to the *Antigone* (written later but chronologically prior), *Oedipus the King*. There we hear of Oedipus's (Antigone's father/brother) fateful encounter with the Sphinx: a monstrous, female, maternal, foreign creature, part woman/part (in the Greek context) vulture. The Sphinx held Thebes hostage and killed all the city's would-be saviors when they failed to solve her riddle. "What crawls on all fours in the morning, walks on two legs midday, and then in the evening on three?," asked the Sphinx (posing what Cavarero calls elsewhere "the riddle of the legs").[22] "Man," replied Oedipus correctly.[23] It earned him his throne—he entered Thebes and became king—because his correct response resulted in the death of the Sphinx, who threw herself over a cliff. Cause of death?

Maybe too much inclination.[24]

The Sphinx's inclination to inclination is evident in her riddle, which shows how temporary is the rectitude that man (mis-)takes for his species-essence when he calls himself *homo erectus*. The Sphinx's riddle teaches that uprightness is only a *part* of a human life, not its essence or *telos*. The key to the riddle is that infancy and old age, figures for natality and mortality (and the enduring relationality of a human life that is rendered unmistakable in these periods of dependence), are on a par with periods of autonomy—all elements of human life, not deviations from it, not preludes or postludes to it, either. That the Sphinx is Egyptian and Oedipus the whitened primogenitor of Western philosophy's rapturous attachment to male autonomy makes all the more poignant the fact that Oedipus triumphs while failing to learn the Sphinx's lesson.

To *know* that man is not just vertical but also inclinational (crawling as an infant, walking with a cane, or leaning on others for support in old age) is Oedipus's rare gift.[25] But to really *understand* the *meaning* of this knowledge, which is the relationality of the human, turns out to be beyond even him.[26] When he pursues the knowledge that will be his tragic undoing, Oedipus listens to no one and accepts no counsel. He is rigid, autonomous, a strict verticalist. The wisdom of inclination was the Sphinx's criterion for ruling. But while Oedipus's reply to her riddle showed he knew about inclination, his knowledge was not experiential. He himself, in his own life, diverges from the norm that is the riddle's solution. He himself presumably did not crawl on four legs as an infant. His father, Laius, frightened by a prophecy that his son would one day kill him, had his infant son's ankles pierced and tied together, leaving Oedipus with a lifelong wound and limp. And in his old age, Oedipus, in exile, will walk with the help and support of one or both of his two daughters, Ismene and Antigone, suggesting he walks on four or six legs in the evening of his life, but not—as the riddle teaches—on three, like most old men, with a cane.[27] Oedipus's tragedy will turn on the temporariness of his two-leggedness, which, as with all verticalists, he mistakes for his life's entirety or its essence. Oedipus puts his faith in his autonomy, and this is what eventually brings him down. His verticalist inflexibility is his undoing.[28] In Cavarero's terms from *Relating Narratives*, we might say he embodies philosophy and not "narration."[29]

Historically, Antigone has been viewed as very much her father's daughter, as the Chorus puts it in Sophocles's play. Stubborn. Willful. Autonomous; obeying a law that is her own. Erect. Even manly.

But there is a case to be made for an inclinational reading of Oedipus's daughters as understanding inclination or relationality—the lesson of the Sphinx—better than their father.[30] In the play's first scene, Antigone whispers confidentially to Ismene, "Ismene, have you heard?"[31] She seeks her sister's help; she cannot act alone. The sisters surely incline as they share a secret, the awful fate of their warring brothers, Eteocles and Polynices, both now dead, and Polynices left to rot, unburied, charged with treason by their uncle, Creon. Together, the sisters narrate their situation and explore the courses of action open to them, considering their obligations.

Antigone is willing to suffer anything to dignify her treasonous brother Polynices in death. Ismene is more cautious, but she is willing to risk herself for the living Antigone, if not for the dead Polynices. While they struggle over how to meet the demands of Creon's edict, the sisters move from murderous rage to adoring mutuality to altruistic self-sacrifice and determined survival, often in an instant. Creon is not paranoid when he wonders what the sisters are doing out of sight, in *his* home. As he says to Ismene, "You—in my own house, you viper, slinking, undetected, sucking my life-blood! I never knew I was breeding twin disasters, the two of you rising up against my throne."[32] He is not wrong. The sisters *are* conspiring; this is their inclination. Not *all* inclination is conspiratorial (inclination may be erotic, maternal, dependent, and so on), but it may well be that *all conspiracy involves inclination*. Breathing together—as conspirators do—postulates that posture. Philosophy's Antigone stands up, alone, for her rights/rites, strong, rigid, unbending. Perhaps it is more accurate to say that our received Antigone *is* Philosophy (no less so than is Oedipus, on Cavarero's account, in *Relating Narratives*).[33]

Cavarero's attention to posture in *Inclinations* invites a different Antigone, the Antigone of agonistic sorority, political theory's Antigone, I would argue, and she is not just vertical.[34] She inclines to Ismene, sometimes in rage, sometimes in love, sometimes in rejection and sometimes extending protection, initiating, responding, planning with and against her sister how to overcome Creon, or sometimes focused on how to protect her sister from his sovereign injustice or cruelty. Such exemplary soroal inclinations are obscured from view by the insistent assumption of verticality.

Then, in the sisters' final scene, the two women speak in code, colluding conspiratorially, in front of Creon but beneath his grasp.[35] Each sister offers to die for, with, or in place of the other. "Let me die with you," says Ismene. "No," says Antigone returning the favor. "My death will be enough."[36] Then she distracts Creon from his plan to kill both of them by calling out, "Hey Creon, what more do you want than my death?" Nothing more, he says. Here a sororal, inclinational altruism powers Antigone's agonism. If she ends in suicide, it is arguably because the violence proscribed by pacifism finds its expression: if not against the tyrant then against his would-be opponent, who takes it in.

Many classicists, influenced perhaps by the philosophers' vertical Antigone, who represents only fidelity to the dead, and not also the care of sororal action in concert, are confused and even enervated by Antigone: she says she is all about family but then seems terribly cold and cruel to Ismene, especially in the sisters' second scene together. For them, "No, my death will be enough," is Antigone hogging all the glory for herself, not a woman sacrificing for her sister, who will go on living.[37] The most common technique used by classicists to make sense of these agonistic sisters is to split the two women characters into two oppositional figures, one who is rigidly vertical versus one who flexibly inclines, one who battles versus one who cares, one who is (in Eve Sedgwick's terms) *paranoid*—"Such, I hear, is the martial law our good Creon lays down for you and me—yes, me, I tell you" (Antigone, 37–38) and one who is *reparative*: "Wild, irrational as you are, my sister, you are truly dear to the ones who love you."[38]

Such splitting normatively heterosexualizes the pair. Antigone is masculinized, treated as a moral and philosophical standard of uprightness, and Ismene is feminized, judged from verticality's perspective as wanting (lacking verticality's virtues) or too caring, the latter an inclinational trait both celebrated *and* criticized by feminists who identify the feminine either with the virtue of care or the feminine flaw of caution when courage is what is called for. One result of the splitting is the destruction of the women's powerful sorority and their agonistic conspiracy.[39]

I argued in detail in *Antigone, Interrupted* what I have in brief suggested here: that the two women are united sororally in conspiracy against Creon.[40] Cavarero's *For More Than One Voice* was a key text for that close reading of the play, which attended not only to the words (*logos*) but also to the various intonations (*phonē*) and sounds alongside which lines mistaken by philosophers to be "arguments" are performed dramatically. But now, Cavarero's more recent focus on *inclination* calls our attention to posture, which, as we saw earlier, is a focus in the play as well, and it opens the play anew.

In the sister's second scene together, the women argue in front of Creon, and Ismene offers to die with her sister, indeed, begs to do so. It matters how the women are positioned, how we visualize them, as they argue, or seem to. Ismene says, "Let me die beside you, consecrating the dead together." Antigone responds, "Never share my dying, don't lay claim to what you never touched."[41] Are they at opposed sides of the stage, rigid and vertical? If so, we might have the Classicists' iconic, cold Antigone, betraying her earlier claim to stand for family, being characteristically cruel to her mewling sister, and guarding all the glory for herself. But if the two women lean in, perhaps even crouch on the ground, cajoling, whispering, touching each other, as Creon, nearby, stands erect and puzzles over what to make of them, then we have a very different sense of things: in such an *inclinational* staging, we see sisters who have fought in the past finding a way to communicate altruistic love, in front of an erect tyrant. With their postures and voices, and not just their words, the sisters combat Creon's tyranny of verticality. Through *logos* and *phone*, and now through *klinē*, their refusal might resound. The sisters' inclined collaboration has not survived, since Hegel, the transformation of Antigone into a solitary dissident. That is why we need the *Bacchae*, too, and its plural and partnered Antgiones.

## Leonardo's Madonna: Inclination as Altruism or Agonism?

*Antigone* and the *Bacchae*, as I have read them here, dramatize inclination as refusal. In both tragedies, the central agency of inclination is not, however, Cavarero's maternity but, rather, sorority. This is important for democratic theory because the sororal relationship is the more egalitarian of the two.[42] We need not prefer one to the other as a political exemplar, but the sororal's claim to be included in inclination's kinship archive surely demands that we at least pluralize the kinship position with which inclination is connected by Cavarero. One of Cavarero's own preferred illustrations of inclination bears this out: sorority is discernible, too, in the painting of the Madonna by Leonardo that graces the cover of her book (See Fig. 1 in Chapter 1 above). As with the *Bacchae* and the *Antigone*, here, too, in Leonardo's Madonna we may detect sorority and agonism alongside Cavarero's maternity and altruism. Indeed, Leonardo's painting is, arguably, both more "Greek" that is to say, more agonistic, *and* more sororal than first appears.[43]

First, as art historians and critics have long pointed out, the two women as Leonardo painted them look more like sisters than mother and daughter. Anne does not appear older than her daughter, at least not old enough to be her mother.[44]

Second, Cavarero points out that the posture of inclination is made possible by Leonardo's "subversive" decision to place "the child *beside* the mother [Mary] and not in her arms, as in the traditional representations." But we may note that there are two mothers here and two children, and one pair is represented in Cavarero's preferred, more subversive way, while the other is actually depicted in the traditional style. Mary is the child of Anne and Jesus the child of Mary. Jesus is on the ground, as Cavarero says, but the other child, Mary, sits in her mother's lap. Thus, Leonardo's painting *cites* the norm with one mother/child while subverting it with the other. This is important because it highlights the exceptionality of the subversive decision, which may not exemplify maternity as such (it obviously does not, given that Mary sits on Anne's lap) but rather the connection of Mary to the awful fate that awaits her child. As Cavarero notes, Jesus is on the ground, playing with a lamb, and the lamb is "a symbol of the passion and the sacrifice that awaits him."[45] That violence is *portended*, as Cavarero says, by the lamb. But it is also portended precisely by the posture of inclination singled out here by Cavarero.

The untraditional distance between Leonardo's Mary and child, which enables the subversive non-holding noted by Cavarero, is not just depicting maternity's inclination but its deprivation, too. Indeed the posture may be more typical of (and may be a citation of) the more perfectly altruistic relation between living and dead, as when Antigone inclines toward/over the dead Polynices (here in this painting by Stillman [Fig. 2],

FIGURE 2. Marie Spartali-Stillman, *Antigone from "Antigone," by Sophocles* (1844–1927), oil on canvas, Simon Carter Gallery, Woodbridge, Suffolk, UK. Source: Bridgeman Images.

pictured with Ismene—giving imagistic support to my sororal reading of the play). Is Leonardo citing this norm of death-care?[46] If the lamb in the Leonardo painting foretells Jesus's sacrificial fate (as Cavarero argues), so too surely does the inclination of mother to child, which cites the posture of care for the dead (for which Antigone, the lamenting sister, is above all known).

Third, Cavarero identifies the mothers in Leonardo's painting only with altruistic care, but she does acknowledge later in her book, with Levinas, that with the capacity to care comes always also the possibility of wounding. This doubled possibility, she explains, is not belied by maternal inclination, for to be inclined is not yet to care or to wound but to be on the cusp, positioned undecidably in response to the call of the exposed other.[47] But the undecidability that joins wounding and caring is to some extent undone by Cavarero when she posits Leonardo's painting as a depiction of the caring inclination of altruism and says we must look *elsewhere* for maternal murderousness: "Alongside Leonardo's Madonna lovingly bent over baby Jesus, consider Euripides's Medea, the infanticide . . . [Medea, who kills her two young sons to avenge wrongs committed against her by their father] reminds us that care is not an automatic or obvious response of maternal inclination."[48] We could say the same of Agave in the *Bacchae*, whose regicide is after all also a filicide: the young king Pentheus is her son. Still, the caring and the wounding of which Cavarero *says* maternity is simultaneously capable are split when Cavarero assigns them to two separate works of art, one Christian, one Greek; one representational, one dramatic; one Madonna, one Medea.[49]

Notably, Freud, whom Cavarero never mentions here (and you have to admire that), saw something more menacing in this very painting: in Leonardo's Mary, Freud saw a phallic mother, the secret repository of the very verticality that Cavarero sees as indexed only by the lone tree that Leonardo put (safely?) in the background of the two loving women. Distant, but there in the painting: a vector of verticality. Cavarero points out the tree, reassuring us of its distance but, still, acknowledging its existence. In so doing, she establishes the heterotopian quality of the women's scene as well as its fragility.

But Freud saw in this painting (with the help of Oskar Pfister) a danger more proximate: the outline of a vulture in the drapery of the women's dress (Fig. 3). The creature represents the capacity to wound, Freud says. And it results from Leonardo's mother's wounding of her son.

Freud was building on Leonardo's own natal recollections. As a baby, the artist had dreamed that (in his words) in his cradle "a vulture came down to me, and opened my mouth with its tail, and struck me many times with its tail against my lips." In his earlier psychobiography of Leonardo, Freud had said the dream was a screen memory of homosexuality whose repression enabled the flowering of artistic genius. Now, by way of the Madonna painting and its hidden bird of prey, Freud says this is actually evidence that Leonardo's mother, "like all unsatisfied mothers, took her son in place of her husband, and by too early maturing his eroticism robbed him of his masculinity."[50] We have here an example of caring and/as wounding, albeit one underwritten by Freud's misogynistic view of the mother.

But the co-incidence of menace and tenderness, the combined capacity to wound and care, might surface here for *different* reasons than Freud's if we note that, were it not for its title, Leonardo's painting could be seen as a detail of the *Bacchae*, the tragedy in which women frolic together among animals in a field. After all, the painting depicts two women, who seem to be about the same age, sisters perhaps, at ease in a field with a baby and a lamb with a slightly forbidding-looking tree standing ramrod straight in the background. Is Pentheus perched up there? The image could have been called "*In the Fields of Cithaeron.*"[51] Were Leonardo's

FIGURE 3. Leonardo Da Vinci, *The Virgin and Child with Saint Anne* (1503–19), on Poplar Wood, Louvre, Paris. Source: Wikimedia Commons. With thanks to Matthew Martin for recreating the vulture outline.

painting recast as Greek, then the future portended here would not be the sacrifice of the baby prefigured by the lamb, as Cavarero argues, but rather the regicide that the tall tree in the background would call to the mind of anyone familiar with Euripides's *Bacchae*.

Is it too much of a stretch to see the outlines of Euripides's women and their soon-to-be toppled tree in Leonardo's painting? No more so than finding a vulture in the women's dress-drapery, surely. And, once we have found that vulture, we are already with the Greeks and surely in the company of the Sphinx, who is in some renderings in the Greek context part woman, part vulture. In any case, this would not be the first time a Christian-themed work by Leonardo was recast as Classical.

In the late seventeenth century, Leonardo's portrait of St. John (here is a different St. John that still remains and likely resembles the one that was painted over, [Fig. 4]) was painted over and made into Bacchus (Fig. 5).[52] It was as if to correct an error.

Leonardo's *St. John* was described as disturbing by some: "suavely beautiful, youthful and slightly androgynous."[53] Beneath the baptism lay the bacchanalia. It was easy to transform "the long-handled cross-like staff of the Baptist to a Bacchic thyrsus" (the thyrsus carried by the men in the *Bacchae* in celebration of the feast of Dionysus) and to turn St. John, himself, into Bacchus or Dionysus.[54] The palimpsest is an invitation to find, beneath the Madonna, Agave the bacchant.

## Toward an Agonistic Inclination

I have been suggesting that inclination may signal not only care and/or wounding or the cusp between them but also refusal, and that, for those interested in a politics of refusal, inclination may be an important part of refusal's repertoire. Refusal as inclination can take the agonistic form of engaging directly with powers that be, and/or it can take a separatist heterotopian form of establishing islands of alternative living, away from such powers, their promises, and their cruelties, where care can be practiced. Cavarero proposes "an imaginary *completely apart* from geometric verticalism."[55] That complete apartness means that inclination is either nourished by forms of life in a space apart or has a kind of gravitational pull that takes us elsewhere.

But inclination might also impel us toward more direct forms of engagement: that is to say, it may be agonistic. In *Antigone*, the sisters defend their right to incline over the dead, and, in *The Bacchae*, Agave and her sisters join with other women to defend their right to *klinē*. In both plays the women succeed, to some extent, but in neither do the women

FIGURE 4. Leonardo Da Vinci, *St John* (1513–16), oil on walnut wood, Louvre, Paris. Source: Heritage Images.

FIGURE 5. Leonardo Da Vinci, *Bacchus* (1510–15), oil on walnut panel transferred to canvas, Louvre, Paris. Source: Wikimedia Commons.

win. Cavarero might say the breadth of the women's promise in the Bacchae is narrowed when they set their sights on toppling a king. That, indeed, is the risk of their agonism. These women's inclination does not serve as an ethics "apart" (which is what Cavarero says she wants to establish), indeed it *cannot*, because the sovereign power won't let it, and because the women's *klinē* is the basis of a political action that enters into agonistic conflict with rectitude and ends with regicide, literally or figuratively; either way, in both plays the king is brought down, repaying perhaps a prior wrong in which a man becomes king as the Sphinx dies.

This suggests both the promise of apartness *and* its limits. To contest verticality means we risk falling into its conceptual clutches, to be judged wanting from its perspective, to be pressed anew to yield to its demand for upright autonomy, to be drawn into its spell. But to leave it be and build elsewhere means we leave verticality empowered to do its work. (This is surely one message of that tree in the distance in Leonardo's painting.) This is the risk of heterotopia, though perhaps not its fate: the strategy of apartness, so necessary to build the world on behalf of which we want to mobilize, may need to risk impurity, too; that is to say, we need to risk partnership with the kinds of agonistic engagement (with each other and with verticality itself, even) that could risk inclination's undoing. At the same time heterotopias—or fugitive spaces such as those explored by Cavarero and by Saidiya Hartman, Fred Moten, Toni Morrison, and others—are where we learn and practice what the world might be.[56] Without such exercises to vivify justice for us, we risk losing sight of what is wrong with an unjust society and can become reconciled to it and habituated to our place in it. Without the agonism to which I want to press inclination here, thinking with and against Cavarero, rectitude is naturalized and becomes an incontestable standard. It has happened before. Indeed, it still is happening. The power of heterotopia must be leashed to a political obligation or determination to return to the city, and, as it happens, that is precisely what the bacchants do in Euripides' play.

## Conclusion

The argument of this chapter has implications for the idea of an ethics of nonviolence endorsed by both Butler and Cavarero in this volume. While not advocating in favor of violence, this chapter has tracked the inescapability of violence in politics, especially in times of political change or transformation. In this respect, I have come to think that the *Bacchae* is more instructive than the *Antigone*, hence my pairing of them here and my references to Antigones, in plural, throughout. Antigone has come to represent the principled stance of a disobedience that disavows violence but insists on political involvement. Antigone positions herself both on the axis of verticality—against Creon—and inclinationally, with her sister, Ismene, and her brother, Polynices. Notably, though, there is no gynocentric heterotopia for Antigone, only the carved-out space and time of the household (a topos but not a heterotopia) in which to conspire with her one lone sister. In the *Bacchae*, by contrast, a play so long received as an account of female madness, we see something else, potentially a powerful political parable of sisters who act in concert to bring down a king.

The bacchants' heterotopia outside the city, Cithaeron, hosts an experiment in living where women renounce conventional domesticity and recreate life on new terms: collective, tribal, mystical, and devoted to pleasure. It is important that the only time the women resort to violence is when they are intruded upon, first by shepherds thinking to betray them and earn the favor of the king and later by the king himself, who thinks he can change costume to pass as a woman and exploit secrets to which he has no right. In both scenes, blood is drawn as the women avenge the violation of their space and defend the world they have built. Without such defense, their heterotopia is vulnerable to the infiltration of those who would destroy it.

In the first violation by the shepherds, the bacchants choose animals as the objects of violence, a warning to the men who thought to attack; and in the second, famously, the women kill and dismember the king. Read as a parable, and freed from the pathologizing receptions that cast the women as mad, the *Bacchae* can be seen as an exploration of how regicide is always what is at stake when people refuse the status quo and invent other ways of living. As a parable, the play does not recommend the literal killing of the king; it teaches that refusal and its heterotopias are as such regicidal.

This instructively prepares those who seek alternatives to the status quo for the likely severity of the inevitable pushback. Butler, who has written about the violence committed against sexual minorities, minoritized for walking with a swish, knows this well, as does Cavarero who also charted the dance of violence in her earlier book, *Horrorism*.[57] The parable of the *Bacchae* is more up front about what is at stake in the challenges issued by radical feminism: rather than suffer a regime's violence in the hope of demonstrating its injustice, the bacchants combat it by modeling a more or less pacifist alternative that does not commit, ethically, to participate in its own destruction. Not only that, they return to the city to loudly claim it. The bacchants' return to the city is a bold move that combines rectitude and inclination. That the tactic fails in the *Bacchae* need not make it uninstructive for us.

## Notes

1. See J. L. Austin, *How to Do Things with Words* (Cambridge, Mass.: Harvard University Press, 1962). Of course, Cavarero herself does things with inclination, applying the concept and perspective to a host of texts and images. My aim is to expand the "how" of "how to do things" in order to show how intimately related inclination and agonism can be seen to be.

2. Adriana Cavarero, *Inclinations: A Critique of Rectitude*, trans. Amanda Minervini and Adam Sitze (Stanford, Calif.: Stanford University Press, 2016). Cavarero's other writings are attentive to Greek tragedy. As my discussion here and in *Antigone, Interrupted* will attest, I have learned a great deal from Cavarero's work.

3. In my forthcoming *A Feminist Theory of Refusal* (Harvard 2021), I offer an extended reading of Cavarero's inclination as a "posture of refusal" and of the *Bacchae* as a fable of inclination as refusal (what I call here "agonistic inclination"). For Cavarero's own reading of the Sphinx, see *Relating Narratives: Storytelling and Selfhood*, trans. Paul A. Kottman (London and New York: Routledge, 2000), where, working with the poetry of Muriel Rukeyser, Cavarero develops a reading of the Sphinx compatible with but different from the inclination-centered one I develop here (though our readings come close to convergence when she refers to the Sphinx's test as "the riddle of the legs," and mine of course conjugates her idea of inclination). The Sphinx, Cavarero says, invites Oedipus "to place Woman next to Man—in the position always denied her of the subject" (51). Oedipus fails to take up that invitation, she says. I will argue that the Sphinx also invites Oedipus to place inclination alongside rectitude as an essential human comportment, no less so than rectitude or uprightness. To this invitation, Oedipus says yes. He knows how to answer the riddle rightly, but he does not know the answer experientially. Or at least so I shall argue here.

4. On agonism and refusal as care, see Bonnie Honig, "Twelve Angry Men: Care for the Agon and the Varieties of Masculine Experience," *Theory & Event* 22, no. 3 (2019): 701–16.

5. See, for example, Cavarero, *Inclinations*, 152, and throughout.

6. Though sometimes the arboreal and the vertical/patriarchal dovetail, as in the image *Adam Pierced by the Arrow of Mercury* in Cavarero, *Inclinations*, 58.

7. Gilles Deleuze and Félix Guattari, *A Thousand Plateaus: Capitalism and Schizophrenia*, trans. Brian Massumi (Minneapolis: University of Minnesota Press, 1987), 151.

8. Jacques Rancière, "Ten Theses on Politics," trans. Davide Panagia and Rachel Bowlby, *Theory & Event* 5, no. 3 (2001): no pagination, https://doi.org/10.1353/tae.2001.0028.

9. That is to say, Cavarero's argument calls to mind Deleuze and Guattari's displacement of the Arboreal (vertical) with the Rhizomatic (inclinational) (though Cavarero's ontology remains humanist) or even recent efforts in Disability Studies to break the assumed neurotypical connections between physical and intellectual ability and deconstruct the binary of able and disabled, to pluralize what counts as "able." Neither of these literatures is mentioned by Cavarero, who stresses she is working "apart," focusing in particular on gender and the discipline of philosophy. There is a third parallel archive, though, the Gilligan-Kohlberg debate about the gendered distinction between an ethics of care (altruism) versus autonomy, and this last one *is* mentioned by Cavarero, who affiliates her project with Gilligan's. These other literatures may help situate the project for those new to Cavarero's *Inclinations*.

10. Giorgio Agamben, "The Glorious Body," in *Nudities*, trans. David Kishik and Stefan Pedatella (Stanford, Calif.: Stanford University Press, 2011).

11. The pentimento of Christian over pagan imagery—here, Agamben's Christian over Deleuze and Guattari's arguably Dionysian approach—is a theme/issue throughout. Agamben has other examples that link inoperativity to sensorial pleasure, such as the whipping cream machine that comes up late in his essay on the Glorious Body. I discuss that as an example of queer inoperativity in Honig, "Is Man a 'Sabbatical Animal'? Agamben, Rosenzweig, Heschel, Arendt," *Political Theology* 20, no. 1 (2019): 1–23, https://doi.org/10.1080/1462317X.2018.1518766.

12. I have elsewhere argued, contra Gilligan, that care may help prop up and not just unsettle the reproduction of autonomy, working as its supplement, undecidably supportive and subversive; Honig, *Political Theory and the Displacement of Politics* (Ithaca, N.Y.: Cornell University Press, 1993), and in Chapter 6.

13. Cavarero, *Inclinations*, 173. Emphasis added. On the question of "complete" apartness: it strikes me that Cavarero is more likely to read drama and literature against the grain to find female voice than she is to approach philosophical texts that way. She cedes Plato and Kant to philosophy where others argue for nonverticalist readings of them. In the case of Plato, for example, see Jill Frank's *Poetic Justice: Rereading Plato's "Republic"* (Chicago: University of Chicago Press, 2018), and for Kant, as a kind of gender/tragic hero who resists the binarism of rectitude versus inclination, see Judith Butler's contribution to this volume. Butler offers a phenomenological deconstruction of the binary: "The inclining figure shadows forth in the upright figure." My own approach generally and in connection with Cavarero in particular is indebted to Derrida, who invited us to read even philosophy literarily and literature philosophically.

14. Cavarero, *Inclinations*, 173–74.

15. But what should we make of this displacement of something like Hegel's eternal irony, away from its first location in the iconic tragic Greek sister/daughter (Antigone), to a new location in the iconic maternal Christian mother/daughter (Mary)? (The pentimento question, again. Though of course in the case of Hegel we are talking about an Antigone that is always already Christian, as I note in *Antigone, Interrupted* [Cambridge: Cambridge University Press, 2013].)

16. Sara Ahmed, *Willful Subjects* (Durham, N.C.: Duke University Press, 2014), 1 and passim.

17. Cavarero, *Inclinations*, 3.

18. Sophocles, *Antigone*, in *The Three Theban Plays*, trans. Robert Fagles and Bernard Knox (New York: Penguin, 1984), 490.

19. Ibid., 743–47.

20. Ibid., 743–47 and 752.

21. The Greek dramas, though enlivened by inclination's perspective, may also divert us from Cavarero's most pointed claims. Thus far, I have focused most on "inclination" as a plane of moral or political geometry, while enlisting it also as a way of *reading*, one that does not go straight to the point (albeit, building always toward the point) but seeks out the curves and declensions of a text, opening up some texts and dramas for new thinking. But, for Cavarero, as already noted, inclination is not just an alternative moral posture or plane, not just a formal geometry, but a posture specific to altruism whose only credibly realist exemplification is maternity. "What other image of radical altruism could serve as a better example, while also remaining

familiar and credible? What infinite responsibility for the other," she asks, "could lower itself, in spite of the self, to lower itself into a more docile hostage? What subjectivity, which figure or character or theme from the real world, could compete with this?" (Cavarero, *Inclinations*, 167). Cavarero chides Levinas for looking elsewhere, including even to the improbable example of Jacob and Esau, those biblical "brothers in arms," as she calls them. "Agonistic sorority" provides an alternative frame, I hope, and is marked also by realism and credibility as well as by a distinguished history in performance and representational art.

22. Cavarero has her own great reading of the myth in *Relating Narratives*, which has two chapters on Oedipus; the second is more centrally on the encounter with the Sphinx. I am suggesting that her argument in *Inclinations* can be extended to generate a third one compatible with, but distinct from, the other two.

23. The content of the riddle is not specified in Sophocles's play, which does, however, have several specific references to the Sphinx. For the specifics of the puzzle, see Apollodorus, *Library* 3.5.8, trans. Sir James George Frazer (Cambridge, Mass.: Harvard University Press, 1963), in which the puzzle appears as follows: *"What is that which has one voice and yet becomes four-footed and two-footed and three- footed?"*

24. Henri Dorra has suggested that in the Moreau painting *Oedipus and the Sphinx*, 1864, the poses of the Sphinx and Oedipus, in which the Sphinx is inclined and Oedipus is vertical, are derived from "the Greek etymological meaning of the word sphinx, which is to clutch, embrace, or cling to"; Dorra, "The Guesser Guessed: Gustave Moreau's Oedipus," *Gazette des beaux-arts* 81 (March 1973): 129–40. Yuan Yuan says "strangle" is the root word in Greek and connects the Sphinx to fears of strangulation by the mother; Yuan Yuan, *The Riddling between Oedipus and the Sphinx: Ontology, Hauntology, and Heterologies of the Grotesque* (Lanham, Md.: University Press of America, 2016).

25. Goux says, "Oedipus alone triumphs through sheer intelligence, with his explanation of the famous riddle that is itself a trial by language"; Jean-Joseph Goux, *Oedipus, Philosopher*, trans. Catherine Porter (Stanford, Calif.: Stanford University Press, 1993). "Sheer intelligence" is not enough. I am thinking it is a trial of life, and the riddle is about life's trials.

26. The Sphinx, a monstrous female or mother figure, provokes attention to the infant who crawls and the elderly or infirm who walk with a cane or who lean on others for support. All incline, their postures slope, and this marks their enmeshment in something like the relationality theorized by Cavarero in *Relating Narratives* and prized by her here, in *Inclinations*, as the basis of an ethics. Are these departures from the norm of rectitude? Or necessary pluralizations of it? This, in essence, is the question posed by the mother/Sphinx to Oedipus. Butler's answer to it (as it were) in this volume is, "All bodies require support to stand on their own . . . and they never outgrow it."

27. On the signifying powers of the cane, see Laurence Ralph, *Renegade Dreams* (Chicago: University of Chicago Press, 2014).

28. Oedipus is unwilling to defer to others, including even Tiresias, the blind seer, who *avows* his dependence on another—always calling attention to the sighted youth who accompanies him in and out of Thebes. The avowal is in both *Oedipus Tyrannos* and in *Antigone*: "This is the way the blind man comes, Princes, Princes, Lock-step, two heads lit by the eyes of one" (*Antigone*). (It is also in the *Bacchae*, where Tiresias

and Cadmus appear together, Bacchus-bound.) Surely, by calling attention to his own inclination, Tiresias aims to inspire others to learn from his example. But Oedipus is unaffected.

29. Cavarero, *Relating Narratives*, 13.

30. In Sophocles's *Antigone*, the Chorus says more than once that the headstrong Antigone is her father's daughter. But this is misleading. Antigone's stubborn "no" to Creon *is* unstinting. But it is worth noting that her head is inclined—Creon says she is looking down—when she is first brought to him, and her communications with Ismene are also inclined.

31. Sophocles, *Antigone*, 11.

32. Sophocles, *Antigone*, 579–600.

33. Cavarero compares Oedipus to Plato to make the point in *Relating Narratives*, Chapter 1.

34. We may see her as "supple," as in Deleuze and Guattari, *A Thousand Plateaus*, 104 and passim.

35. When Eurydice—Creon's wife and the play's only living mother—kills herself using a knife, her manner of suicide is perhaps inclinational—she leans into the blade—and this may express and perhaps also cite her inclination to her lost sons. She blames Creon for their deaths. Indeed, it may be that when Eurydice kills herself to join the sons for whom she would certainly have died, her maternal altruism is on display in this violent act.

36. Sophocles, *Antigone*, 614–16.

37. Their agonistic sorority is itself a refusal of Creon's demand, which is, in effect, that each obey him. One key to this reading, as I have argued, is not to jump to conclusions about Antigone's seeming rejection of her sister's warm declarations of love and solidarity in their last scene together. See, for example, Simon Goldhill, *Sophocles and the Language of Tragedy* (Oxford and New York: Oxford University Press, 2012), and my reply in *Antigone, Interrupted*, 166–67.

38. Ismene, *Antigone*, 115–16; Eve Kosofsky Sedgwick, "Paranoid Reading and Reparative Reading, or You're So Paranoid, You Probably Think This Essay Is about You," in *Touching Feeling: Affect, Pedagogy, Performativity*, ed. Adam Frank (Durham, N.C.: Duke University Press, 2003), 123–52, and Sophocles, *Antigone*, 37–38 and 115–16.

39. We can highlight the care with which Antigone's "cold" utterances to Ismene are suffused, as well as the courage with which the supposedly cowardly or nervous Ismene allies with her sister. True, when Ismene says, "Oh no, my sister, don't reject me, please, let me die beside you, consecrating the dead together" (*Antigone*, 544–45). Antigone responds, "Never share my dying, don't lay claim to what you never touched" (*Antigone*, 546–47). But these words can be said vertically or inclinationally: they may be the words of a rivalrous sister, still angry over earlier betrayals and eager to hoard all the glory for herself; and/or they may be the words of a doomed sister, tenderly expressing care for the one she will leave behind, seeking even now to protect her beloved from sharing her awful fate. When Ismene says, "Why abuse me so? It doesn't help you now," Antigone reassures her, "You are right." This is the only time in the play that Antigone says anyone other than she is right about anything. Surely it is significant. "You are right" may mean that Ismene is right that nothing will stop Creon from putting Antigone to death. But it may also mean that Ismene, who began the play valuing life over death, should accept the gift of life

that Antigone now offers. Antigone fought with her sister about that very point, in their first scene. But she has come around. Her whispered message says she has shifted. She was willing to risk both their lives earlier, but not now: now she wants her sister to live. Hence, Antigone's not at all churlish "Save yourself. I don't grudge you your survival" (552). Should we assume she says it grudgingly? So many classicists see here a final dig at the sister who refused her. But why not read it as kindness? Care? Altruism? Perhaps even maternal (but why not call it sororal)?

40. Honig, *Antigone, Interrupted*, Chapter 6.

41. Sophocles, *Antigone*, 544–47, 614–16.

42. Also the mood of inclinational refusal in these plays is not, per se, altruistic, but agonistic, which melds altruism and conflict and so is, again, important for *political* theory *and* possibly connected to the sisters' relative equality. I note here the similarity to and difference from Mark Devenney's essay in this volume. We agree on the ambivalence of the mother-child relationship, but he concludes it cannot provide the basis for an ethics for this reason. I would argue such ambivalence is precisely what an ethics could be built upon.

43. I choose to multiply the interpretative possibilities of Cavarero's own chosen art object by exploring in detail various *Bacchae*-like readings to which the painting is hospitable. This is in contrast with the approach taken by Clare Woodford in this volume. Woodford asks why Cavarero chooses this Madonna rather than the many others on offer. Where she decenters I pluralize.

44. One could argue, however, that maternity is a better model for politics for *that* very reason. In democratic politics, after all, we are always contesting inequalities in the current partition of the sensible, as Rancière would say. But that is not Cavarero's argument, perhaps because, for her, the aim is not political, but ethical: maternity rather than sorority is privileged because it better, in her view, exemplifies the relationality that is needed for an ethics of altruism that can counter Levinas's egoism. Thus, if Cavarero neglects the classical sources here, that may well be precisely because they steer us more toward politics than ethics and because the mothers in the dramas are seldom altruistic; they are often vengeful and violent. Is this why, here, Cavarero prefers the Christian over the classical and the representational over the performing arts? For a different reading of the painting, also in response to Cavarero, and also pointing out the sorority of the two women, see Alison Stone's "The Ontology of the Maternal: A Response to Adriana Cavarero," *Studies in the Maternal* 2, no. 1 (2010): 2. For Stone, "In his 1910 essay on Leonardo da Vinci, Freud pointed out that there are two mothers in the painting. Reciprocally, there are two *children* in the scene—not only Jesus but also Mary. Mary is in her mother's lap (indeed, she completely fills it). Although now an adult and mother herself, Mary comes to her adulthood and mothering from having been a vulnerable infant cared for by her mother, a vulnerable child that, psychically, Mary will always in part remain. [In her essay in this volume Butler makes the point that the child remains, through all developmental stages.] Mary has grown to occupy a space delimited by the body of her own mother. Thus the painting shows us that Mary as mother—any mother—is always also the daughter of her own mother." Queering Mary also opens some interesting interpretative possibilities, as Woodford's essay in this volume shows.

45. Cavarero, *Inclinations*, 97. This untraditional distance from the mother(s) is what sets the scene for Mary to incline *toward* her child. Also, traditionally, this

mother and child do *not* "look at one another," and yet here they do. Diego Millan suggested to me that we could see the leaning of the mother in the painting as a leaning out and not as a leaning in—a sign of distancing, rather than closeness. That is, we cannot tell decisively if she is reaching for the child to scoop him up, or if she has just set him down and is leaning back and away from him, toward her own mother (sister).

46. Thinking of the inclinational as better represented by the relation between living and dead also addresses another problem: Cavarero's desire to insulate altruism from economism, a move criticized in detail by Derrida, who argues that every (altruistic) gift inaugurates and postulates the economism it is supposed to transcend; see Jacques Derrida, *Given Time*, vol. 1, *Counterfeit Money*, trans. Peggy Kamuf (Chicago: University of Chicago Press, 1992).

47. Cavarero, *Inclinations*, 105

48. Ibid., 105.

49. Projecting maternal murderousness onto the Greek Medea, Cavarero insulates Leonardo's Christian maternity from implication in Freud's (Greek, ambivalent) maternity, characterized at once by "'the promise of unbounded tenderness' and 'sinister menace'"; Miriam Leonard, "Freud and the Biography of Antiquity," in *Creative Lives in Classical Antiquity*, ed. Richard Fletcher and Johanna Hanink (Cambridge: Cambridge University Press, 2016). This is what George Shulman refers to as "the Klein moment" in which caring and wounding coincide in the figure of the phallic mother, a model of a powerful woman who is not castrated. Does Cavarero bury the phallic mother to make a safe maternity: all care, no wound?

50. Quoted in Leonard, "Freud and the Biography of Antiquity," 319. We may note that Medea, too, took her son(s) in place of her husband when she killed *them* to avenge the wrong for which she wanted to kill *him*.

51. Does Cavarero invite the work done here to theatricalize painting when she says in *Inclinations* about the unique signification of the Levinasian face that "the face [that] summons me and commands me not to kill" emerges "from a theater without backdrop" (165)?

52. Notably, as Miriam Leonard says, "Freud thinks that the picture of Bacchus/St John is just a compulsive repetition of the St. Anne picture with its enigmatic androgynous smile" which "leads one to guess [at] a secret love"; Leonard, "Freud and the Biography of Antiquity," 320.

53. Said Pozzo, quoted in Angela Ottino della Chiesa, *Leonardo Pittore* (Milan: Rizzoli, 1967), 109, from a document in the Vatican Library; and Marilyn Aronberg Lavin, "Giovannino Battista: A Study in Renaissance Religious Symbolism," *Art Bulletin* 37, no. 2 (June 1955): 85–101, sourced at Wikipedia, https://en.wikipedia.org/wiki/Bacchus_(Leonardo).

54. Also added was a "vine wreath"; S. J. Freedberg, "A Recovered Work of Andrea del Sarto with Some Notes on a Leonardesque Connection," *Burlington Magazine* 124, no. 950 (May 1982): 285, sourced at Wikipedia, https://en.wikipedia.org/wiki/Bacchus_(Leonardo).

55. Cavarero, *Inclinations*, 173, emphasis added.

56. Saidiya Hartman, *Wayward Lives, Beautiful Experiments: Intimate Histories of Social Upheaval* (New York: W. W. Norton, 2019); Fred Moten and Stefano Harney, *The Undercommons: Fugitive Planning and Black Study* (Wivenhoe: Minor Compositions, 2013); and Toni Morrison, *Home* (New York: Alfred A. Knopf, 2012).

57. On the swish, see Gayle Salamon, "Passing Period: Gender, Aggression and the Phenomenology of Walking," in *Performance and Phenomenology: Traditions and Transformations*, Routledge Advances in Theatre & Performance Studies, ed. Maaike Bleeker, Jon Foley Sherman, and Eirini Nedelkopoulou (New York: Routledge, 2015); on new iterations of violence now, see Cavarero, *Horrorism: Naming Contemporary Violence* (New York: Columbia University Press, 2011).

# Scherzo

# Thinking Materialistically with Locke, Lonzi, and Cavarero

OLIVIA GUARALDO

> Laughter helps one to find a place in the world, but ironically, which is to say, without selling one's soul to it.
> —HANNAH ARENDT, *MEN IN DARK TIMES*

In what follows I would like to perform a feminist "scherzo" in bodily materialism. In Western classical music a "scherzo" (the Italian word for "joke," "jest") is a movement from a larger work (a symphony or sonata) that usually retains the "triple meter time signature and the ternary form of the minuet, but is considerably quicker."[1] It is often, but not always, of a "light and humorous tone."[2]

This feminist scherzo has a light intention and a ternary pace. It touches three different authors, somehow distant from one another, yet all significantly concerned with the body. These authors are John Locke, Carla Lonzi, and Adriana Cavarero. I shall endeavor a combined reading of a few key passages of their most influential texts, hoping to do two things.

First, through the lens of a gendered materialism, enabled and legitimized within the humanities by Second Wave feminism, to analyze three different ways of utilizing the body within philosophical-political discourse to argue that while Lonzi and Locke both emphasize the conflictual element of the sexual encounter—Locke to domesticate it, Lonzi to emphasize it—Cavarero's way of casting the body moves beyond conflict and entails the claim that to experience one's unique being in relation to another's uniqueness is a pleasurable, erotic, and empowering experience that as such need not comprise appropriation (Locke), control, or domestication (Lonzi).

Second, to exhibit, through the materialist reading strategy, the specificity of the feminist perspective grounded in the thought of sexual difference, as expounded in the work of Ariana Cavarero. To a certain extent this perspective diverges from other gendered perspectives that tend to reduce sexuality and the body to a discursive or cultural dimension (thereby further reducing sex to gender), and it aims instead at giving relevance to bodily differences insofar as they tell a different story regarding sex and pleasure. My claim is moreover that the "pleasure discourse" inherent in the thought of sexual difference is not simply another (militant) discourse on the body, but aims instead at altering the ontological-political perspective on the subject.

In order to give an example of this specificity, I recur to Adriana Cavarero's reflection on sexual pleasure, hoping to show how her creative reappropriation of the sexual difference perspective does exactly this: through an embodied and materialist approach to sex, while deconstructing a conventional narrative on eros, it provides elements that contribute to a rethinking of the subject in ontologically relational terms.

1

The first character in this scherzo is Carla Lonzi, an Italian radical feminist activist and a very influential feminist theorist in the early days of Italian Second Wave feminism. A pioneer in tackling political questions by moving from the body and from the political implications of sexual pleasure, she is the author of a provocative book entitled *Sputiamo su Hegel: La donna clitoridea e la donna vaginale* (Let's Spit on Hegel: The Clitoridian Woman and the Vaginal Woman),[3] a text that has been pivotal for the Italian Thought of Sexual Difference.

The second character in this scherzo, John Locke, is among the most influential political thinkers of modernity, the recognized father of liberalism, an undoubtedly crucial thinker in shaping the political mind of an epoch. By virtue of his central position in the Western canon of political theory and his treatment of issues such as political freedom and rights, the social contract, and patriarchal power, he has also become a prominent figure in the "short but intense" history of feminist thought. Often put under scrutiny by feminist political thinkers, Locke has been both celebrated and criticized for providing at once "a language of rights and individuality that early liberal feminists found attractive ... and ... a distinctly modern vehicle of patriarchal oppression."[4]

Yet, as I shall hope to demonstrate in this essay, my brief reading of Locke goes in a slightly different direction than that proposed by feminist political theory.

Finally, the third character, Adriana Cavarero, is a feminist theorist and political philosopher who has been able to creatively combine political theory and radical feminist discourse in the direction of an innovative ontological discourse on the body and the sexed subject (*soggetto sessuato*). Their appearing together in this essay has been inspired by the perhaps trivial attempt of comparing different ways of nominating the body. Not simply the body as such, but the body in its connection to sexual practices. And in spite of the fact that this connection might seem quite obvious for Lonzi and Cavarero—two explicitly feminist thinkers—I shall hope to show that Locke, as well, when speaking of the body as a source for property, is also, implicitly but crucially, speaking of sex. Hence the liberal order of property ownership is itself gendered, rather than just a field in which gender relations operate. This indicates that feminism must always target the order of property.

2

Materialism plays a central role in this analysis, yet with a caveat: it is a materialism that "departs from the economic sphere to consider other forms of materiality."[5] In their 2007 anthology on the body, Margaret Lock and Judith Farquhar, the editors, claim that there is no such a thing as "the body proper" that "stands in a tidy contrastive relationship with the mind."[6] Through a selection of writings that span from Marx to Merleau-Ponty, from Evans-Pritchard to Judith Butler, from Gabriel Marcel to Bruno Latour, the editors of this book are moved by the idea of deconstructing the ethnocentric idea of a proper body (white, masculine, autonomous, productive) by way of exploring ways of embodiment that are plural and irreducible to one another. They explicitly aim at endorsing a materialistic approach to embodiment and carnality. In order to do so, though, they only reluctantly admit some complicity of feminism in this deconstruction of the body:

> Recent scholarship in the human sciences, led *perhaps* by gender, ethnic and rights activism in postmodern popular culture, has turned away from the commonsense body, however, learning to perceive more dynamic, intersubjective, and plural human experiences of carnality that can no longer be referenced by the singular term *the body*.[7]

And again:

> It still bears pointing out that everywhere bodies are somehow gendered. Families, communities, and societies are crossed by inequalities that are often taken to be rooted in forms of embodiment; thus it was feminist scholars who *perhaps* most powerfully in the twentieth century forced a political anthropology of the body.[8]

In line with the spirit of this interesting collection of writings on the body, I advocate a materialistic approach to a "political anthropology of the body," yet I do not share the reluctance with which the editors acknowledge the contribution of feminism to this field of research and this way of thinking. I would, to be frank, take away the two instances of "perhaps" used in the passages regarding gender and feminism. It has been feminist scholarship—initiated and sustained by feminist activism—that contributed to the deconstruction of the idea of a proper body, separated from mind; an inert matter to objectify, measure, control, possess.

When speaking of materialism in feminism I refer explicitly to Italian feminist thought as it developed from feminist activism in the early '70s and later evolved and became theoretically relevant as the thought of sexual difference.[9] Strongly influenced by Luce Irigaray, the Italian *pensiero della differenza sessuale* elaborates an innovative way of thinking the materiality of the body in relation to its sexed dimension. For Irigaray bodily difference is not intended as something biologically fixed, but rather as "the process and relations through which the complexity of matter generates (at least) two ways of forming oneself in relation to the world."[10]

The perspective I seek to enhance in this scherzo is one that, in following a feminist materialist perspective on the body, could be deemed "essentialist" according to certain standards of hegemonic critical discourse. Irigaray herself has often been dismissed as "dangerously essentialist."[11] Yet recent debates over this issue, raised especially by authors who belong to the so-called new materialism—Elizabeth Wilson, Susan Oyama, Jane Bennet, and Karen Barad, among others[12]—have finally put an end to the academic stigma on essentialism.

As Susan Oyama points out, for example, incredulity toward the real and anxiety about essentialism are part of the legacy of Cartesian dualism and sometimes function as traps that shut off paths of intellectual inquiry.[13] Again, in an ironic formulation, Elizabeth Wilson claims that "compulsive antiessentialism" is a disciplining force that has "been naturalized not simply as good critical practice, but as the sine qua non of criticism itself."[14]

## 3

It was indeed Carla Lonzi—a nonacademic theorist who famously wrote the feminist manifesto *Let's Spit on Hegel*, advocating for an anatomical reconsideration of women's bodies in order to perform a truly feminist revolution—who was the mother of this specific form of feminist materialism. In a 1977 collective text significantly entitled *E' già politica* (It's Already Politics)—where she reflects, a posteriori, with others of her group *Rivolta femminile* on their feminist experience—Lonzi affirms that only clitoridean femininity can resist cooptation and functional domestication of women within patriarchy. But what did she really mean by clitoridean femininity? Did she intend it as a biological feature, a cultural one, or both? It is interesting to note that Lonzi described this specific feminine posture as the "assumption of a non-compliant sexual identity." In her own words:

> The identity that stems from the clitoris starts from a "nothing," a cultural void and progressively constitutes itself through an acceptance of oneself that becomes one's own destiny, but cannot fix itself in a role, lest falling back into vaginality. And it cannot reveal itself in the cultural word, but in the identity that stems directly from the assumption of a non-compliant sexual identity which, alone, enables the authentic and complete utterance of the word "I." This "I" as cultural void is the premise for a rediscovery of our body, and therefore of a culture of our own.[15]

In a strongly politicized, separatist sense, Lonzi turns to the body, its material feminine anatomy, as a contrast to patriarchal discourse, to produce a liberating dimension for female subjectivity. The clitoris as a *bodily given* can signal the way toward women's freedom, insofar as it is an anatomical part that can resist cooptation within masculine sexual discourse. According to Lonzi, the clitoris, a source of pleasure naturally present in women's bodies, indicates the possibility of their bodily and symbolic autonomy from men.

For Lonzi, the feminist political issue at stake in the early '70s was that of reflecting, within a consciousness-raising group, on what she called the "void" of a nondomesticated body (the clitoridean woman was not necessarily lesbian, as Lonzi often repeated): the aim was to investigate ways of imagining women as "unpredictable subjectivities."[16] This is why the grounding of women's identity in the clitoris is defined by Lonzi as a "shared risk" that she and her companions of the group wanted to take:[17] to *see what happened* if they dared to ground themselves in their bodies and claim pleasure for themselves; the clitoris understood as a site of undomesticated pleasure that could foreground undomesticated freedom— that was their challenge.

What characterized Italian feminism within the broader Second Wave feminism was a politicized relation to the body, a militant—separatist— politics of the body that immediately contaminated thinking, theorizing a provocative bodily materialism. On this, Lonzi strenuously criticized Hegel—to the extent that she even dared to "spit" on him—because he "naturalized" sexual difference and understood it as an inferiorization of women, the "passivity" in accepting male rule being nothing else than the full realization of their "nature."

On the contrary, Lonzi enhances bodily differences not to naturalize them but to claim that they can be the point of departure for women's creativity and freedom. The clitoris is the medium for female freedom insofar as it is a "void" and as such an "*impensato*"—"unthought"—of patriarchy. The clitoris is not the vagina; the clitoris is not the uterus. The clitoris is the sign of a specific feminine difference—namely, that of a sexual, bodily pleasure separated from both coitus and reproduction.

4

Given this feminist premise, let me now turn to John Locke.

Consider the famous passage on the origin of property in John Locke's *Second Treatise on Government*:

> Every Man has a *Property* in his own *Person*. This no Body has any Right to but himself. The *Labour* of his Body and the *Work* of his Hands, we may say, are properly his. Whatsoever then he removes out of the State of Nature hath provided, and left it in, he hath mixed his *Labour* with, and joyned to it something that is his own, and thereby makes it his *Property*.
>
> It being by him removed from the common state Nature placed it in, it hath by his *labour* something annexed to it, that that excludes the common right of other Men. For this *Labour* being the unquestionable Property of the Labourer, no Man but he can have a right to what that is once joyned to, at least where there is enough, and as good, left in common for others.[18]

Locke establishes a direct and undeniable relationship between labour and property, as it is well known. Yet the primary relationship, the one that enables the emergence of property, is above all the relationship between a self and his body. It is the property of his body—a property that immediately translates into an indispensable bodily freedom—that enables the individual to claim as his own the parts of nature he has, with his body, labored. What was "common" can become *proprius*, or proper, because it has been "joyned" with "something that is his own." Therefore, through a labor that is a joining between the self (his body) and that which is outside the self—namely, something that belongs to nature—man can claim something as his own, as his property.

The body understood as property is at the basis of modern individualism and, as we all know, of modern capitalism. This body that I own allows me to separate something from nature and keep it all for me. This body that I own allows me to think of myself as a commodity: I can voluntarily sell parts of my own body or shares of its energy as labor. Much has been said on this specific Lockean anthropology and its ambiguities: on the one hand it allows us to think of humans as individuals that are autonomous and free, by nature. On the other this autonomy and freedom can easily lead to voluntary servitude insofar as it can be "sold." We are all familiar with the contradictions of liberalism.

Yet, I would like to draw attention to another, perhaps marginal, aspect of this Lockean formulation of property, one that departs from the traditional liberal perspective and digs into a different approach: one that is at the same time "aroused" by Locke's explicit reference to "the body" and canceled out from his discourse immediately. As Terrell Carver has pointed out, there is both a "covert" and an "overt" gender discourse at work in Locke, and when he appears to be gender neutral, "a covert gendering is nevertheless at work."[19] This discursive strategy is indeed typical of Locke's argumentation on matters regarding the sexes, which is, to say the least, ambiguous. Also in other passages of the *Second Treatise*, for example, he "acknowledges women as equals of men in the family," in matters regarding childcare, custody, and divorce, yet at the same time he claims "'a foundation in nature' for women's subjection and inferiority to husbands in the family."[20]

But let us return to the passage quoted previously regarding property. What is this "mixing" and "joining" that he refers to when causally justifying the right to "own" something? There is a body—which is "his"—and an act of joining that body with "something" else. Is it possible to read this famous aboriginal scene of property as an almost unambiguous exemplification of *coitus*?

The way in which Locke defines property by grounding it in "his" body is, in fact, a mimicry of the sexual act of copulation, not exactly aimed at sexual pleasure, but clearly finalized at fertilization, generation: the "he" of the story mixes something of himself (labor) with an entity that is outside himself, and as a result that entity becomes his own, his proper, his property. Significantly, the verb Locke uses to explain this mixing is "to joyn," which etymologically refers to the Latin verb *jungere*: *unite, connect, attach, fasten*. *Jungere* derives from the indo-European root *\*jewg*, which is attested in many languages with the same meaning: to "yoke," "harness," and secondarily to "couple" and "wedlock."[21] The word "conjugal" derives from the same root.

It is not by chance that, as Carole Pateman has pointed out, to think of the human in terms of an individual who is the owner of *his* own person leads us directly to the "fraternal social contract"—namely, to the affirmation of men's equality and freedom and women's submission by way of the concealed, untold "sexual contract."[22] So, inadvertently, while speaking of labor and body and hands, Locke is referring to sex, in the sense of "fertilization": the "he" of the story mixes his own sperm with something else, and then the result of the labor of "mixing" and "joining" is his property.

It is in the nature of this feminist scherzo to undo Locke's famous narrative on property as a mimicry of coitus, and I would claim that the possibility of this very reading arises because there has been a feminist discourse—initiated in activism—that has taught us to think the body and sex in a materialistic—even anatomical—sense. Without any "perhaps."

The Lockean tale of the origin of property—a feminist materialist reading suggests—is profoundly gendered, rooted as it is in a male bodily perspective (and in a masculine notion of sex—namely, *coitus*).

5

Let me in conclusion turn to the third part of this scherzo—namely, Cavarero's digression on eros in her 2000 book *Relating Narratives*. There she provocatively claims that a specific patriarchal or phallogocentric myth has told us for millennia that eros entails a fusion into unity, a disappearing of the self in the annihilating experience of sexual pleasure.

According to this myth, says Cavarero "the two uniquenesses, fusing into the one-all, disappear into a whirlpool of nowhere—the very same place, says a well-known variant of the myth, from which they emerged, namely, the mother. Birth and death, the eternal seduction of the inorganic, would therefore amount to the same thing—provided that the finite, if it is allowed some fleeting shimmer of glory, burns out in the act of its annihilation; provided that the infinite conserves its supremacy, and death its voracity."[23]

This myth is false, continues Cavarero, "because it is false to celebrate existence in rites of dissolution, turning the impulse to love into a desire for death." In fact lovers, despite the myth, do not want to die. They want "the full splendour of the finite according to the reciprocal uniqueness that exposes them and distinguishes them. Loving each other, they are simply reborn into the inaugural fragility of their existence." The joy of love, in other words, "lies indeed in the nakedness of a shared appearance that does not tolerate qualifications but simply exposes two uniquenesses to each other."[24]

According to this different way of narrating the body, the "sexual rite" therefore is not "one of a fusion, which would nullify uniqueness, frustrating the act itself. It is, if anything, the rite of repeating the beginning: exposing once again the naked exposure, not yet covered by any 'what,' that inaugurates the appearance of every human being as unique, because only in the moment of birth is every human being a pure who, to which is in no way added any what. Put another way, the one who has just been born is exemplarily without qualities."

Sex therefore qualifies as an "appearing to each other with indifference regarding qualities—an indifference which finds its height in the orgasm" in which lovers come to repeat the beginning of their existence. They do not return into the womb of the mother, as the myth claims; on the contrary, they are ousted again into the "inaugural nudity of an appearance—one which now has the perfect relational character of a co-appearance."[25]

Whereas orgasm is mythically identified with death—a pleasure that coincides with self-annihilation within an impersonal logic of the flesh—Cavarero claims we can perhaps think of orgasm as a *reenactment of birth*, intended as the naked appearance of a who: "Lovers undress themselves in order to caress their naked bodies, and yet only in the orgasm is the nakedness of the existence truly such, in so far as it is stripped of every quality."[26]

What eventually dies in the experience of orgasm told differently is the *subject* inflated of its qualities: "The loss of meaning of *what* one is—and knows oneself to be—the total oblivion of one's own personal qualities and social markers—thus gets mistaken for the death of the self."[27]

In this scene of sexual pleasure—marked by nakedness and exposure—the body is prevalent, since "existence inheres to the body," while the nudity of each body is here presented in a symbolic dimension of relationality: Cavarero qualifies it as a "spirituality of flesh and fleshiness of the spirit which makes their indiscernibility the miracle of uniqueness."[28]

In this original redescription of eros and orgasm, Cavarero furthers the kind of feminist thinking inaugurated by Carla Lonzi, a thinking that is profoundly rooted in bodily materiality. From her early writings on Plato to the latest work on "inclination," Cavarero's thinking always takes its bearings from a bodily materiality that is the situated point of departure of any theoretical endeavor. According to Cavarero, there cannot be thinking without a body, and the body is a "given" that as such cannot be exhausted by discourse, since it always *exceeds* the sociocultural frames that aim at entrapping it. The body for Cavarero is a "given"—both a celebrated source of vitality and an undeniable *limit* of the self—and in its materiality influences our way of thinking, our ethics, and our politics.

The thought of sexual difference as initiated by thinkers such as Luce Irigaray and Carla Lonzi has proven crucial in both a political and theoretical way. Politically it furthered the legacy of Second Wave feminism: women as subjects historically reduced to their "mere bodies" turned the disadvantage into a positive element, seeking a way to liberation and freedom that had to be grounded in the body. This political point has been translated by the thought of sexual difference into a radically innovative theoretical posture: thinking had to be contaminated by the body, the material elements of the flesh had to be incorporated into the immaterial dimension of theory, in order to disrupt a mechanism of exclusion, of both women and the body.

Cavarero elaborates along this line of thinking by claiming that thinking the body materialistically means to articulate alternative meanings for the given, irreducible fact of embodiment, thereby telling our bodies differently from the way they have been told—or negated—by the Western tradition, patriarchal, phallogocentric, or simply egalitarian.

## 6

To conclude this feminist scherzo, let me sum up its main points: Locke, Lonzi, and Cavarero present three ways of narrating sex: implicitly, explicitly, creatively. Locke aims at disciplining sex by including it in a property discourse; Lonzi aims at openly politicizing sex, in a separatist way; and Cavarero instead aims, more subtly, at providing a provocatively creative account of orgasm that is one with her effort of rethinking the subject: exposed and relational, profoundly dependent upon a bodily materiality that cannot be removed. Orgasm results in relationality at its purest, an instant of pleasure that does not include death or annihilation. This way of casting the body, its nakedness and exposure as orgasm, entails the claim that to experience one's unique being in relation to another uniqueness is a pleasurable, erotic, and empowering experience that as such must not necessarily entail appropriation (Locke), control, or domestication (Lonzi).

By exploring the possibilities of *the given* of our bodily condition—an anatomical *destination* to pleasure—Cavarero gives a creative account of orgasm, one that enables us, perhaps, to start from the very bodily experience we share in order to sketch possible ways of understanding our coexistence. To refer to relationality as carnal pleasure is a provocative materialist move Cavarero takes from the Thought of Sexual Difference, but also moves the stakes of this thinking further.

If then Locke presents us with a domesticated, even masked, notion of sex as marital coitus, finalized at fertilization and property, if, again Lonzi presents us with a notion of sex as politicized anatomy finalized at deconstructing patriarchy and opening the way for a liberated female subjectivity, Cavarero offers us a variant of sex that is somehow deprived of the conflictual elements Locke seeks to tame and Lonzi tends to emphasize.

In the orgasm scene I have evoked, at stake is what I would call a "postcoital" version of eros: the bare nakedness of the bodies surely recalls their unavoidable gendered nature, but the orgasm as such—understood as a reenactment of birth—is imagined as an almost nongendered experience: certainly not masculine, insofar as it is postcoital, perhaps not even strictly feminine, in the way in which, for example, Irigaray imagined and described female sexuality in *Speculum*.[29] In Cavarero's *Relating Narratives* bodies appear in their uniqueness. Pleasure is here understood in its essentially relational form, and anatomy plays a role only insofar as bodies are the vehicle of relationality and pleasure. Neither coital nor clitoridean, orgasm is here a possible figure of relationality that has the oxymoronic traits of a "spirituality of the flesh."[30]

Proposing eros as an experience of joyful reciprocal appearance of two naked uniquenesses reveals the specific Cavarerian methodology, one she applies often in other works: it consists in taking a very stereotypical scene to dismantle it from within. Yet the dismantling process is not an end in itself, it is not exhausted, so to say, by its own critical intent. The dismantling process provides an opening to test possible different meanings for the stereotype, different narrations of it.

The effect, in this specific case, is that of dismantling a coital version of orgasm—a phallocentric orgasm, one that has always been identified with "death," dissolution of the self inside the womb, drive toward self-annihilation—in order to recast it as the naked appearance of the lovers in their uniqueness. There follows a definition of love that does not fade into dissolution and death but into the reciprocal gaze of a couple.

Through the dislocation of orgasm from the *eros-thanatos* (love and death) dimension of the male-dominated narrative, a new space is opened:

one that helps rethinking subjectivity in its purely relational/orgasmic/pleasurable dimension.

Cavarero's insightful reading of scenes that can be considered familiar, common, even stereotypical—in ways that depart radically from their commonness—has a strong feminist appeal. Underlying her philosophical and political effort to rethink subjectivity there is always a feminist intention, and a feminist outcome, as well: the relational narrative of orgasm provides women with a different frame in which to think of themselves as sexual subjects outside the male-dominated narrative of orgasm as death. By virtue of this reframing of sexual pleasure, women—as well as other subjects who prefer noncoital sexual practices—can find a space of meaning for their own sexual pleasure, without figuring as "void," "incomplete," "castrated" but instead as viable, possible, if not even *real* subjects. Narrating orgasm differently contributes, in other words, to taking the feminist endeavor a step further: from sex to self, the step is a decisive one, as Carla Lonzi never tired of repeating.

Notes

1. "Scherzo," *Classical Cat*, https://www.classiccat.net/genres/scherzo.info.php; retrieved Feb. 8, 2019.

2. T. Russell and H. Macdonald, H, eds., "Scherzo," *Grove Music Online*, retrieved Feb. 8, 2019, from http://www.oxfordmusiconline.com/grovemusic/view/10.1093/gmo/9781561592630.001.0001/omo-9781561592630-e-0000024827.

3. Carla Lonzi, *Sputiamo su Hegel: La donna clitoridea e la donna vaginale e altri scritti* [Let's Spit on Hegel: The Clitoridian Woman and the Vaginal Woman and Other Writings] (Milan: Scritti di Rivolta Femminile, 1974). For the English translation of this text, see http://blogue.nt2.uqam.ca/hit/files/2012/12/Lets-Spit-on-Hegel-Carla-Lonzi.pdf, retrieved Feb. 23, 2019.

4. Nancy J. Hirschmann and Kirstie McClure, "Introduction: Johnny, We Hardly Knew Ye," in *Feminist Interpretations of John Locke*, ed. Nancy J. Hirschmann and Kirstie McClure (University Park: Pennsylvania State University Press, 2007), 2.

5. Margareth Lock and Judith Farquhar, "Introduction," in *Beyond the Body Proper: Reading the Anthropology of Material Life*, ed. Margareth Lock and Judith Farquhar (Durham, N.C.: Duke University Press, 2007), 10.

6. Ibid.

7. Ibid., 2, my emphasis.

8. Ibid., 9, my emphasis.

9. See, for an overview on Italy's vivid feminist landscape, Paola Bono and Sandra Kemp, *Italian Feminist Thought: A Reader* (Oxford: Blackwell, 1991).

10. Claire Colebrook, "Materiality: Sex, Gender and What Lies Beneath," in *The Routledge Companion to Feminist Philosophy*, ed. A. Garry, S. J. Khader, and A. Stone (London: Routlege, 2017), 196.

11. Ibid.

12. For a very clear and useful assessment of the impact of new materialism for feminist thinking, see Samantha Frost, "The Implications of the New Materialisms

for Feminist Epistemology," in *Feminist Epistemology and Philosophy of Science: Power in Knowledge*, ed. H. E. Grasswick (Dordrecht: Springer 2011), 69–83.

13. Susan Oyama, *Evolution's Eye: A System's View of the Biology-Culture Divide* (Durham, N.C.: Duke University Press, 2000), quoted by Frost, "Implications," 75.

14. Elizabeth Wilson, *Neural Geographies: Feminism and the Microstructure of Cognition* (New York: Routledge, 1998), 1–2, quoted by Frost, "Implications," 75n14.

15. Maria G. Chianesi et al., *È già politica* (Milan: Scritti di Rivolta femminile, 1977), 21–22, my translation.

16. Lonzi, *Sputiamo su Hegel*, 60. See also, on the notion of unpredictable subjectivity, Ida Domijianni, "Un/domesticated Feminism," *Soft Power* 6, no. 2 (2018): 13–26.

17. Chianesi et al., *È già politica*, 22.

18. John Locke, *Two Treatises of Government*, ed. Peter Laslett (Cambridge: Cambridge Univerity Press, 2005), 5, 27, 287–88, italics in the text.

19. Terrell Carver, "Gender and Narrative in Locke's *Two Treatises of Government*," in Hirschmann and McClure, *Feminist Interpretations of John Locke* (2007), 192; see also Hirschmann and McClure, "Introduction," 11.

20. Hirschmann and McClure, "Introduction," 3–4.

21. "Join," *Online Etymology Dictionary*, https://www.etymonline.com/word/join, retrieved Feb. 11, 2019.

22. Carole Pateman, *The Sexual Contract* (Stanford, Calif.: Stanford University Press, 1988).

23. Adriana Cavarero, *Relating Narratives: Storytelling and Selfhood*, trans. Paul Kottman (London: Routledge, 2000), 111.

24. Cavarero, *Relating Narratives*, 111.

25. Ibid.

26. Ibid., 112.

27. Ibid.

28. Ibid.

29. Luce Irigaray, *Speculum of the Other Woman*, trans. Gillian C. Gill (Ithaca, N.Y.: Cornell University Press, 1985).

30. Cavarero, *Relating Narratives*, 112.

# ÉTUDES

# Cavarero, Kant, and the Arcs of Friendship

CHRISTINE BATTERSBY

My underlying concern in this étude is the extent to which Adriana Cavarero's relational ontology can provide us with a suitable opening for the important task of reimagining the grounding principles of political and ethical theory in ways that help us reconcile the ideals of free choice and individualism with the recognition that all humans are vulnerable, and that the individual's choices are subject to manipulation. This is an urgent question, since we find ourselves living at a time when power inequalities and states of dependency are increasing rather than diminishing. The so-called tech giants (including Facebook, Google, Microsoft, Amazon, Apple) play on our weaknesses as they manipulate our needs, our friendships, and our desires, and there is increasing evidence that these technologies are themselves being exploited in order to distort the operation of democratic systems of government. There is a pressing need for a political and ethical framework that can adequately address issues relating to power imbalances, along with bodily and psychological frailties. I will, however, approach this topic in a sideways fashion: through a consideration of Cavarero's criticisms of Immanuel Kant in her recent book *Inclinations: A Critique of Rectitude*.[1]

There we discover that Cavarero is highly critical of Kant for privileging a self that positions itself as solitary, as upright and always under the control of the head and of reason, and for developing an "autarchic and egoistic model" that makes "verticality" key to the "postural geometry of Kantian ethics."[2] As such, Cavarero places Kant in opposition to her own relational ontology and her own alternative ethics and politics, which emphasize interpersonal relationships, vulnerability, and modes of inclination and subjectivity linked to maternity. Cavarero's argument against Kant is important to that of the book overall, as well as to her philosophical position more generally, as Judith Butler also shows in her chapter, "Leaning Out."[3] We see this in Chapter 2 of *Inclinations*, entitled "Kant and the Newborn," and in comments on Kant scattered throughout that book, as well as in a related essay, "Rectitude: Reflections on Postural Ontology" (2013), which focuses almost entirely on Kant.[4]

*Inclinations* opens with the observation that it was when writing about what is missing from Kant's philosophy that Walter Benjamin came up with the idea that moral philosophy would be radically transformed if we gave inclination (*Neigung*) a positive moral value.[5] For Kant, famously, moral worth is tied to obedience to the moral law and, more especially, to duty (*Pflicht*); by contrast, inclination is either morally neutral or morally harmful. Cavarero regards Kant's low esteem for inclination as symptomatic of a more general failing in our culture and develops Benjamin's hint about inclination—and about Kant—as she seeks to expose the bias toward the upright and the perpendicular that dominates Western thought. In *Inclinations*, it is the maternal that takes center stage, and Cavarero shows how Kant, along with many other writers, fails to register the ontological and ethical imbalances that result from the fact that a human fetus is dependent for its growth on a mother, and that infancy is also a state of dependence on an adult—and usually female—carer. Neglecting ontological dependencies and power inequalities, philosophers and political theorists overprivilege fully autonomous, and ideally equal and adult selves. Cavarero provides a pithy critique of such a cultural bias, and seeks to counterbalance it by stressing the visual, metaphoric, and philosophical importance of being off-balance, with one self inclining toward another. As such, Cavarero is seeking to provide an alternative imaginary not only to an ontological schematism that has a dominant and solitary "I," but also to any ethics or politics that is erected on such a basis.

Much of her critique of Kant is well-founded, but Cavarero neglects Kant's privilege of friendship and his account of "unsocial sociability" (*ungesellige Geselligkeit*) as integral to human civilization. In what follows I will look at this gap. I will be critical, but the criticisms are offered in a spirit that does, I hope, reflect my longstanding friendship with Adriana Cavarero. Indeed, the criticisms are not meant to detract from the power of this, her most challenging, original, and important book—at least as far as I am concerned. My criticisms will be detailed insofar as they relate to Kant; but at stake is a broader issue, in that it seems to me that Cavarero's ontology, with its emphasis on asymmetrical relationality, needs a further swerve so as to include arcs of dependence that are appropriate to friendship between individuals, states, and other social groupings.

And here I need to start by saying that Cavarero is not entirely fair to Kant. Relationality does, for example, play a larger role in his philosophy than she allows. She suggests, for example, that Kant is a solipsist, relying on Hannah Arendt's *Book of Thoughts* to establish this claim.[6] But this is rather misleading, insofar as solipsism is usually defined as the view or theory that the self is all that can be known to exist. Kant's position, by contrast, as it emerges in the *Critique of Pure Reason*—and, more especially, in the "Refutation of Idealism" of the second (1787) edition—is that we cannot have direct inner knowledge of the self, and that we are only able to say "I" insofar as we are able to locate an object in space and time to which we stand in a *relationship* of negation. Cavarero's reading of Kant elides the positions of Descartes and Kant; but, for Kant, Descartes is an idealist, and precisely the type of idealist that he sets out to "refute."[7]

Cavarero and Arendt are on stronger ground when together they suggest that Kant's moral philosophy goes astray insofar as it neglects other human beings with whom we share the space-time world. But even here there is a degree of exaggeration. Cavarero quotes Arendt as claiming that "'it is most surprising that in *The Critique of Practical Reason*, and in his other moral writings, Kant hardly can speak of *other people* [*Mitmenschen*]. It is really just about the Self and Reason functioning in isolation.'"[8] But the I and reason are never isolated in Kant, at least on the level of the space-time world, which is, Kant insists, the only world that it is possible to *know*. Cavarero reads Kant as adopting a "two-world" ontology that reaches back to Plato.[9] Kant is, however, even more critical of Plato and Platonism than he is of Descartes.[10] He does not claim that we can have *knowledge* of the world of the noumenal in which freedom, God, and the soul exist as ontological entities; but only that in our moral dealings with others—and also in terms of the relation that the self has with itself—we have to act *as if* that were the case. Ascribing moral responsibility in the empirical (phenomenal) world does, Kant argues, require treating the "I" *as if* it were autonomous and also a unity, and *as if* it were responsible for its own freely chosen actions. As such, Kant does not fit straightforwardly into the "two-world" view of human reality that Cavarero describes in terms of an "immobile and ecstatic verticalization" that is entirely hostile to inclination and the "curled-up posture" of those who are trapped within Plato's cave of sensory illusion.[11]

There is a caricature of Kant as an isolated individual who did not much like other people—especially children. And, to some extent, Cavarero recycles this view. But we now know this to be a historical mistake. Kant's closest friend was Joseph Green, an English merchant, originally from Hull, also unmarried, but three years younger than Kant. Green lived his life in accordance with strict rules and maxims, timetabling his day-to-day activities with scrupulous attention to detail—so much so that it has been argued that he provided the model for the main character, Orbil, in Theodor Gottlieb von Hippel's satirical play *The Man of the Clock or the Orderly Man* (1765).[12] Kant is also often mocked for leading a similarly routinized life; but this was not a feature of his daily life as a young man, and it was Green who persuaded Kant to change his ways.

The two men spent so much time together, and were so close, as to lead one German scholar to suggest that it was potentially *schwul*—a slang term for homosexual or "queer."[13] Earlier in this volume, we saw Judith Butler playing with a similar idea, although her mischievous comments are made on the basis of narrative and philosophical and physical instabilities, rather than through awareness of Kant's male friendships and their associated routines.[14] The two friends ate together, went on trips together, discussed books and politics together, and were also said to take an afternoon doze together—also with other male friends—side by side, in easy chairs.[15] Kant was said to have read every sentence of the *Critique of Pure Reason* to Green and discussed each sentence with him.[16] After Green died in 1786, Kant went into a kind of mourning and stopped going out to eat in the evenings. He did, however, keep up his relationship with Robert Motherby, another of the Hull merchants and the business partner of Green. Kant was a frequent guest for Sunday lunch, and was treated as a family member as he played with the nine surviving children and helped with the education of the older boys.[17] Thus, if we follow Kant into the labyrinths of his moral philosophy and look more closely at his private life, we end up not with an isolated self and reason, but with an intimate circle of friends who care for each other, mostly in male friendship circles, but also within the domestic and family sphere.

In testimony to Kant's close friendships, I was excited to stumble across the image of an engraved glass goblet, inscribed with the date August 30, 1763, together with a motto (in English) and the names of Kant and six of his friends, including Green, Motherby, and Charles Staniforth (brother-in-law to Green, and also closely linked to the shipping merchants of Kingston-upon-Hull). (See Fig. 1a.)[18] The motto reads, "Secrecy in love and sincerity in Friendship / all Happy together notwithstanding what happend [*sic*] in the World." (See Fig. 1b, which contains the complete transcription of the inscription on the glass.)[19]

The discovery was made on the website of the "Friends of Kant and Königsberg" [*Freunde Kants und Königsbergs*], an organization that ar-

FIGURE 1A. *Kant Glass Friendship Goblet* (1763), © 2013 Freunde Kants und Königsbergs e. V. Source Image by Viktor Haupt, supplied by Freunde Kants und Königsbergs e. V.

ranges an annual trip to the Russian exclave of Kaliningrad—formerly Königsberg—to honor Kant on his birthday, in the city where he spent his whole life. Since the existence of this goblet is absent from recent scholarly biographies of Kant, I have investigated its pedigree, and looked further into its history. Correspondence with the Motherby family assured me of its legitimacy, a conclusion very recently confirmed by Simon Wain-Hobson, a connoisseur of Georgian glass, whose attention had also been drawn to the image on the website, and who had also been in correspondence with the family and the owner of the glass. Wain-Hobson has no doubt that the goblet itself, with its "triple series opaque twist stem," was made in Britain, and that the "*diamond* point inscription of dubious quality" would most likely have been executed in Königsberg. As he indicates,

*Secrecy in love and sincerity
in Friendship*

*Emanuel Kant M. A.
Anthony Schorn
Joseph Green
Robert Motherby.*

*all Happy together notwithstanding what happend in the World*
=
*August of 30<sup>th</sup>
1763*

*Joseph P... [?]
John Chappoll
Charles Staniforth*

FIGURE 1B. *Kant Glass Inscription* © 2013 Freunde Kants und Königsbergs e. V.

the stem of the glass has been broken and "repaired using a soldered tin collar"; in addition, "a gold plaid ribbon" of unknown significance and date was knotted around the stem.[20]

My historical research also revealed that August 1763 was the time of a global banking crash that economists have compared to that of September 1998.[21] Triggered by the ending of the Seven Years War—and the signing of the Treaty of Paris that initiated the series of international realignments that triggered the American War of Independence in 1775—financial ruin faced many merchant banking companies, across Europe and beyond. The firm of Motherby and Green survived the banking crash in good shape, as did that of Charles Staniforth—so much so that his son, John Staniforth the younger, would later become the M.P. for Hull and then also the Director of the Bank of England.[22] Kant clearly benefitted from having a competent firm of merchant bankers looking after his finances at this time of economic catastrophe. Not all the signatories were so fortunate, however. Thus, for example, it seems likely that the name "Anthony Schorn" refers to Anton Schorn, son of Michael Schorn—a fabulously wealthy wine and shipping-merchant (and collector of "luxury" goods)—who traded out of Braunsberg (present-day Braniewo in northeast Poland), sourcing wines from right across France, and trading also in salt, limes, sugar, coffee, yarns, and huge quantities of window glass. In July 1765 Michael Schorn's enterprise suddenly and unexpectedly collapsed, "like a house of cards," its owner having been forced into bankruptcy by the Königsberg shipping firms with whom he had long-standing and trusted trading relationships. This catastrophe did, in its turn, lead to the financial ruin of Anton Schorn's own business.[23] Given this outcome, not quite two years after the drinking party, it's important not to sentimentalize the reasons each of the friends allowed his name to be scratched with a diamond onto the surface of the drinking glass. The goblet does, nevertheless, emblematize an ideal of friendship across national borders and the mutual dependence of one adult self on another in a time of crisis, shifting national borders, and political and economic instability.

The glass and its historical background show very clearly how we can be led astray if we treat Kant as a solitary individual, cut off from friendships and disconnected from those around him. We have seen Cavarero agreeing with Arendt when she claims that Kant hardly speaks of other humans anywhere in his writings on morality. But although it's true that other humans have a quite subsidiary role in Kant's *Critique of Practical Reason* (1788), in his later *Metaphysics of Morals* (1797) other human beings are certainly spoken about—not only in volume 1, which focuses on justice and "the doctrine of right," but also in volume 2, which focuses on what it is to be a virtuous individual. This volume starts with "a Human Being's *Duties to Himself*" (as Arendt and Cavarero might lead us to expect); but it then moves on to the topic of our "Ethical *Duties to Others*" [*ethischen Pflichten gegen Andere*]—an extended, but also condensed, section of Kant's ethics that Arendt seems not to have known.[24] These duties are, first, our duties to other humans simply insofar as they are human beings; second, our duties to those humans whom we should love [*Liebespflicht*]; and, third, our duties pertaining to those humans we should respect [*der Pflicht der Achtung für Andere*].[25] Kant treats friendship under this third heading—that of respect for others—while nevertheless adding an extra chapter on the intimate link between love and respect in friendship.

Here, Kant focuses on the distinction between modes of friendship that have the capacity to fizzle out when circumstances change and "moral friendship," which consists in "the complete confidence of two persons in revealing their secret judgments and feelings to each other, as far as such disclosures are consistent with mutual respect."[26] Underlying Kant's disquisition on friendship in these pages is his insistence that a "human being is a being meant for society (though he is also an unsociable one)." On the one hand, his social drive means that "he feels strongly the need to *reveal* himself to others (even with no ulterior purpose)." On the other hand, "hemmed in and cautioned by fear of the misuse that others may make of his disclosing his thoughts, he finds himself constrained *to lock up* in himself a good part of his judgments (especially those about other people). He would like to discuss with someone what he thinks about his associates, the government, religion and so forth, but he cannot risk it."[27]

Here Kant is describing a kind of dialectic of friendship. On the one hand, there is loneliness that is a kind of "prison"; but an individual can escape from being "shut up" inside himself by finding a close friend who shares the individual's "general outlook on things." With such a friend, "secrets" will be shared, and the friend then has an obligation never to divulge what he or she has been told.[28] This means, Kant argues, that it is important not to place the friend in the position of knowing things about one's self that would present the friend with a moral quandary or undermine the two friends' feelings of mutual respect for each other.[29] It's a duty to others, as well as to oneself, "not to *isolate* oneself," Kant insists, as he constructs an imaginary "circle," with the self with its moral principles at the center. This "all-inclusive circle" should include "those who, in their disposition, are citizens of the world" and who share a "disposition of reciprocity—agreeableness, tolerance, mutual love and respect."[30] As a corollary to this duty, Kant also insists that we should exclude from this social and moral circle those who reveal a "vicious" character, and the section ends with a barb against anyone who "is rich enough to bribe parasites with the pleasures of luxury."[31]

The motto on that friendship goblet of 1763—"Secrecy in love and sincerity in Friendship"—would seem thus to prefigure Kant's much later account of moral friendship, which keeps the tension between "the need to reveal" oneself and secrecy in play. The phrase "secrecy in love" was probably taken from Samuel Butler's *Hudibras* (1663–78), a mock-heroic satirical poem that had been translated from English into German and that Kant refers to elsewhere.[32] In it, Butler's anti-hero and a Dame debate whether oaths respecting the secrecy of love should be respected, given that love itself is a "treason" that wrenches the lover away from sociality, especially since oaths about love often serve as a cover for disputes about money.[33] *Hudibras* took aim at the Protestant sects that emerged during the English civil war. It was subsequently much used by rebels against the English crown and others contesting civil authority.[34] As such, it seems as if the German philosopher and his English merchant friends were not only vowing secrecy in love, but probably also about money, as well as about political and religious allegiances that might mitigate against their friendships. Kant was a strong opponent of the British monarchy—a view probably not shared by his English friends—which he accused of conducting a war without consulting the British people.[35] Kant and his friends also needed to be careful not to offend the Prussian state, which exercised political censorship over what could be written and said. The motto on the engraved glass goblet positions friendship as a remedy for political and financial uncertainties: "all Happy together notwithstanding what happend in the World."

Elsewhere in this volume we have seen Bonnie Honig look to sorority as a means of extending Cavarero's argument about the importance of inclination.[36] Sisterhood does, however, suggest a *biological* or *natural* relationship that does not start in "unsociality," and, as such, Honig's argument leads in a different direction—and one that does not foreground the fragilities and hazards of friendship that I am concerned to emphasize here. Unlike sisterhood, friendship has to start *from scratch*; friends need to *work across time* to negotiate disparities in power, personal situation, inclinations, and beliefs. As Clare Woodford also points out, friendship does not entail shared inclinations or consensus, although Kant's account of "moral friendship" does privilege those modes of friendship in which inclinations are shared.[37] Importantly also, friendships can be abusive—and often do involve modes of bullying and of seduction.

At a global level, there are the bullying relationships that exist between global superpowers and their client states. At a more individual level, there are issues relating to sexual abuse, or the abuse involved in turning a young and vulnerable human being into a potential terrorist, willing to kill and maim civilians for the "greater good" of a religious or political cause. In these dangerous times of political populism, of Brexit, Trumpism, and of manipulation of "friends" via social media, it is worth looking again at Kant's account of human and civic relationality to see how the arcs of *friendship* between civil societies and also between persons can be developed in ways that involve a reimagination of autonomy, but without subjection or abuse. The development of cosmopolitanism—and also its occasional setbacks—depends on this dialectic between the one and the many. This is not to say that we should accept Kant's account of the dialectics of friendship without questioning the assumptions on which it is based. But it is to add into Cavarero's argument in *Inclinations* the point that she makes in *Relating Narratives: Storytelling and Selfhood*, where we encounter a self "that belongs to the world, in the relational and contextual form of self exposure to others," and where friendship is also given an important role in allowing the "I" to discover itself and reveal itself to itself.[38]

In a recent essay entitled, "All of Us Are Vulnerable, But Some Are More Vulnerable than Others," Alyson Cole has explored some of the political and ethical problems that stem from overemphasizing dependence and vulnerability as part of the human condition.[39] If all of us are vulnerable, how can we adequately theorize those who are most vulnerable?

And—to extend Cole's analysis—if all of us are vulnerable, how do we go about defending the minds of those who are most vulnerable from those political fanatics or those with political power who would seek to take over their choices and their inclinations by turning them into terrorists or cogs in some political machine? Of course, there are weaknesses in the Kantian position that posits autonomy, freedom from constraint, and equality as ideals for moral behavior. But there are also problems with a position that emphasizes vulnerability and asymmetrical relationships of dependency as the basis for a new ethical and political ideal.

In this étude I have offered a limited defense of Kant (whose ideas of sexual, racial, and ethnic differences I have strongly criticized elsewhere),[40] as a way of pointing to other models of relationality that could serve as a counter to the overidealized account of autonomy and of equality so often associated with Kant's philosophical system. I strongly believe that we need a new type of political and ethical framework that can adequately address issues of trust and mistrust, along with the pervasiveness of bullying and other abuses of power. However, if we are to confront the particular political dangers of our time, it seems to me that the mother-child relationship is a perilous starting point, and that we should also look back at Kant's dialectics of friendship, together with Cavarero's emphasis on friendship in her earlier book, to discover how the arcs of relationality can best be developed with the goals of democratic freedoms and cosmopolitanism in view.

Notes

1. Adriana Cavarero, *Inclinations: A Critique of Rectitude*, trans. Amanda Minervini and Adam Sitze (Stanford, Calif.: Stanford University Press, 2016); first published in Italian (2014).

2. Ibid., 129, 33, 121.

3. Judith Butler, "Leaning Out, Caught in the Fall: Interdependency and Ethics in Cavarero," in this volume.

4. Cavarero, *Inclinations*, 25–33. Cavarero, "Rectitude: Reflections on Postural Ontology," *Journal of Speculative Philosophy* 27, no. 3 (2013): 220–35.

5. Cavarero, *Inclinations*, 1, 177n1; Walter Benjamin, "Zur Kantischen Ethik," *Gesammelte Schriften*, ed. Rolf Tiedemann and Hermann Schweppenhäuser (Frankfurt: Suhrkamp, 1974–99), 6:55, https://archive.org/stream/GesammelteSchriftenBd.6/BenjaminGs6#page/n5.

6. Cavarero, *Inclinations*, 31, 181n22, citing Hannah Arendt, *Denktagebuch: 1950 bis 1972*, ed. Ursula Ludz and Ingeborg Nordmann (Munich: Piper, 2002), 818.

7. Immanuel Kant, *Critique of Pure Reason*, trans. and ed. Paul Guyer and Allen W. Wood (Cambridge: Cambridge University Press, 1997), 326–29 [B274–79]; 121n.–22n. [Bxxxix–xli]; and see also 425–31 [A367–80]. The 1781 page numbers are marked "A"; the 1787 page numbers are marked "B." See Kant, *Gesammelte Schriften*,

ed. der Deutschen [formerly Königlich Preussischen] Akademie der Wissenschaften (Berlin: Walter de Gruyter Verlag, 1902–), vol. 3 (B edition) and vol. 4 (A edition). Further references to this Akademie edition will be prefaced Ak., followed by the volume and page numbers.

8. Cavarero *Inclinations*, 31, quoting Arendt, *Denktagebuch*, 818.

9. Cavarero, *Inclinations*, 27.

10. Kant, *Critique of Pure Reason*, 140 [A5/B8–B9]; 395–98 [A312–19/B368–76]. See also Kant, "On a Recently Prominent Tone of Superiority in Philosophy," in *Theoretical Philosophy after 1781*, ed. Henry Allison and Peter Heath (Cambridge: Cambridge University Press, 2002), 431–45 [Ak. 8:389–406].

11. Cavarero, *Inclinations*, 54, and see 33.

12. Theodor Gottlieb von Hippel, *Der Mann nach der Uhr oder der ordentliche Mann*, ed. Erich Jenisch, 4th ed. (Halle: M. Niemeyer, 1928), http://www.zeno.org/nid/20005071739. And see Manfred Kuehn, *Kant: A Biography* (Cambridge: Cambridge University Press, 2001), 154–57.

13. Hans-Peter Gensichen, "Wie schwul war Kant?," *Forum für Politik, Gesellschaft und Kultur* 234 (March 2004): 43–47, http://www.forum.lu/pdf/artikel/5189_234_Genischen.pdf.

14. Butler, "Leaning Out."

15. Alfons Hoffmann, ed., *Ein Lebensbild nach Darstellungen der Zeitgenossen Jachmann, Borowski, Wasianski* (Halle an der Saale: Hugo Peter, 1902), 57, https://archive.org/details/immanuelkanteinloohoff. And see Kuehn, *Kant*, 273.

16. Kuehn, *Kant*, 240–41.

17. Marianne Motherby, "Kant and the Motherby Family," trans. Terence Coe, Freunde Kants und Königsbergs, 2020, www.freunde-kants.com/kant-and-the-motherby-family.

18. Figure 1a. The goblet remains in the Motherby family, and I am indebted to Marianne Motherby, as well as to its current owner, the photographer Viktor H. Haupt, and Freunde Kants und Königsbergs e. V., for permission to reproduce it here. See also Motherby, "Kant."

19. Inscription can be viewed online at http://www.kant-online.ru/en/?p=191; © 2013 Freunde Kants und Königsbergs e. V. Motherby, "Kant" includes a "corrected" version of the inscription, but Marianne Motherby has been unable to determine which version is correct, and I have chosen to remain with the original deciphered text.

20. Simon Wain-Hobson, "To See a World in a Glass Engraving," *Glass Matters: Journal of the Glass Society* (forthcoming). I have corresponded with Wain-Hobson, and his essay incorporates some of my conclusions. It does, however, include additional detailed information about this 21.6 cm-tall glass and the names inscribed on it. In particular, he identifies John Chappoll as John Chappell (1739–76), the son of the master of a ship that traded between Hull and Königsberg, and who always took to sea with him books of poetry by Milton and Edward Young.

21. Isabel Schnabel and Hyun Song Shin, "Liquidity and Contagion: The Crisis of 1763," *Journal of the European Economic Association* 2, no. 6 (Dec. 2004): 929–68.

22. See The History of Parliament: The House of Commons, 1790–1820, ed. R. G. Thorne, online ed., accessed September 25, 2018, https://www.historyofparliamentonline.org/volume/1790-1820/member/staniforth-john. This records that Joseph Green's brother, Philip Green, was a shipowner based in Hull, as was also John Staniforth (d. 1798), the brother of Charles Staniforth, a merchant

trader with offices in London. Charles's son, John Staniforth (1771–1830), became M.P. for Hull in 1804 and Director of the Bank of England in 1807.

23. Franz Buchholz, "Braunsberg im Wandel der Jahrhunderte: Festschrift zum 650jährigen Stadtjubiläum am 23. und 24. Juni 1934, http://www.braunsberg-ostpreussen.de/buchholz-ges.htm.

24. Immanuel Kant, *The Metaphysics of Morals* [1797], in *Practical Philosophy*, trans. ed. Mary J. Gregor (Cambridge: Cambridge University Press, 1996), 602–3 [Ak. 6:491–93].

25. Ibid., 603 [Ak. 6:493].

26. Ibid., 586 [Ak. 6:470–71]. Kant also outlined some modes of instrumental friendship in his *Lectures on Ethics*, as recorded in the notebooks of his students between 1774 and 1777. See Lara Denis, "From Friendship to Marriage: Revising Kant," *Philosophy and Phenomenological Research* 63, no. 1 (July 2001): 3; and Lara Denis and Oliver Sensen, eds., *Kant's Lectures on Ethics: A Critical Guide* (Cambridge: Cambridge University Press, 2015).

27. Ibid., 586 [Ak. 6:471–72].

28. Ibid., 587 [Ak. 6:472].

29. Ibid., 585 [Ak. 6:469–70].

30. Ibid., 588 [Ak. 6:473].

31. Ibid., 588 [Ak. 6:474].

32. Kant, *Lectures on Anthropology*, ed. Allan W. Wood and Robert B. Louden, trans. Robert R. Clewis and G. Felicitas Munzel (Cambridge: Cambridge University Press, 2012), 391–92 [Ak. 25:1268–69]. See also Kant, *Dreams of a Spirit Seer Elucidated by Dreams of Metaphysics* (1766), in *Theoretical Philosophy, 1755–1770*, ed. David Walford and Ralf Meerbote (Cambridge: Cambridge University Press, 1992), 336 [Ak. 2:348].

33. Samuel Butler, *Hudibras: Poem*, new ed. (London: Suttaby, Evance, Fox, and Crosby, 1812), 1:248, Part 2, Canto 1, lines 415–45, https://catalog.hathitrust.org/Record/005641486.

34. Bruce Ingham Granger, *Political Satire in the American Revolution, 1763–1783* (Ithaca, N.Y.: Cornell University Press, 1960), 12–15.

35. Kant, *The Conflict of the Faculties* (1798), trans. Mary J. Gregor, in *Religion and Rational Theology*, ed. Allan W. Wood and George Di Giovanni (Cambridge: Cambridge University Press, 2001), 305–6, 306 n. [Ak 7:90].

36. Bonnie Honig, "How to Do Things with Inclination," in this volume. I am less interested than Honig (or also Cavarero in her "Coda" to this volume) in "doing things" with inclination. This links to my criticism of Carol Gilligan and her "feminine" ethics of care in Christine Battersby, *The Phenomenal Woman: Feminist Metaphysics and the Patterns of Identity* (Cambridge: Polity Press, 1998), 206–8.

37. Clare Woodford, "Queer Madonnas," in this volume.

38. Cavarero, *Relating Narratives: Storytelling and Selfhood*, trans. Paul A. Kottman (London and New York: Routledge, 2000).

39. Alyson Cole, "All of Us Are Vulnerable, But Some Are More Vulnerable Than Others: The Political Ambiguity of Vulnerability Studies; An Ambivalent Critique," *Critical Horizons* 17, no. 2 (2016): 260–77, https://doi.org/10.1080/14409917.2016.1153896.

40. See especially Christine Battersby, *The Sublime, Terror and Human Difference* (London and New York: Routledge 2007), 45–99.

# Bad Inclinations

*Cavarero, Queer Theories, and the Drive*

LORENZO BERNINI

## Cavarero in European Sexual Difference Feminism

Cavarero is one of the putative founders of European sexual difference feminism and continues to be one of its main exponents. However, because of the originality of her views, she cannot be considered an emblematic representative of this branch of thought. To start with, one of the main frictions between Cavarero and other well-known European feminist thinkers rests in her refusal to use psychoanalysis as a tool to understand humanity in general and femininity in particular. Over a kind of knowledge that, in her view, is bound to erase the singularity of the human by subsuming it under pseudo-universal categories, Cavarero prefers to stay within the philosophical tradition in order to give a radical critique of it. In *In Spite of Plato*,[1] Cavarero presents her theoretical practice as an act of theft: depriving philosophy of some of its key figures and endowing them with new meaning from the unexpected point of view of a woman practicing philosophy.

Through the rereading of Plato, Descartes, Hobbes, Locke, and Kant, Cavarero points out that the subject of knowledge, ethics, and politics that the philosophical canon describes as neutral is actually male individual, conceived of by male philosophers in their own image. As Cavarero argues in *Stately Bodies*,[2] only men would resort, as Hobbes did, to the fiction of individuals springing "out of the earth, and suddenly, like mushrooms, com[ing] to full maturity without any kind of engagement to the other."[3] And, as she purports in an essay from 1999,[4] only men would magine, as Descartes did, to be brought into the world without the help of others, by means of thinking alone.[5]

On the other hand, Cavarero draws on twentieth-century philosophy to think of what the canon left unthought. More specifically, her main interlocutors are Levinas in the field of ethics and Arendt in the field of politics. Yet, she does not exempt them from her feminist critique. Levinas, in Cavarero's view, is to be praised for conceptualizing the primacy of the other over the self. The other, for him, is always already present, and the other's face is always already hailing the self. In the ethical scene he sketches, however, there is no room for the asymmetrical, original relationship that involves the mother and the child she gives birth to, nor for her inclination toward the baby for caring purposes. In his account, the subjects of ethics are two adults who confront each other face to face: two Hobbesian mushrooms, or better two male warriors whose task is to resist the impulse to kill one another. As in most parts of the philosophical tradition, also in Levinas, morality—its origins, horizon, and background—is marked by death and killing more than life or birth.[6]

According to Cavarero, Arendt's importance lies precisely in, instead, underscoring the dependence of human singularity on the plurality before which humans appear and in interpreting the act of appearing in terms of natality: for Arendt, only by acting before a plurality of humans, a human is recognized as a singular subject, and in so doing, in a certain sense, gets born as a proper human. At the same time, however, Arendt is also complicit with the philosophical tradition when forgetting to sexuate the subjects of politics. According to Cavarero, she overlooks that the second birth, through political action, is preceded by a first birth: that of the infant from the woman's body. *This* event inaugurates the dependency of human beings, first, on those who generated them, and second, on their caregivers. Humans are thus not self-standing individuals, or beings whose existence is only determined by the act of thinking, or creatures that pop up from the ground like mushrooms; and they do not come into being when they appear in the public sphere, either. As *Relating Narratives*,[7] *Horrorism*,[8] and *Inclinations* recount, humans are born unarmed, and their bodily existence is made possible by the inclination of others (traditionally their mothers) who take care of them. Furthermore, their sense of themselves is made possible by the inclination of others who are the witnesses of their existence, available to collect their life stories and renarrate such stories to them, and to others.

## Cavarero and Butler

In line with her roots in sexual difference feminism, Cavarero turns the relationship between mother and child into the foundation of her ontology of the human. The acknowledgment of the humans' constitutive dependency, of the defenselessness of the newborn, and of the existence of altruistic human inclinations such as those of maternity is the starting point for Cavarero to construct an ethics of nonviolence and promote a new relationship between the self, the other, and the common world. However, her insistence on the maternal does not translate into a heterosexist stance. Within sexual difference feminism, Cavarero takes on a highly original position: not only because she does not restage psychoanalytic definitions of femininity and masculinity, but also because she engages with lesbian feminism and queer theories. Indeed, it was thanks to Cavarero that Judith Butler's work was introduced to Italian audiences in 1996, in the translation of *Bodies That Matter*,[9] just six years after the groundbreaking publication of *Gender Trouble*.[10] In her introduction to this text, Cavarero presents Butler "as one of the most well-regarded representatives of American lesbian thought, ingenious philosopher and crucial figure in the international feminist scene," "gay and lesbian studies," and "queer theory."[11] A tribute to Butler's theory of gender performativity can also be detected in the second part of *For More Than One Voice*, where Cavarero reflects on the predominance, in opera, of vocals over semantics—hence of femininity over masculinity—and in this predominance she finds the reason "opera has an irresistible tendency to stage drag."[12]

A more intense dialogue between Butler and Cavarero began after 9/11, when vis-à-vis the new global war, both authors radicalized their critique of the philosophical canon and of its methodological individualism. Drawing on one another, they both developed an ethics of nonviolence, grounded on the awareness of shared human vulnerability. Cavarero is quoted in *Precarious Life*,[13] *Giving an Account of Oneself*,[14] and *Notes toward a Performative Theory of Assembly*[15]: Butler makes use of Cavarero's *For More Than One Voice* to frame both Lévinas's theory of responsibility and Arendt's theory of plurality and natality. On the other hand, Butler appears in *Horrorism, Thou Shalt Not Kill*,[16] and *Inclinations*, where her work is not only praised, but also, to some extent, challenged. Cavarero, in fact, argues that Butler's theory of vulnerability puts too much emphasis on negativity. Even when dwelling on the relationship between babies and their caregivers, Butler's insistence is more on the *vulnus* (that is, the wound that the other may inflict on the baby) than on the altruistic inclination of the other on the baby. Additionally, when analyzing the care relationship, Butler seems to forget, in Cavarero's view, that the caregiver is generally a mother and that the position of men and women in the birth scene is unequal.[17]

In 2005, the Italian journal *Micromega* featured a dialogue between Cavarero and Butler on the theme of violence. There, a further difference between the two authors emerges. This is the text where Cavarero makes her stance on psychoanalysis more explicit and blames Butler, not without irony, for adopting it. As when someone pushes a friend to side with her, Cavarero starts by paying all due respect to Butler's critique of Freud's and Lacan's heterosexism, which, in her view, "targets" "one of the founding elements of psychoanalysis, if not its very foundation." She then adds that what makes psychoanalysis irretrievable from a philosophical point of view, in her understanding, is its "mythicizing of childhood," which restages naturalistic necessity into the interpretation of human action.[18] To this, Butler replies that most contemporary psychoanalysis rejects being labeled as science and, as such, rejects an understanding of psychic processes as natural. By doing so, Butler pushes Cavarero to admit that, rid of "its clinical pretension," psychoanalysis can be considered "one of the most interesting theories of the twentieth century," which "allows [us] not only to deconstruct the classical subject, but also to think the category of relationship."[19] These benevolent words are, quite obviously, addressed to Butler's specific use of psychoanalysis. Yet, here I recall them to legitimize my attempt to complement Cavarero's relational ontology of the human with a trend in contemporary queer thought, which often takes distance from Butler's theory of gender performativity—namely, so-called antisocial theories.

## Cavarero and Antisocial Theories

In *Inclinations*, Cavarero makes one last "brief mention" of queer theories, introducing them as a fundamental critique of "the hegemony of the hierarchizing *dispositif* of heterosexuality that turns 'right' and 'straight' into synonyms."[20] Queer theories, she claims, challenge "*Homo erectus*"—that is, the aforementioned rational individual/mushroom of the philosophical tradition—"and consign him to his own 'bad inclinations,' which are 'abnormal' and as a consequence 'unnatural.'"[21] The reference to the "inclining" force of sex and its power to carry humans away from their nature is quite brief here. Resorting to her method of stealing from the philosophical canon, Cavarero's discussion operates in terms of "sins of the flesh against nature (*crimina carnis contra naturam*)"[22]—a category that Kant inherited from Thomas Aquinas.[23] Antisocial queer theorists, instead, adopt the concept of "drive" (*Trieb* in German, *pulsion* in French), introduced by Freud and reinterpreted by Lacan and Laplanche—two authors that Butler quotes, in the aforementioned dialogue with Cavarero, as good examples of nonscientific psychoanalysis.[24] And the concept of drive is precisely what I want to quickly scrutinize now.

In *Freud's Drive*,[25] Teresa de Lauretis follows Laplanche and explains that, in Freud's interpretation, the sexual drive is not natural and does not coincide with the sexual instinct, for it is a perversion of it.[26] Indeed, in his *Three Essays on the Theory of Sexuality*,[27] Freud contends that, despite surfacing at an early stage, sexual drives do not emerge directly from the infant's biological needs, but rather from the arousal that the infant experiences while being fed, washed, and touched by caregivers.[28] The drive does not originate from the body, Laplanche and de Lauretis conclude, but it is "implanted in" the bodily surface,[29] thereby configuring an intermediate region between the inside and the outside, the somatic and the psychic. This region does not properly belong to the subject: the subject rather loses itself through it.

More than a decade earlier than de Lauretis, Leo Bersani, another reader of Laplanche, in his *The Freudian Body*[30] and *Is the Rectum a Grave?*,[31] claims that the drive is unnatural and perverted, that it undermines both the instinct of procreation and that of self-preservation. For him, the sexual drive comes to coincide with the death drive—the latter understood not as the search for physical pain and suicidal tendencies, but as a *jouissance* produced by what he calls "self-shattering"[32]: the symbolic dissolution of identity, the erasure of the boundaries that separate the subject from the other and the world.

For Bersani, as well as for Lee Edelman, who in *No Future* reinterprets Bersani's thought within a Lacanian framework,[33] the drive is what properly defines what is sexual for both straight and queer subjects. However, within the heterosexist symbolic order, the negativity of the drive, its disturbing uncanniness, is transferred onto homosexual intercourse only, which cannot be rescued by reproductive ends. Heterosexual sex is invested with the political meaning of perpetuating society and the human species, hence it is perceived as "natural," whereas homosexual sex constitutes a threat to meaning itself because of its infertility and as such becomes "unnatural," "abnormal." Butler would say "abject"[34]; and Butler would partake in the struggle of sexual minorities for the recognition of their gender identities and affective relationships—for the subversion and redefinition of kinship. She would give voice to the aspirations of sexual minorities to subvert the heterosexual norms and become intelligible as humans. On the contrary, Edelman urges queers to give up their struggle for recognition and to remain where they are, outside signification and intelligibility. He invites them to occupy the dark space of negativity that they have always inhabited, with no hope that social recognition, laws for marriage or adoption, and access to artificial reproduction will suffice to do away with it.[35] This is the main reason the branch of queer theory to which Edelman and Bersani may be ascribed has been qualified as "antisocial."

To summarize: so-called antisocial theories interpret the human by means of tools that are drawn from psychoanalysis. Additionally, they insist on the negativity of the sexual drive, understood as the death of subjectivity and as the rupture of all social relationships. Finally, they invite queer subjects to welcome such negativity and embody it publicly. If one thinks of the critiques in *Horrorism*, where Cavarero moves to Bataille's "voluptuous overlap of death and eros,"[36] these theories may seem very distant from her feminist portrayal of the caring mother's inclination onto the child. And they certainly are. Edelman even argues against the centrality of the Child in social life as the matrix of meaning, a disciplinary device for adult sexuality, and a political vehicle to spread homo-trans-biphobia—referring to this with the startling phrase "the fascism of the baby's face."[37] However, this is not the same as the "obsessive insistence on eroticism understood in terms of violence and violation,"[38] which Cavarero detects in Bataille.

In *Relating Narratives*, Cavarero explicitly contests the comparison of Eros and death, and she describes the scene of two lovers making love, appearing naked to one another and reaching orgasm as a new birth.[39] But here I am not talking about a romantic couple, and I am not even talking about orgasm. I am not talking about love, making love, and pleasure, but about sex, about fucking and excitement. And here—this is important to clarify—death is not taken literally, but as a metaphor for the suspension of consciousness through arousal. What I propose is to explore, next to vulnerability, violence, and dependency on care, an additional side of the exposure of human beings to one another. My point is to establish connections between the perspective of a woman whose philosophy centers on women's generative power and that of queer subjects—especially gay men like Bersani, Edelman, and myself—who reflect upon the sterility of their own sexual acts. Cavarero herself acknowledges the importance of this operation, as highlighted in the previous quote from *Inclinations*. However, the tools that she steals from the box of the philosophical canon, while refusing to do so from that of the psychoanalytic tradition, in my opinion, are not enough for this task.

The sexual drive, as it is interpreted by psychoanalysis, represents the obscene double of maternal care. Every human comes to the world unarmed, defenseless, and totally dependent on the other. Through inclination, adults—usually, but not exclusively, mothers—take care of a child's needs, yet at the same time deviate them. As Kant said before Freud, adults turn a child's needs *"contra naturam,"* hence make them properly human. On the one hand, maternal care responds to the infant's instinct of self-preservation, quest for utility, self-affirmation, and pleasure. On the other hand, it raises a bad inclination—that is, an aptitude for defeating self-affirmation by means of a *jouissance* that goes far beyond the pleasure principle by which "the subject is momentarily undone."[40] The understanding of the undoing of the subject through excitement is a fundamental contribution of so-called antisocial queer theories to the critique of individualism and its male, right, straight, violent, utilitarian, and competitive interpretation of the human. By complementing Cavarero's relational ontology with the psychoanalytic concept of the drive, new aspects of human vulnerability may emerge, where care and sex are perversely enmeshed and the subject, through inclination, abandons itself to the other.

### Notes

1. Adriana Cavarero, *In Spite of Plato: A Feminist Rewriting of Ancient Philosophy*, trans. Serena Anderlini D'Onofrio and Áine O'Healy (Cambridge: Polity, 1995).

2. Cavarero, *Stately Bodies: Literature, Philosophy, and the Question of Gender*, trans. Robert de Lucca and Deanna Shemek (Ann Arbor: University of Michigan Press, 2002).

3. Thomas Hobbes, *De cive* (1642), cap. VIII.

4. Cavarero, "Il pensiero femminista: Un approccio teoretico," in *Le filosofie femministe*, ed. Adriana Cavarero and Franco Restaino (Milan: Bruno Mondadori, 1999), 78–115.

5. Obvious reference is the well-known motto "cogito ergo sum," by René Descartes, in *Discours de la methode* (1637).

6. Cavarero, "Coda: Adieu to Lévinas," in *Inclinations: A Critique of Rectitude*, trans. Amanda Minervini and Adam Sitze (Stanford, Calif.: Stanford University Press, 2013), 133–75.

7. Cavarero, *Relating Narratives: Storytelling and Selfhood*, trans. Paul A. Kottman (London and New York: Routledge, 2000).

8. Cavarero, *Horrorism: Naming Contemporary Violence*, trans. William McCuaig (2008; repr. New York: Columbia University Press, 2011).

9. Judith Butler, *Bodies That Matter: On the Discursive Limits of Sex* (London and New York: Routledge, 1993).

10. Butler, *Gender Trouble: Feminism and the Subversion of Identity* (1990; repr. New York and London: Routledge, 1999).

11. Cavarero, "Prefazione all'edizione italiana," in Butler, *Corpi che contano: I limiti discorsivi del sesso*, trans. Simona Capelli (Milan: Feltrinelli, 1996), vii, my translation.

12. Cavarero, *For More Than One Voice: Toward a Philosophy of Vocal Expression*, trans. Paul A. Kottman (Stanford, Calif.: Stanford University Press, 2005), 129. Cavarero's analysis starts from the phenomenon of so-called opera queens—that is, gay men who are fond of opera—as described in Wayne Koestenbaum's book *The Queen Throat: Opera, Homosexuality and the Mistery of Desire* (New York: Poseidon, 1993). On the use of drag codes in opera, the author concludes, "By use of the categories of Judith Butler, one could . . . say that in addition to stabilizing the stereotypes of sexual identity through their apparent transgression, operatic drag confuses them and unleashes all the unsettling effects of parody"; Cavarero, *For More Than One Voice*, 129.

13. Butler, *Precarious Life: The Powers of Mourning and Violence* (2004; repr. New York and London: Verso, 2006).

14. Butler, *Giving an Account of Oneself* (New York: Fordham University Press, 2005).

15. Butler, *Notes Toward a Performative Theory of Assembly* (Cambridge, Mass., and London: Harvard University Press, 2015).

16. Cavarero and Angelo Scola, *Thou Shalt Not Kill: A Political and Theological Dialogue*, trans. Margaret Adams Groesbeck and Adam Sitze (New York: Fordham University Press, 2015).

17. "Contemplating the natal scene, Butler holds it important to specify the relation 'by which we are, beyond ourselves, implicated in lives that are not our own,' can take the form, in the case of a baby, of an essential need for sustenance, which is however followed by a reply of abandonment, or violence, or starvation [that gives it over] to nothing, or to brutality, or to no sustenance." The emphasis is thus placed on a vulnerable being who is consigned above all to the *vulnus*, to the wound that the other may inflict on it. That this other, given the setting, is identifiable with the maternal figure is more than obvious. But, perhaps because she is convinced that "there is no reason to assume that these caregivers must be Oedipally organized as 'father' and 'mother,' Butler does not foreground this question"; Cavarero, *Horrorism*, 22. Quotations are taken from Butler, *Precarious Life*, 45, 28, and 31.

18. "In criticizing the heterosexual paradigm, you target one of the founding elements of psychoanalysis, if not its very foundation. I wonder then, precisely because I trust your radicality, whether it is possible to cast a similar critique to the psychoanalytic narrative of the self, as its process of formation, articulated in stages of differentiation with different degrees of necessity, requires childhood to be foundational (and mythological, in my view)"; Butler and Cavarero, "Condizione umana contro 'natura,'" in *Differenza e relazione: L'ontologia dell'umano di Judith Butler e Adriana Cavarero*, ed. Lorenzo Bernini and Olivia Guaraldo (Verona: Ombre corte, 2009), 131, my translation; *Micromega*, no. 4 (2005): 135–46.

19. Butler and Cavarero, "Condizione umana contro 'natura,'" 131, my translation.

20. Cavarero, *Inclinations*, 63. I am honoured to be quoted here: "As Lorenzo Bernini observes, 'queer' is the opposite of 'straight' . . . since heterosexuality is traditionally associated with moral rectitude, which is also, in turn, heterosexual'";

Cavarero, *Inclinations*, 63; the quote is taken from Bernini, *Queer Apocalypses: Elements of Antisocial Theory*, trans. Julia Heim (Basingstoke: Palgrave Macmillan, 2017), 3–4.

21. Cavarero, *Inclinations*, 63.

22. Cavarero, *Inclinations*, 63–64.

23. The category appears in Immanuel Kant's The *Metaphysics of Morals* (1797), in *Practical Philosophy*, trans., ed. Mary J. Gregor (Cambridge: Cambridge University Press, 1996); and Thomas Aquinas' *Summa Theologiae* (1265–74). Kant, *The Metaphysics of Morals*, trans., ed. Mary J. Gregor, in *Practical Philosophy*, trans., ed. Mary J. Gregor (Cambridge: Cambridge University Press, 1996), 353–603.

24. "Followers of Jean Laplanche would agree on this too, as they would counter both the natural status of the self and the drive, and the scientificity of psychoanalysis. Even Lacan made it clear that all human desire is, by definition, non-natural, as it only emerges in the context of language or, more specifically, in the hailing scene"; Butler and Cavarero, "Condizione umana contro 'natura,'" 128, my translation.

25. Teresa de Lauretis, *Freud's Drive: Psychoanalysis, Literature and Film* (Basingstoke: Palgrave Macmillan, 2008).

26. Jean Laplanche, *Vie et mort en psychanalyse* (Paris: Flammarion, 1970); Laplanche, *La révolution copernicienne inachevée (Travaux 1967–1992)* (Paris: Aubier, 1992).

27. Sigmund Freud, *Three Essays on the Theory of Sexuality*, trans. Ulrike Kister (New York and London: Verso, 2016).

28. To provide an example: according to Freud, "sucking with delight" is a masturbatory activity of the infant, which reactivates the arousal of the oral area initially stimulated by the mother's breast and/or bottle. The oral drive, therefore, leans onto the feeding instinct, not on that sexual instinct that Freud deems "natural." To him, the latter aims at the heterosexual coitus for procreative purposes and surfaces only in puberty, without ever erasing once and for all other perverse (hence nonreproductive) drives.

29. De Lauretis, *Freud's Drive*, 50.

30. Leo Bersani, *The Freudian Body: Psychoanalysis and Art* (New York: Columbia University Press, 1986).

31. Bersani, "Is the Rectum a Grave?," in *Is the Rectum a Grave? And Other Essays* (Chicago and London: University of Chicago Press, 2010); Bersani, *Homos* (Cambridge, Mass.: Harvard University Press, 1996).

32. Bersani, "Is the Rectum a Grave?," 30.

33. Lee Edelman, *No Future: Queer Theory and the Death Drive* (Durham, N.C., and London: Duke University Press, 2004).

34. Butler, *Gender Trouble*, 133–34.

35. "So Antigone may well depart from her tomb at the end of Butler's argument, returning to life in the political sphere from which she was excluded, but she does so while preserving the tomb itself as the burial place for whatever *continues* to insist outside of meaning, immune to intelligibility now or in any future yet to come. She emerges from her tomb, that is, only to claim, for those condemned to unlivable lives on account of unintelligible loves. . . . Ironically, Butler's reading thus buries Antigone once more—or buries in her the *sinthomo*sexual who refuses

intelligibility's mandate and the correlative economy that regulates what is 'legitimate and recognizable'"; Edelman, *No Future*, 105.

36. Cavarero, *Horrorism*, 49.

37. Edelman, *No Future*, 75.

38. Cavarero, *Horrorism*, 53.

39. "Appearing to each other with indifference regarding qualities—an indifference which finds its height in the orgasm—lovers therefore come to repeat the beginning of their existence. They do not return into the womb of the mother; on the contrary, they are ousted again into the inaugural nudity of appearance—one which now has the perfect relational character of co-appearance"; Cavarero, *Relating Narratives*, 112.

40. "Overwhelmed by stimuli in excess of the ego structures capable of resisting or binding them, the infant may survive that imbalance only by finding it exciting. So the masochistic thrill of being invaded by a world we have not yet learned to master might be an inherited disposition, the result of an evolutionary conquest. This, in any case, is what Freud appears to be moving toward as a definition of the *sexual*: an aptitude for the defeat of power by pleasure, the human subject's potential for *jouissance* in which the subject is momentarily undone"; Bersani, *Homos*, 100.

# Querying Cavarero's Rectitude

MARK DEVENNEY

I am inclined to agree with Adriana Cavarero.[1] Inclination, as an archetypal posture, knocks the "I" from its supposed center of gravity. It lends support to a relational ontology and recognizes the constitution of human beings as vulnerable subjects. The human, in order to be, depends upon others. It is a dependency in which the biological and the political overlap. There is no way back to an original nature or reason to ground humanity independently of the symbolic and relational mediation of all we do.[2] Yet, in agreement lurks danger. Agreement disguises a policing of words, of passions, of inclination and its inclinations. If agreement presupposes the symmetrical relations that Cavarero's *Inclinations* undermines, then my agreement is a poisoned chalice. As Macbeth, wrestling with his conscience, knows, the "instructions of the chalice return to plague their inventor commending its ingredients to our own lips." This analogy is forced, perhaps violent. However, it reflects my concern that Cavarero's "new fundamental schematism," premised on maternal inclination and natality, too knowingly introduces a new form of propriety. While Cavarero deliberately deploys a method of exaggeration to contrast the two *dispositifs* of verticalization and relationality, her text is haunted by what it tries to expel. Her ethics reintroduces the rectitude she so cogently dismantles. In this case, the line between her ontology, her politics, and her ethics is too straight. If the "relational model does not in fact allow for any symmetry at all," rendering the protagonists unbalanced, then the lines of flight from ontology into ethics and politics cannot be quite so straight. I aim to render inclination improper—to read Cavarero so consistently that her consistencies unravel. This improper gesture is the best compliment to a text that seems always already to have anticipated every objection. I contend that her inclined reading too quickly glosses over promises that lurk in the texts she analyzes. In particular, Hobbes's *Leviathan* hides an improper promise that Cavarero's fundamental schema must ignore. It is inclined in ways that the focus on (e)rectitude glosses over.

## Cavarero's Inclined Politics

Cavarero's *Inclinations* develops an "ontological, ethical and political model," an other *dispositif* of inclination. She contrasts inclination with the *dispositif* of rectitude and verticalization, of the upright erect male figure, committed to the life of reason. Cavarero is the first to admit that the *dispositifs* are stereotypes. There is deliberate politics in her pushing the stereotypes to their very limit. She overlays the *dispositif* of verticalization with its other, inclination, bearing witness to the perturbation it causes to the dominant forms of reason, ontology, and ethics. The performativity of her text effects a shift in worldview. The geometry of reason is shown to be wobbly, uncertain in its erectitude, insistent on maintaining a rigor mortis that Cavarero renders comical. It comes to resemble an impossible, parodic, but nonetheless hegemonic logic that renders inclinations and passions as other—as objects to be (ab)used and as liminal borders invoked to discipline the proper bounds of reason. In the Preface to the second edition of the *Critique of Pure Reason*, for example, Immanuel Kant writes:

> Speculative reason threaten[s] . . . to make the bounds of sensibility coextensive with the real, and so to supplant reason in its pure [practical] employment. Critique limits speculative reason . . . and it thereby removes an obstacle which stands in the way of the employment of practical reason and threatens to destroy it. . . . To deny that this is positive . . . would be like saying that *the police are of no positive benefit*, inasmuch as their main business is to prevent the violence of which citizens stand in mutual fear, in order that each may pursue his vocation in peace and security.[3]

In policing the proper limits of reason, Kant's *Critique* demonstrates that human beings are free. Yet he compares his critique to the police who protect the community by monopolizing violence. Reasoned violence is deemed necessary to protect the community against itself. In policing the limits of reason, Kant legitimates, like the police, a violence intrinsic to reason. Cavarero contests both the proper bounds of reason and the policing of sensibility that secures the rectitude of Kant's version of practical reason. What is the politics of this argument? How does it practice a politics, and what shape does it give to politics? How does this practice and this form shift what counts as politics? Let me begin by focusing on Cavarero's practice of reading before turning to the lines linking ontology, politics, and ethics.

## The Politics of Reading

Cavarero engages in "an emphatic forcing of maternal inclination" against the individualistic ontology and epistemology epitomized by Locke and Kant. Her inclining of the subject presupposes a relational ontology, one that does not "fragment the subject but bends it and gives to it a different posture."[4] Her forced reading identifies two postural paradigms. It aligns these with two sexes, two models of subjectivity, and two discordant ontologies. It deploys, in her words, an "accentuation of the emotional and sentimental baggage [of maternity] to *exploit it properly*"[5] (italics added). What could it mean to exploit maternity properly? Does Cavarero, perhaps deliberately, echo Kant here? Or does this proper exploitation indicate a certain limit to this text, one that we might destabilize at just that point where it marks its own boundaries? There are advantages to this forced reading. First, it sets out in stark form the dominant ethos, an individualist ontology that Cavarero terms evil in its refusal of inclination. Second, it enacts another ontology, another way of being and living together that any individualistic ontology must rely upon while simultaneously denying. In this respect at least Cavarero performs an immanent critique. She demonstrates that rectitude presupposes what it simultaneously abjures. Yet, third, she is not quite patient enough for such a painstaking form of critique. Her purpose is not to effect a shift from within the dominant paradigm. Rather, she showcases its morbidity. She deploys sly humor, wry jokes, art, literature, and reason both as critique and as a performative enactment of inclination. Here Cavarero's tones are black and white. Unlike the inclined works of art she analyzes, Cavarero draws stark lines extinguishing all life from the vertical posture, even as she exhumes its body. There is something odd about this exercise—the ontology of inclination she defends abjures such stark lines. In fact, her model of relationality recasts rectitude as just another inclination—not a *dispositif* with any ontological warrant. It is a form of inclination that may have its moment—as *Bob Marley and the Wailers* reminds us in calling on the oppressed to "Get up, stand up, stand up for your right; Get up, stand up, don't give up the fight." Recast as a particular inclination, rectitude may have its virtues, as Honig and Woodford argue in this volume. Why then does Cavarero insist so strenuously on its rigidity? Does her methodological commitment to "extremization" poison her new fundamental paradigm? Does the poisoned chalice of "extremization" return to the lips of its purveyor? In "properly" exploiting the sentimental baggage of the relational paradigm, must Cavarero police a new form of the proper, one that all too quickly disguises its own exclusionary and proprietary gestures? The method of reading that Cavarero employs opens onto a question about the politics performed in the reading of texts. I turn shortly to her reading of Hobbes. Let me be blunt, though—there is a hermeneutic violence at the center of this strategy. This violence is at odds with the ontology and ethics Cavarero defends. She cannot reincorporate the texts she reads because as archetypes of rectitude their possible inclinations are obscured. Cavarero misses the impropriety that plagues these texts. Let me turn to a second set of questions. These concern the all-too-"straight" lines that tie Cavarero's ontology to an ethics and a politics.

## *Dispositifs*: Ontology, Ethics, Politics

Cavarero performs an embodied ontology that is simultaneously a new humanism. It is universal in impulse premised on a particular version of the common—what is common to the human is exposure, vulnerability, and dependence on others. It is tempting simply to note that Cavarero draws on a long line of theoretical work about embodiment and relation. However, this would do an injustice to her text. Cavarero, uniquely, insists on a mode of relationality that begins in the uneven inclination of the mother and child. Communicative dreams of symmetry or ego psychological accounts of the growth of autonomy are upended. Cavarero thus extends the relational model in ways that Arendt, Jonas, and others seemed to resist. The condition of humans in the world is one of congenital vulnerability and dependency. "In this framework," she writes, "birth holds vulnerability and relationality together in an inseparable ontological bond."[6] The questions this raises touch on the links between biology and politics. It forces us to ask if this is a new universalism that acts as the foundation for politics and ethics. Such an investigation refuses the ridiculous penchant for evolutionary theory in contemporary political studies. Such approaches naturalize biology and thus neutralize politics. Cavarero is aware of the risks. However, in reprising her account of natality and appearance, we see that all too straight lines link the starry night of ontology to her ethics and politics.

I have already noted Cavarero's celebration of inclination as a *dispositif* that articulates together ontology, ethics, and politics. The choice of the word *dispositif* here is important—but it betrays an uncertainty. Foucault had conceptualized *dispositifs* as "heterogeneous ensembles consisting of discourses, institutions, architectural forms, regulatory decisions, laws, administrative measures, scientific statements, philosophical, moral and philanthropic propositions—in short the said as much as the unsaid."[7] An analysis of a *dispositif* traces the connections between these heterogeneous elements and its modalities of formation and transformation in a specific conjuncture that responds to particular demands, crises, or apparent needs. Foucault views philosophical and moral propositions—ontological and ethical positions—as elements of such ensembles. On this reading philosophy does not reconstruct what is foundational or universal. Rather, ontological claims attain their value in relation to the ensemble. They are contingent, emergent, relational—not merely descriptive of the object they claim to know. Foucault, we might say, proposes a philosophy in the middle voice. The philosopher is implicated in the ensemble and cannot stand outside of it assuming the position of the neutral observer. This is a middle voice in which statements follow lines of flight that disturb the philosophical attempt to render words and propositions, ethics and politics proper to themselves.

Cavarero's version of the *dispositif* is somewhat different. Focuault's account might be deployed to describe the verticality that Cavarero mocks, but this requires stretching the notion of *dispositif* beyond Foucault's account. Cavarero bestrides the history of philosophy, demonstrating the erect analogies that link Plato to Locke or Augustine to Kant. However, the use of the word *dispositif* loses all meaning if applied to her account of inclination. Cavarero proposes a new humanism, a foundational vulnerability that is constitutive of what it is to be human. She asks:

> What might happen to the horizontal relation of reciprocity, which defines politics as the scene of appearance, if it is the unbalanced relationship between the newborn and the mother that serves as a *premise* for securing *the ontological root for action*?[8]

This quote is deceptively simple, but it indicates the scope of Cavarero's argument. She rejects the invocation of symmetrical reciprocity as the basis for an ethics or a politics. This is a familiar argument, made often by poststructuralist critics of deliberative democracy. It is compatible with Mouffe's agonistic account of democracy, among others. However, Mouffe's critique of communicative ethics as too formal, as disguising substantive claims about the good life in the guise of a neutral universality, now comes back to bite. Cavarero characterizes this post-foundational approach as too abstract. She adds to it two elements. First, the foundational place of the mother-child relationship in every life; second, the necessary inequalities in all relationships as a backdrop to thinking about any ethics or politics—and concomitantly the disguised violence of an approach to politics that begins with the assumption that all are equal. In this case dependency lends weight to an ethics that begins in inclination. Vulnerability is not an external imperative but is the very condition in which any human action takes place. For the present, though, note the slightly odd phrasing of this claim: the unbalanced relationship between the newborn and the mother serves as *a premise* for securing the ontological root for action. What is the status of this premise, and what exactly is the relationship between the premise and the *ontological root* for action? The notion of a *dispositif* does not help here. In a *dispositif* the relation of forces between elements is uneven. The claim to priority of one or other element is contingent and open to shifts and changes. Cavarero goes further and lays claim to an ontological root for action. She echoes, with a twist, word for word what Arendt writes about action: "The miracle that saves the world, the realm of human affairs, from its normal 'natural ruin,' is ultimately the fact of natality, in which the faculty of action is ontologically rooted."[9] Cavarero insists upon the relation between mother and child in this scenario, resisting recourse either to an essentialist biology or to the assumption that the possibility of action lies in symmetrical equality. The one who enters into the scene of action is already an inclined subject, a vulnerable subject in relation. What is important is not the mere fact of birth—rather, it is that no matter what body one is born with she will enter into relation with others upon whom she is dependent.

Before I turn to the particularity of this argument, let me return to the question of the *dispositif*. Cavarero sacrifices the contingency that was central to Foucault's use of this concept. Her invocation of ontology aims to present a neutral standpoint that can serve as the premise of an ethics. She cannot have it both ways. Whatever one makes of Foucault's happy positivism, he never framed it in terms of a prior ontology that would provide warrant for particular ways of acting. The question Foucault might have posed back to Cavarero would query the place of her ontology and ethics within the play of *dispositifs*. How does it relate to law, administration, and science? What forms of discipline, subjectivization, and policing does it engender? What possibilities does it open up, even as it closes others down? If with Foucault we view the philosophical text as imbricated in an ensemble of practices from which it cannot be disassembled, we may want to reconsider the very particular claim that Cavarero makes about the inclined relationship of mother to child.

## Mother and Child Reunion

Cavarero privileges the mother-child relation highlighting its role in Christian iconography. It is this argument that I find most problematic—why should inclination, passion, or relationality in itself open on to an ethics or a politics? Cavarero is aware of the risks. It is for this reason that she devotes much energy to demonstrating the limits of the Hobbesian account. Hobbes too relies on an ontology that invokes passions and inclination. Yet he assumes, contrary to Cavarero, that the individual is driven by inclinations that are not reasonable. Hobbes's subject is ruled by inclination *ab initio*. Life in a state of nature is nasty, brutish, and short—precisely because human beings are inclined to pursue their own passions. Although Hobbes posits a radical equality, it is founded on the possibility of homicide, or so Cavarero avers. Hobbes's individualist ontology founds the equality of individual proprietors of the self.

Cavarero is right to demonstrate the limits of both the individualistic and narcissistic assumptions that characterize this anthropology. She is right, too, that it cannot ground an inclined ethics. However, we might read Hobbes from a different angle, an angle that undermines Cavarero's quick dismissal of his homicidal equality. Hobbes recognizes that human beings are vulnerable. Such vulnerability is the other side of the violence that they may inflict, or have inflicted, on themselves and others. The equality found in the state of nature is precisely an equality of vulnerable bodies, bodies that wish to avoid the threat of death. This vulnerability explains why such selfish proprietors would give up so much. They forsake radical equality in making a contract that founds that great Leviathan.

There are some strange twists here that Cavarero does not note. First, the sovereign does not make a contract—the contract is between the subjects of the new state who transfer their right to protect their own lives to a Leviathan that remains radically outside any contract, and continues to abide in a state of nature.[10] As a consequence the obligations of citizens no longer hold if the sovereign threatens their lives. For this reason, Hobbes, unlike Rousseau, for example, allows that citizens may resist the threat of violence to their own lives. Hobbes provides one of the classic defenses of the right to refuse military service and allows that someone who has committed a crime may rightfully avoid sovereign punishment to save their own life. There is a further twist. The Leviathan is constituted, as

Cavarero rightly notes, by the bodies of all those who contract together. Its body—that of the body politic—is vulnerable to an infinite array of possible threats. Every time the Leviathan harms a citizen, he injures himself. His constitutive vulnerability acts as a check on the violence that he might—as the exception to the rule that implements the rule—carry out.[11] This reading of Hobbes—at very least a plausible one—points to a question we would need to put to Cavarero. Humans are constituted as vulnerable subjects, as subjects who come into being as a consequence of inclinations that situate everyone as dependent. Yet such dependency is also the possibility of violence. The ontological condition with which we begin—even if premised on the mother-child relationship that is central to Cavarero's account—does not a priori rule out possible violence. The invocation of the fact of this asymmetrical relation cannot in itself found an ethics unless one has already presupposed that human lives are valuable in themselves. To put this differently, there is always another argument that must be made before we can jump from the relational ontology to an ethics. Ontology and ethics do not presuppose each other. One reason for offering this reading of Hobbes is that it points to the skewed paths that lead from first premises to ethical or political conclusions. We might solve this apparent problem by insisting with Levinas on the priority of ethics—insist that we are constituted in relations that are ethical first, that place a primordial demand on all subjects before the face of the other. But this solution too is abstract, as Cavarero notes—even though it emphasizes the face of "the other," this is not the face of an other. At the point at which it does become the face of an other—as when Levinas considers the politics of Israel—problems arise.

My point is most clear if we turn to Melanie Klein, for whom the relationship between mother and child is ambivalent from the beginning. It cannot act as the basis for an ethics. Consider her account of envy. Envy, she argued, arises from a primary destructiveness that is initially directed against the feeding breast. The inclined mother is a source of possible relations of love, but also of oral and anal-sadistic relations constitutive of the self.[12] The issue is not that Klein is correct—rather it indicates that Cavarero too quickly excludes other possible consequences of the uneven, inclined relation between mother and child. The internal objects essential to the adult self are more ambivalent than Cavarero allows. One response is simply to assert that inclination points to a primary vulnerability to which we must respond. However, this misses the point. For Klein it is vulnerability and loss that may result in violent impulses. In this case, an ontology of vulnerability is unpredictable and uncontrollable. It may have consequences injurious to both self and other. To assert that vulnerability grounds an ethics is to abstract from the situational specificity of the mother-child relationship. Importantly, the anger that may be experienced arises regardless of the mother's actions. The primary relationship that grounds Cavarero's relational ontology is messier than she allows. As Clare Woodford emphasizes in her étude, the Christian iconography that underpins it relies on an idealization just as abstract as the presupposition of symmetrical equality found in those traditions to which Cavarero objects. How so? Cavarero herself notes that Jesus is born to a mother without sexual intercourse having taken place. Joseph must accept the rather far-fetched story that Mary bears the child of God. A more complex story of this family might reject the idealized fiction of the mother-and-child reunion, questioning the role of the father Joseph in this story. Cavarero pushes the iconic story to its limits in order to found an ethics of vulnerability. Is this abstraction any better than that of Arendt, who grounds action in natality, in the possibility of continual renewal, while ignoring the constitutive role of the mother in giving birth to the new? Perhaps Arendt resisted just such an invocation of the mother-child relation because its introduction raises a set of substantive questions that trouble the all-too-easy distinctions between labor, work, and action and the account of politics that relies upon these distinctions. Cavarero asks, "What happens if we begin with the unbalanced relation between mother and child?" The consequences are indeed radical—but they do not give any warrant to a particular ethics unless a set of further, contestable decisions are taken. Whatever ontological presumptions we begin with the lines of flight into an ethics or a politics are complex, unpredictable, and contingent. A relational ontology night accurately describe how it is that human beings come to be. However, there is a radical contingency about that coming in to being that cannot be solved by invoking an ethics it cannot ground.

## Conclusion: Toward an Improper Relationality

I accept with Cavarero that the human is constituted in relation and that an individualistic ontology is nonsensical. Rather than invoke an ontology, however—whether it be a Spinozist version of infinity, a new materialism, a Lacanian notion of the real—an improper politics probes the exclusions constitutive of particular ontological claims. It does not assume that there is a proper way to be and is not tempted to turn this impossibility into a negative theology, or indeed an ethics of caution against rectitude. Rather, it recognizes that being is always articulated within particular forms of proprietary order; let us call these *dispositifs*. The

Greek term *ousia* is variously translated as being, substance, and property. Fundamental ontology aims to determine what exists in and of itself without further need of predicates, to determine what is proper to itself. The hierarchy of *Being* moves from the particular ontologies to a general ontology and then to a fundamental ontology. Cavarero, despite herself, replays this classical account of the hierarchy of Being that distinguishes ontic particularity from the question of what is common to Being in general. This allows her to identify that nonpolitical space beyond contestation, the new humanism that grounds her relational ethics. In keeping with the etymology of *ousia*, I ask how what is proper to being comes to be accepted—and then ask what the consequences are of such policing of the proper bounds of being. I do not hold that human beings are by nature violent, loving, or otherwise inclined. Rather, in line with a radical anti-humanism, I argue that the human comes to be in an overdetermined complex and cannot be known outside of this complex. It is precisely for this reason that we must engage in hegemonic struggle to secure the nonviolent ethics that Cavarero proposes. However, this is a work and a labor without prior warrant. In seeking to give it prior warrant an unspoken violence is committed—one that requires that we close our eyes to the complexity of the initial relationships so crucial to the becoming of any child.

Notes

1. Adriana Cavarero, *Inclinations: A Critique of Rectitude*, trans. Amanda Minervini and Adam Sitze (Stanford, Calif.: Stanford University Press, 2016), 155.

2. This was recognized by Freud in his distinction between "Instinkt" and "Triebe" (drive.) The English translations of Freud's texts too often use the word "instinct" for what are in fact distinct concepts.

3. Immanuel Kant, *Critique of Pure Reason*, trans. Norman Kemp Smith (London: Macmillan, 1929), 26.

4. Cavarero, *Inclinations*, 11.

5. Ibid., 14.

6. Ibid., 122.

7. Michel Foucault, "The Confession of the Flesh," in *Power/Knowledge*, ed. Colin Gordon (New York: Harvester Wheatsheaf, 1980), 194–95.

8. Cavarero, *Inclinations*, 120.

9. Hannah Arendt, *The Human Condition* (New York: Doubleday, 1959), 222.

10. Much has been made of this argument in the biopolitical arguments that followed the publication of Georgio Agamben's *Homo Sacer: Sovereign Power and Bare Life* (Stanford, Calif.: Stanford University Press, 1998).

11. Thomas Hobbes, *Leviathan* (London: Penguin, 2012).

12. Melanie Klein, *Envy and Gratitude: A Study of Unconscious Forces* (London: Hogarth, 1957).

# From Horrorism to the Gray Zone

SIMONA FORTI

For those who are, like me, interested in redefining the relationship between evil and power[1]—given that political philosophy cannot do without this rethinking—Adriana Cavarero's *Horrorism* is a "necessary" text.[2] First of all, because it helps us to accomplish a fundamental theoretical passage: to look at the scene of evil, orienting our attention not toward the abyss of perverse liberty of the violent perpetrators, but in the direction of the final result of that violence: the helpless victim. This perspective, that of the victim, has long been ignored.

Even those who maintain that they have radically reframed the field of inquiry from the point of view of the Freudian "discovery" of *Todestrieb* are in fact still wearing, at least to a certain extent, the habitual lenses. Isn't pointing one's finger toward that incandescent nucleus of the subject that consists of destructive *jouissance*—as Lacan and the post-Lacanians do to indicate the nature of evil—isn't that an ancient gesture? Don't they restate, though in a secularized and nonmoralistic form, the centrality of that diabolic will-to-nothing that, in the Christian vision, expresses itself in the sin of omnipotence of a creature who, as an act of rebellion against the creator, destroys what the creator created? What is certain is that even the most careful interpreters of the death-drive have continued to afford visibility only to *one* of the characters occupying the theater of violence and destruction: he who, monopolizing all the power, undertakes destruction. Cavarero has shifted the focus from the "pleasure of cruelty" to the pain of the victim, reduced to total passivity: the totally helpless vulnerable.[3]

Taking as its point of departure the transformation of conflicts in the contemporary world, which emptied of significance the concepts of war, terror, and enemy, *Horrorism* redraws the political place of the victim. But Cavarero's perspective is so radical that it brings into one tangle ethics and ontology.

First, I will parse out the radicality of Cavarero's perspective that enacts this tangling. It is by reflecting on the genocidal legacy of the twentieth century that Cavarero brings to completion that discourse that, from Levinas to Butler, through Arendt and Agamben, has *philosophically* interrogated the historical and ontological specificity of the new figure of the helpless victim, the one I call "absolute victim."[4] The laboratories of the regimes of the twentieth century—not just Auschwitz—have managed to produce together, with an absurd amount of psychic and physical suffering, a new form of life—a new reality that is an unprecedented configuration of being, existential and biological.

Second, I will delve into this ethical-ontological view by putting forward a comparison between Cavarero's idea of ontological crime and Primo Levi's tale of the process of annihilation endured in the camp.

Finally, I will address Levi's reflections on power, arguing that these reflections mark the distance between a political philosophy of the "normality of evil" and the so called post-Auschwitz philosophy of "radical evil,"[5] to which *Horrorism*, to some extent, still belongs.

The general thesis in the background of *Horrorism*—similar to Judith Butler's most recent stances[6]—is that the vulnerability that constitutes us—a permanent status of being human—exposes our bodies, because of our mutual dependence, to two alternative responses: *care* or *wounding*. Some situations of total dependence are given in which the relationship is transformed into a practically unilateral position—for example, in early infancy and in some of the adversities of old age. Such relationships therefore entail a deep disparity of power: to the almost complete passivity of one of the actors (the newborn or the incapacitated elder) corresponds an almost unlimited responsibility of the other.

Now, why do some blows dealt by a violent and unilateral response trespass the field of ethics to reach into the domain of ontology? Because, we could answer, if becoming a victim of another's intentional violence is a constitutive possibility of vulnerability, nonetheless violence and victimhood are declined in many ways. Hence, we face the distinction between a crime that is, so to speak, purely ethical and one that becomes ontological.

Adriana Cavarero's first move is clearly Arendtian: "The horrorist crime," unlike various forms of political violence, acquires an ontological dimension in that it aims at the heart of the constitutive structure of that being we call the "human animal." We enter into the realm of *horrorism* when we strike at the uniqueness of "singular plural beings"—when that uniqueness becomes undone, which is as much a phenomenal and corporeal given rooted in our biological birth as it is a trait that repeats itself incessantly, inscribing our actions and our identities in the ontological category of natality,[7] in the very possibility of beginning and changing.

It is then not by chance that as an extreme and at the same time paradigmatic example of ontological offense to a "singular plural being," Cavarero looks to those bodies who, in order to destroy other bodies, transform themselves into explosive weapons. In this act, the horror provoked by the deflagration "disfigures bodily integrity to the point" that "it mixes shreds of the flesh of the victim with those of the perpetrator" and brings organic matter back to shapelessness,[8] thus transgressing at the same time the "fact of birth" and "the law of natality."

Certainly the history of political horror does not begin with the "random victims" of terrorist attacks: torture has always been an effective training ground for horrorism. It is the most ancient and elementary instance of the "*construction* of the helpless." Torture is not an emotional and impulsive response of aggressiveness: it is methodic, organized, controlled violence. The relationship between the torturer/tormentor and the tortured is one of the quintessential scenes of evil: a situation in which the *relationality* of power is erased because the torturing subject retains all the force, physical and symbolic, in order to transform himself into some kind of inverted God, whose sovereign omnipotence is measured on the total impotence of the other. The sovereign torturer owns the body of the other, who—reduced to aching flesh—is almost always unable to use even his last resource of freedom and resistance: giving himself to death. The tortured is literally in a trap, can open himself to nothing and no one; and as a consequence of this, no power transits through his body. Even language loses structure and is reduced to a scream.[9] Totally at the mercy of the other's dominion, the victim of torture becomes a metonymic figure of that total asymmetry of power that congeals into domination and represents in my eyes the emblematic scene of the coincidence between evil and power.

Because of the residual subjectivity of the victim, however, who at least can look his torturer in the face, perhaps we are not yet fully in front of that process of depersonalization and dehumanization that has become the subject of political philosophy in the last few decades. It is in fact reflecting on the genocidal legacy of the twentieth century that Cavarero, in the wake of Levinas, Arendt, Agamben, and Butler, pushes further, *philosophically*, the interrogation on the figure of the helpless victim.

Not only "the perverted, degenerated helpless"[10]—as Cavarero puts it—denies the singularity derived from natality, but it even erases the temporal difference between life and death. We could then say that horrorism implies that death is no longer the end of someone's life, the transformation of a living body into a corpse, but rather becomes the passage from one to the same body, but separated from the previous body by a radical process of desubjectivation. We are no longer in the presence of a subject who is located in a temporal sequence of becoming, connecting substance to attributes and predicates, but of a body who, because of the accidents it endured, survives its destitution, but no longer reestablishes the circularity of meaning. And it is horrorism, I want to add, because it is something for which our ontology has not at all prepared us: if it has allowed us to think the change of form into the permanence of substance, it has prevented us somehow from thinking the change of substance into the permanence of form.

*Zoe, homo sacer*,[11] absolute victim, degenerated helpless: it is of this chain of synonyms that Adriana tries to think, starting from the disorientation they induce because of their divergence from the usual ontological axis.

It is then not by chance that one of the most powerful chapters of *Horrorism* focuses on Primo Levi's tale of the process of annihilation endured in the camp,[12] read as a kind of "ontological" proof—we could say *more Auschwitz demonstrata*—of the presence or absence of the boundary between what abides by the "order of being" (of being human) and what transgresses it.

There is no doubt, then, that Primo Levi's work describes the process of desubjectivation with more acumen and sensitivity than any philosophical treatise on the topic. Levi, in fact, does not want to evoke his suffering, but tries, as a chemist, to point the microscope with precision on his experience. In the pages of *If This Is A Man*[13] (published for the first time in 1947), and of *The Drowned and the Saved* (published in 1986, one year before his death),[14] Levi moves as a naturalist, as a clinical observer. Step by step, he describes the process of transformation that the human animal endures in a state of maximum deprivation until the last stage of that annihilation, the *Muselmann*; the man in decomposition that the writer describes with these words: "One hesitates to call them living; one hesitates to call their death death—in the face of it they have no fear, because they are too tired to understand."[15]

The path to the *Muselmann* begins with the first alienating experience of the train journey, and, insult after insult, over the course of just a few days, the habits and clothes of civility are dismissed. One finds himself being—Levi tells us—what the Germans want to believe we are: nothing but "pieces," *stücke*, as the brutal count recites, according to the morbid adoration of numbers of the Germans.

I have been working for a while on Levi as a political philosopher,[16] and not just writer, and I have to admit that in no philosophical text the "absence of world" has been better articulated. As in the case of torture, absence of world means absence of comprehensible human relationships, of habits, from a home to clothing; it means deprivation of everything that protects us from the brutality of external agents and allows us to take on a position of our own, though never fixed once and for all. Now, so Levi reflects, "a life without world" will be an empty man. Another will then be able to decide lightheartedly of his life or his death outside the scope of any human affinity. Hence the question of the title, "If this is a man," and hence the true meaning, for Levi, of the term "annihilation camp."

It is clear that Levi is studying, first of all in himself, the consequences of the progressive disintegration of identities. He reports the results of the experiment of being drawn to "the bottom,"[17] where the victims fight for what is for many of them the last battle for survival. The *Muselmann*—"the image of all the evil of our time"—is the one who gives up, who does not resist the undertow, who cannot stay at the bottom, who cannot engage in the struggle with the arrogant violence of the camp's law. All it takes is to follow all the orders, Levi says, and in very little time you transform into the *Muselmann*: into the figure in which the *agon* becomes agony.

But if *If This Is a Man* were only this, were only—that is—the description, as Adriana Cavarero suggests, of that process of destitution of a form of life, of the subject, and the production of that unprecedented new form that is the construed defenseless, Levi's text would be a terrific analysis, but would not be that great philosophical lesson on power that it is for me. And here is the difference between Cavarero's reading and mine. A difference, ours, that is not so much an interpretive question over Levi's text, but rather a different perspective from which to look at the relationship between evil and power.

*If This Is a Man* is not only a treaty of *thanatopolitics*,[18] as Agamben suggests and Cavarero herself seems to imply. The concentrationary universe described by Levi is not simply the laboratory—of which Arendt also spoke—in which the plurality of human beings is transformed into an indistinct mass of victims, identical and interchangeable. Primo Levi does describe the process of decomposition of a complex aggregate (the subjectivity of life before the camp), but he also narrates the process of reaggregation of the human matter in another subjectivity, which, though reassembled in the worst possible conditions, still responds to the law of the plurality of forms of life and with it to the law of the incessant dynamic of the energy of power.

*The Drowned and the Saved*, written by Levi a few months before his death, confirms a posteriori the complexity of that horror of which he brought testimony in the 1947 text. For those who, having looked the Gorgon in the face, manage to resurface, a new process of subjectivation, of recomposition of identity, cannot but impose itself and start again. Certainly this happens in a context heavily marked by necessity, by terror and violence, which remain to mark a break from the previous life. But the enormous suffering does not remain mute and indistinct: it becomes the suffering of someone who can use it to enter again the *agon* of power.[19]

In other words, there is power circulating among the bodies and the subjectivities *before* they reach the bottom, and, if one resists at the bottom, power and the struggle for it start again. A new form of life stitches the fragments, bringing them back together in a violent collective dimension, in the vortex of a struggle for survival no longer mitigated by the many barriers with which civilization protects us.

For this reason, the relationships of power portrayed by Levi appear as primary structures, in a sort of pure state hardly ever observable in civil society. And though the new collectivity of the camp represents a sort of Hobbesian state of nature, upside down and perverted, it discloses to us in its folds dynamics "we find," though less savage and violent, "in any relation of power."[20]

The originality of Levi's reading, so complementary to Cavarero's *Horrorism*, consists in making of the *Muselmann only one* of the many outcomes of the power of the Lager. There have been too many readings, even quite recently, according to which the scene of evil, of horror, to say it with Cavarero, consists of only two figures: the SS and the *Muselmänner*. For Levi, plurality endures even in the lager, which has never been a simple universe with a dualistic topology.

This is why, if inserted in an ideal history of political thought, *If This Is A Man*, read in light of *The Drowned and the Saved*, belies that manicheistic understanding of power that thrusts an abyssal distance between the feverish will to power of the leaders and the indistinct passivity of the mass. It is true, he will admit in his last work, that the structure of the lager makes almost impossible any control from the bottom. But the real challenge for the writer is this: never doubt that the *Muselmann*, the "helpless constructed," as Cavarero would say, is "the image of all the evil in the world," but also wonder about the dynamics of "our own reality" that brought the *Muselmann* about. So if Levi's message is never ambiguous—there are victims and persecutors, no judgment ought to ever keep them in one embrace—nevertheless he never tires of repeating, "As in front of any relation of power, even more in the *Lager*, if one wants to really understand, one cannot stop at the two blocks of the victims and the persecutors. One must mercilessly investigate "that gray zone," "that hybrid category of inmate-functionaries" that "is both its framework and its most disturbing feature": "This category is a gray zone, with undefined contours, which both separates and connects the two opposing camps of masters and servants. It has an incredibly complicated internal structure, and harbors just enough to confound our need to judge."[21]

Many are the ways to rebound from the bottom. It is a sort of cynical and violent struggle for recognition, to which the "fit," the strong, the astute participate, who not only cleverly dodge the toughest blows of power coming from above, but who also intertwine with it relationships of complicity. About this, Levi's words cut like a knife: "If a position of privilege, a degree of comfort, and a reasonable probability of survival are offered to a few individuals in a state of slavery, in exchange for the betrayal of a natural solidarity with their comrades, someone will certainly accept. He will be removed from the common law and will become untouchable; hence the more power is granted, the more hateful and hated he will be. When he is given command of a group of unfortunates, with the right of life or death over them, he will be cruel and tyrannical, because he will understand that, if he is not sufficiently so, someone else, judged more suitable, will take over his post. Moreover, his capacity for hatred, which remains unfulfilled toward the oppressors, will spill over, unreasonably, onto the oppressed; and he will be satisfied only when he has heaped onto his underlings the abuse received from above."[22]

In the deprived world of prisoners, we find all the ingredients that modulate power: from power exercised through expedients to power as a long-term strategy; from power as brute force to power as seduction; from the quest for prestige—"an unquenchable need of civilization"—to the resentment of those frustrated and in search of social redress; the desire of those who stand on the last steps of the social ladder to shed humiliation and contempt, and to throw them upon the new arrivals, thus inventing a new category of inferior rank on which to unload the weight of the offenses pressing them from above. Unlike what a hagiographic *postbellum* literature would want, the camp does not sanctify the victim, but rather degrades it. It corrupts it to the point of making it coincide—for psychic and physical violence—with the image held of them by the guardians.[23]

The "gray zone," present in all human cohabitation, from the totalitarian regime to "a big industrial complex," is the backbone upon which power stands, whose figures, though various and ill-defined, represent a "common sample of humanity."[24]

If these men were numerous in the camp, even outside those boundaries, they always are and always will be. We will not understand the enormous power of evil if we keep our sight only on the SS and the victims. From Eichmann to the *Sonderkommandos*—that "band of half consciences" in which hierarchs big and small place themselves—they *all* collaborate with *horrorism*, that evil that is constructed in normality: it feeds off of unaware signatures and shrugs, of complacent smiles and deference.

There isn't an essence, a truth that defines once and for all what is power and what is evil. There are only ways to exercise power and differences in these ways. This is because power is not something that arrives after, like a supplementary attribute, which adds itself to the substance of our life. It is part of the modalities of expression and organization of our life, which in strict continuity with matter can be riven by forces that sustain it or forces that threaten it, marked as it is by the agonism between life and death. That's why I am convinced that Levi's extraordinary texts—*If This Is A Man* and *The Drowned and the Saved*, rightfully read and reread all over the world—are among the most important philosophical-political works of the last century. They contain the soberest, but also perhaps the most effective confutation of all the substantialist conceptions of power: of Nazi power, for sure, but most of all of power in general.

Very close to the path opened by Foucault, Levi too thinks of power as an energy of matter—and for him we are matter—which relates in many ways: sometimes virtuous, many times problematic, and in some cases ferocious, a bringer of domination. Levi is the boldest author of a microphysics of power. He could probe—without mercy and without ideological or doctrinal prejudices—the motor of the dynamics of power: from its extreme phenomenologies—the drowned and the masters of death—to its multiple intermediate degrees, in their diverse tones.

But if Levi offers to us this deconstruction of the classical view of power, which divides in two opposite poles the field of action between those who command and those who obey, it is first of all because he dismantled the very structure of metaphysical dualism; from the dualism between soul and body to that between good and evil, a dismantling that reaches to the most untouchable of them all: the dualism between victim and perpetrator.

In conclusion, bringing again Levi to meet Cavarero, the horrorist scene is not constituted only of terrible erect men who draw the greatest pleasure from contemplating the victims, lying prostrate and powerless, as the imagination of Canetti would have it and as Cavarero criticizes.[25] The gray zone, that intertwinement of so many threads and inclinations, while revealing to us one of the secrets of "voluntary servitude," discloses also that horror can emerge from a nonerect position.

Notes

1. See Simona Forti, *New Demons: Rethinking Evil and Power Today*, trans. Zakiya Hanafi (Stanford, Calif.: Stanford University Press, 2015).
2. Adriana Cavarero, *Horrorism: Naming Contemporary Violence*, trans. William McCuaig (New York: Columbia University Press, 2011).
3. See Wolfgang Sofsky, "The Paradise of Cruelty," in *Violence: Terrorism, Genocide, War* (London: Granta, 2004), 15–55.
4. See Forti, *New Demons*, especially 125–79.
5. See for all, Richard J. Bernstein, *Radical Evil: A Philosophical Interrogation* (Hoboken, N.J.: Blackwell, 2002).
6. See Judith Butler's *Precarious Life: The Powers of Mourning and Violence* (2004; repr. London: Verso, 2006); and *Giving an Account of Oneself: A Critique of Ethical Violence* (New York: Fordham University Press, 2005).
7. Natality, here, is used in the way in which the concept is thematized by Hannah Arendt; see *The Human Condition* (1958; repr. Chicago: University of Chicago Press, 1998).
8. See Cavarero, *Horrorism*, 89–97.
9. On this see also Elaine Scarry, *The Body in Pain: The Making and Unmaking of the World* (Oxford: Oxford University Press, 1985), 27–59.
10. Cavarero, *Horrorism*, 39.
11. The reference here of course goes to Giorgio Agamben's *Homo Sacer: Sovereign Power and Bare Life* (Stanford, Calif.: Stanford University Press, 1998); and *Remnants of Auschwitz: The Witness and the Archive* (New York: Zone, 1999).
12. Cavarero, *Horrorism*; see in particular the chapter "Those Who Have Seen the Gorgon," 33–40.
13. Primo Levi, *If This Is a Man*, in *The Complete Works of Primo Levi*, ed. Ann Goldstein (New York: Liveright, 2015), 1:1–207.
14. Levi, *The Drowned and the Saved*, in Goldstein, *Complete Works of Primo Levi*, 3:2405–2575.
15. "All the *Muselmänner* who go to the gas chambers have the same story, or, more exactly, have no story; they have followed the slope to the bottom, naturally, like streams running down to the sea. Once they entered the camp, they were overwhelmed, either through basic incapacity, or through misfortune, or through some banal incident, before they could adapt; they are beaten by time, they do not begin to learn German and to untangle the fiendish knot of laws and prohibitions until their body is already breaking down, and nothing can save them from selection or from death by exhaustion. Their life is short, but their number is endless; they, the *Muselmänner*, the drowned, form the backbone of the camp, an anonymous mass, continually renewed and always the same, of non-men who march and labor in silence, the divine spark dead within them, already too empty to truly suffer. One hesitates to call them living; one hesitates to call their death death—in the face of it they have no fear, because they are too tired to understand"; Levi, *If This Is a Man*, 85.

16. See at least, "Poor Devils Who 'Worship' Life: Us," in Forti, *New Demons*, 307–22.

17. *On the Bottom* is the title of a fundamental chapter of Primo Levi's *If This Is a Man*, 18–33.

18. As it is also, for example, for Agamben, *Remnants of Auschwitz*.

19. See Giunia Gatta, "Suffering and the Making of Politics: Perspectives from Jaspers and Camus," *Contemporary Political Theory* 14, no. 4 (2015): 335–54, https://doi.org/10.1057/cpt.2014.52; Bonnie Honig, *Antigone, Interrupted* (Cambridge: Cambridge University Press, 2013).

20. See Levi, *Drowned and the Saved*, 3:2561.

21. Levi, *Drowned and the Saved*, 3:2435.

22. Levi, *If This Is a Man*, 1:86.

23. Levi, *Drowned and the Saved*, 3:2435 and Levi, *If This Is a Man*, 1:86.

24. Levi, *If This Is a Man*, 1:13.

25. See Elias Canetti, *Crowds and Power* (New York: Viking, 1962); and Cavarero, *Inclinations: A Critique of Rectitude*, trans. Amanda Minervini and Adam Sitze (Stanford, Calif.: Stanford University Press, 2016), 81–87.

# Violence, Vulnerability, Ontology

*Insurrectionary Humanism in Cavarero and Butler*

TIMOTHY J. HUZAR

When a person writes, no matter the claims she makes in this writing she also, ineluctably, manifests a sense of the world. Indeed, this sense of the world may be more important than any discrete claim she makes. It may reinforce how the world is predominantly understood, or it may challenge this received understanding, or it may even call for the end of the world (as we know it); particularly if this world is constituted in violence.[1] Over the course of their recent work, Adriana Cavarero and Judith Butler offer a sense of the world centered around vulnerability: what Cavarero has called a "new relational ontology of the vulnerable" and what Butler has called a "new bodily ontology" or a "relational social ontology."[2] Much attention has been paid to this work in the secondary literature, especially concerning the relationship of this ontology to ethics, politics, and humanism.[3] In this étude I argue that the account of humanness that emerges from this ontology should be understood as an *insurrectionary humanism*.[4] This insurrectionary humanism can be thought as an example of what Jacques Rancière has called the "poetics of politics": Cavarero and Butler manifest an insurrectionary account of humanness that is disruptive of dominant conceptions of the human and the world that sustains him.[5] Their work is generative of another conception of what it is to exist with others, one at odds with prevailing conceptions of existence. This is not posited in the abstract, however. Cavarero and Butler's work responds to scenes of violence; what motivates the poetics of politics that is their insurrectionary humanism are, in part, these scenes of violence. As a consequence, the "imaginary of hope" that Cavarero calls for in her "Coda" to this volume can be understood as a form of nonviolence in a precise sense: the manifestation of, as Bonnie Honig conceptualizes it in her contribution, "heterotopian" refusals that are nonviolent in their amelioration of extant violence, even when these imaginaries adopt the inclined posture of refusal.

As an *insurrectionary* humanism it is a humanism that is marked by uprising, revolt, and mutiny, which is not posited in the abstract but intervenes in an always already given set of power relations and violences; it redistributes who and what is visible and sayable, decoupling certain bodies from certain capacities and creating the conditions for the apprehension of new forms of existence. As an insurrectionary *humanism* it enacts this insurrection around the locus of the human. I describe Cavarero and Butler's work as an insurrectionary humanism rather than a mere humanism, antihumanism, or posthumanism (Butler in particular has been associated with all of these) because none of these conceptions prioritize the deployment of humanness as an intervention in dominant conceptions of the human.[6] This is not to say that insurrectionary accounts of humanness cannot be thought as anti-, post- or mere humanisms; rather, it is to say that the notion of an insurrectionary humanism stresses intervention as its primary frame of analysis and thus makes clear something that is not overt in the other conceptions. It could in this way be described, following Honig, as an "agonistic humanism," if the accent of this agonism falls on the imbrication of the political, ethical, and ontological, rather than the valorization of the political first and foremost, which, I would argue, we see in Honig.[7] This point should not be belabored, however: it is not my intention to offer a fifth term alongside anti-, post-, mere- or agonistic humanism (to say nothing of Honig's charge of mortalist humanism).[8] Rather, I am using the term to delineate an aspect of Cavarero and Butler's thought that I think is important, in that it helps make apparent the ethicopolitical stakes of their respective interventions.[9] No doubt an insurrectionary humanism shares something of a mere humanism, an antihumanism, a posthumanism, and an agonistic humanism, even if it is not fully congruent with any of these terms.

Following Fred Moten, who himself follows Nahum Chandler, it may be more productive to understand Cavarero and Butler's respective ontologies of humanness as paraontologies, signifying that these ontologies not only operate *beside* ontology ("an insurrection at the level of ontology") but also are *distorted* ontologies and further *distort* prevailing ontologies: a parataxic parody of ontology.[10] The disruption of prevailing ontologies of humanness matters because of the attendant violences associated with these prevailing ontologies. As Olivia Guaraldo notes in relation to Cavarero and Butler, "Politics and ethics must be thought of within the context of an undeniable violence that, at the same time, is the cipher of an undeniable relationality."¹¹ In this sense, scenes of violence become a negative foundation conditioning the urgency of the staging of an insurrectionary account of humanness. Further, however, these scenes of violence—enacted in the name of the mythical figure of the purportedly universal subject of history and against those who do not conform to his implicit morphology and ontoepistemology—do not finally determine the form of this insurrectionary humanness, even if they make its staging urgent. Instead, this insurrectionary humanism takes as its resources the everyday experiences of those who live despite their abjection from a proper accounting of the world; what Cavarero calls an "imaginary of hope."

For Cavarero, both her own and Butler's work "focuses on the need to radically re-examine violence, connecting it to an ontology that demonstrates an ontology ingrained in humanity."¹² In this way, relational ontologies of vulnerability do not simply rearticulate the human but intervene in violences. In Cavarero's words

> the true target of [the relational model] is not, in fact—or not only—the philosophical genealogy of the subject; it is the violent practices of domination, exclusion, and devastation of which the subject itself is an accomplice. . . . The emphasis on vulnerability, in the relational model invoked here, is therefore first of all an accent on politics, ethics, and the social. The choice of assuming vulnerability as a paradigm of the human, far from an abstract speculative move, is instead rooted in the analysis of concrete situations.¹³

This aspect of Cavarero's work comes out most forcefully in her discussion of the Holocaust. In her essay "Narrative Against Destruction," Cavarero suggests there is an ethical valence in narrating the life stories of those who have been exposed to extreme violence. This narration does not suggest "a universal value" of the human. Instead, it is a "restitution of a possible sense for humanity itself, through the tale of the injured and the wounded."¹⁴ Cavarero highlights that as a "restitution" this humanity can only be figured in the light of its attempted destruction and, further, that what is offered is only a "possible sense" for humanity. These qualifications are important, as they make clear that to determine an account of the human from and yet separate to the destruction of humanness would be a mistake, in that the "possible sense" of the human preserved in the face of its destruction can only be made sense of in this context and not apart from it. To detach this "possible sense" of the human from the scene of its destruction would be to lose both the provisionality of this sense of the human and the urgency of its articulation: these qualities are not incidental to the "possible sense" of the human that Cavarero posits but on the contrary are central to its meaning. If "narrating life stories" is a process of "rehumanization," then this is not a positing of the human apart from its destruction, but rather is a process of "redeeming the meaning of the human from the ruins of the inhuman": for Cavarero, "the humanity that is recovered is a lacerated humanity." As a consequence, "what remains of the human consists precisely in this capacity of questioning the inhuman." The "scandal" of the inhuman sets the "infinite task . . . to radically rethink the human in light of its unspeakable destruction."[15] In this way, Cavarero insists that "there is an ethical and even ontological urgency in the necessity of . . . narration, almost as if every recounted story, snatched from oblivion, saves a possible sense of the human from its absolute negation and destruction."[16]

Biographical narration thus not only directly opposes the destruction of life stories, but can only be understood when considered in the light of this destruction:

> When it comes to biographical writing, and even more so, when history is produced through extreme horror, narrating is not merely "reconstructing" the thread of a life story; it is above all opposing the work of destruction that has devoured life itself. It is ultimately a making against destroying, a creating against demolishing, a doing against undoing.[17]

Something is missed if processes of making, creating, and doing are thought apart from the destroying, demolishing, and undoing that warranted them in the first place. These scenes operate almost as a negative foundation, conditioning the urgency of a project that is concerned with recovering not just the stories of people whose lives would otherwise be forgotten, but the ontological status of humanness as such (tied up as it is with the possibility of the storying of these lives). An account of what it is to be human, invariably composed of histories, narratives, and ontologies, is important precisely because humanness itself was the target of the horror of the camps; it is humanness that was destroyed, demolished, and undone.[18] As such, the end goal of such accounts is not primarily attempts at descriptive accuracy; they are improvisatory, performative interventions; accounts of humanness—that is, the *making, creating*, and *doing* of humanness—that struggle with and against the fact of the *destroying, demolishing*, and *undoing* of humanness. As I have suggested, one could therefore describe these accounts as insurrectionary humanisms.

Of course, these insurrectionary humanisms—or perhaps, accounts of insurrectionary humanness (or even insurrectionary accounts of humanness)—are themselves motivated by certain "normative aspiration[s]," and simply opposing the destruction of humanness offers one few clues as to what these aspirations should be.[19] This does not mean that one either cannot, nor should not, stage such accounts. Nor does it mean that one will not have good reasons for the form that these accounts take, reasons born out of the lived experience of those who demonstrate the absurdity of universal Man. Rather, it is to recognize the provisionality of these stagings, their contingency, their poeticity, and, significantly, their historicity; that is, the scenes of destruction from which they emerge. In saying that these accounts of humanness emerge from scenes of destruction one has to be careful: they do emerge from such scenes, but in their emergence they are also acting on these scenes themselves. Indeed, how one makes sense of destroying, demolishing, and undoing is mediated by particular expressions of humanness. In some extreme cases the destroying, demolishing, and undoing can only be recognized after the entity that has been exposed to these processes has become apparent, a point that Judith Butler makes forcefully.[20] The emergence of the human, then, at the same time becomes a way of manifesting a certain sense of violence, a violence that itself mediates how humanness is made sense of (as well as, so often, obscuring itself in the process).

In this way it would be a mistake to read Cavarero's account of humanness apart from destroying, demolishing, and undoing because her account is inextricably intertwined with said destruction. To do so would be to reduce her account to a mere humanism grounded in its appropriate human ontology. And while Cavarero's account maintains an ontology, the motivating ground for her account of humanness is not this ontology but rather destroying, demolishing, and undoing: that is, violence and violation.[21] Cavarero's ontology of uniqueness is an ontology stripped of its metaphysics: it is concerned not with *what* being *is*, but *who* beings *are*. It is premised not on an abstract account of being but on the mundane, banal recognition that everyone is different from every other one. Narration rather than philosophy would, for Cavarero, be its proper mode of articulation, a narration that, as we have seen, is especially pressing in the wake of scenes of violence.[22] Further, the meaning and significance of this uniqueness are utterly expositive: uniqueness does not reside *within* but emerges *between*, either between those who comprehend one another in the sociality of furtive co-appearance or between the one apprehending the life of another through narration.[23] In Cavarero's words,

"The ontological status of the *who*—as exposed, relational, altruistic—is totally *external*."[24] In this way, as Elisabetta Bertolino notes, it is Cavarero's very use of ontology that paradoxically "de-essentializes ontology."[25] "Ontology" may not even be the correct word for what Cavarero is describing: for Cavarero, "it is necessary to use words with bad intentions (*cattive intenzioni*), situating them in a different context that can overwhelm and recodify them, pushing those terms towards unpredictable meanings."[26] Ontology would precisely be such a word for her: her claiming of it with bad intentions is as much about deconstructing a metaphysical system that is complicit in the violent exclusion of the singular existence of people as it is about being philosophically rigorous. One can see then that despite her reticence about the notion of performativity as it is found in Butler's work, Cavarero's approach to theorizing, narrating, and storying is grounded in a recognition of their performatively efficacious qualities, an aspect that is pressing precisely in the context of the destruction wrought on the ontologies, narratives, and histories of those who have been exposed to extreme violence.[27]

Just as Cavarero's account of humanness is staged in relation to violence, so too is Butler's. For Butler, her account of vulnerability—that, as socially embodied beings, we are of necessity vulnerable, even if this vulnerability is differentially distributed—is not so much an ontology but rather an "insurrection at the level of ontology."[28] This suggests that charges of humanism leveled at Butler miss the mark: as Fiona Jenkins has argued, Butler's positing of vulnerability cannot simply be substituted in as a type of intellectual upgrade for our presumed self-sufficiency, "whereby one hegemonic conception of the subject succeeds another."[29] This would miss the transformational power that the poetic operation of Butler's theorizing maintains; its "poetics of politics."[30] If we imagine Butler's account of humanness as substituting and succeeding a demonstrably defunct conception of the human, then the schemas and rationalities that sustain this defunct conception remain unchanged.[31] Instead, when Butler stages an embodied relationality, it is not simply offered as a replacement, precisely because it suspends or renders inoperative the rationality that sustains the concept it would be replacing, creating a social imaginary that could be inhabited by those who do not see themselves reflected back in the figure of Man, even as it draws on their lived experience in its articulation.

The insurrectionary humanism that Butler stages is premised on a particular account of violence. This can be seen, as Cavarero indicates, in the etymology of the word "vulnerability": the *vulnus* in the word signifies "wound" in the Latin.[32] For Butler, a central aspect of violence is its varying visibility: violence can be recognized, misrecognized, or can evade recognition entirely, even by the person who is undergoing violence; one's violation depends upon schemas of recognizability, intelligibility, and normalization to be recognized as violence.[33] Since, following Butler, these schemas "not only organize visual experience but also generate specific ontologies of the subject," this potential failure to recognize violence also extends to one's own recognition of personal violation.[34] This means that while violence is the backdrop to almost all of Butler's work, an account of what it is—when something counts as violence and when something does not—is necessarily not to be found.[35] Nonetheless, Butler is politically and ethically motivated by a desire for a less violent world, and her analyses are replete with examples of violent injustice. She does not shy away from questions of violence and does not elide the problems violence poses through a purely theoretical analysis. For Butler, the problems violence poses are precisely what motivate her account of ethics and her ontology of vulnerability that refuse to rest on an ontology of sovereignty, autonomy, and invulnerability. What Butler's work suggests is that violence varies in its visibility precisely because when one makes claims about what it is, one is also making a claim about the entity exposed to violence (that is, that it is properly violable). One might want to resist this (refusing the argument that property damage equals violence), or one might want to affirm it (insisting that the "corrective surgery" enacted on intersex infants is a form of violence), but in either case there is a constitutive politics to any account of violence, one that imbricates violence with accounts of humanness and oppressive processes of racialization, gendering, and disablement.[36]

If we accept that Cavarero and Butler stage an insurrectionary humanism in their respective works, then we could argue that this helps furnish a social imaginary that offers a counterhistory of what it is to be-with-others while also disrupting dominant accounts of existence. These dominant accounts are shored up through the violation of forms of life that are incongruent with a conception of Man as sovereign and autonomous, and it is these histories of violence that give an urgency to the insurrectionary humanisms that Cavarero and Butler stage, revealing the project of nonviolence that both are committed to. My concern is that losing sight of this can too easily mean that the "poetics of politics" of Cavarero and Butler's stagings are downplayed, and thus so too are their particular political interventions.[37] It is this aspect of their work that can temper critiques focused on their ethical or humanist impulses: this is not to downplay their emphasis on the ethical or the human, but to insist that there is already a politics operative here; that in a world where extant humanness is constituted in violent abjection, the politics of their ethics (and the ethics of their politics) are not only crucial, but inevitable. Finally, although their work is made urgent by histories of violence, these histories do not determine the form that their insurrectionary humanisms take. Cavarero and Butler share a rigorous engagement with the category of vulnerability, and both are attentive to the *vulnus*'s ambivalence of wounding *and* caring, even if this emphasis is stronger in Cavarero. For both, the critique of the subject needs to be enacted through the articulation of an alternative, whose form is made apparent in the precarious lives lived in sociality despite these histories of violence.

Notes

1. On the end of the world as a response to violence, see Denise Ferreira da Silva's "Toward a Black Feminist Poethics: The Quest(ion) of Blackness toward the End of the World," *Black Scholar* 44, no. 2 (Summer 2014).

2. Adriana Cavarero, *Inclinations: A Critique of Rectitude*, trans. Amanda Minervini and Adam Sitze (Stanford, Calif.: Stanford University Press, 2016), 129; Judith Butler, *Frames of War: When Is Life Grievable?* (London: Verso, 2010), 2, 184.

3. See, for example, Jodi Dean, "The Politics of Avoidance: The Limits of Weak Ontology," *Hedgehog Review* 7, no. 2 (2005); Samuel A. Chambers and Terrell Carver, *Judith Butler and Political Theory* (London: Routledge, 2008); Ann V. Murphy, "Corporeal Vulnerability and the New Humanism," *Hypatia: A Journal of Feminist Philosophy* 26, no. 3 (2011) and *Violence and the Philosophical Imaginary* (Albany: State University of New York Press, 2012); Bonnie Honig, *Antigone, Interrupted* (Cambridge: Cambridge University Press, 2013), 17–31; Susan Heckman, "Vulnerability and Ontology: Butler's Ethics," *Australian Feminist Studies* 29, no. 82 (2015); Michael Feola, "Norms, Vision and Violence: Judith Butler on the Politics of Legibility," *Contemporary Political Theory* 13, no. 2 (2014); Sina Kramer, "Judith Butler's 'New Humanism': A Thing or Not a Thing, and So What?" *philoSOPHIA* 5, no. 1 (2015); and the essays that comprise Moya Lloyd, ed., *Butler and Ethics* (Edinburgh: Edinburgh University Press, 2015).

4. On insurrectionary humanism, cf. Judith Butler's "insurrection at the level of ontology," in her *Precarious Life: The Powers of Mourning and Violence* (London: Verso, 2006), 33; and comments made in her "Soulèvement," in *Soulèvement*, ed. Georges Didi-Huberman (Paris: Gallimard, 2016). Cavarero's relationship to an insurrectionary humanism may need to be complicated by her insistence on the posture of inclination in her *Inclinations*: the Latin root of "insurrection" is *īnsurgō*, which signifies "rising up," with its roots in the Latin *regus*, "to lead" or "to rule." Cf. Bonnie Honig's contribution to this volume for Cavarero's refusal of verticalist representations of refusal: Honig, "How To Do Things with Inclination: Antigones, with Cavarero."

5. Jacques Rancière and Davide Panagia, "Dissenting Words: A Conversation with Jacques Rancière," *Diacritics* 30, no. 2 (Summer 2000): 113–16.

6. For example, see Butler as offering a humanism in Bonnie Honig's "Antigone's Two Laws: Greek Tragedy and the Politics of Humanism," *New Literary History* 41, no. 1 (2010); an antihumanism in David Weberman's "Are Freedom and Anti-Humanism Compatible? The Case of Foucault and Butler," *Constellations: An International*

*Journal of Critical & Democratic Theory* 7, no. 2 (2000); and a posthumanism in Mari Ruti's "The Posthumanist Quest for the Universal," *Angelaki: Journal of the Theoretical Humanities* 20, no. 4 (2015).

7. Honig, *Antigone Interrupted*, 10.

8. On Honig's charge of mortalist humanism, see ibid., 17.

9. It should be noted that there are important differences in Cavarero's and Butler's thought, in particular their engagement with the issue of sexual difference; nonetheless, for the purposes of this étude I engage their thought together, recognizing both the way they have each been influenced by the other's thought and together have influenced contemporary debates on vulnerability.

10. Butler, *Precarious Life*, 33. On paraontology, see Fred Moten's "Blackness and Nothingness (Mysticism in the Flesh)," *South Atlantic Quarterly* 112, no. 4 (2013): 742, and his "The Subprime and the Beautiful," *African Identities* 11, no. 2 (2013): 240; and Nahum Dimitri Chandler's *X—The Problem of the Negro as a Problem for Thought* (New York: Fordham University Press 2014). See also Cavarero's account of inclination, which is precisely the distortion of the rectitudinous ontology of the Western political subject; *Inclinations*. For more on Butler's account of vulnerability as an ontology, see Stephen White's "As the World Turns: Ontology and Politics in Judith Butler," *Polity* 32, no. 2 (1999): 156, where White reads Butler's work for what he describes as a weak ontology. While some of my discussion of Cavarero and Butler's insurrectionary humanism resonates with White's "weak ontology," I differ in insisting on the importance of the disruptive aspects of these ontologies and the scenes of violence that make their staging urgent.

11. Olivia Guaraldo, "Re-locating Politics in the Age of Globalization," in *The Ashgate Research Companion to the Politics of Democratization in Europe: Concepts and Histories*, ed. Kari Palonen, Tuija Pulkkinen, and José María Rosales (Farnham: Ashgate, 2008), 113.

12. Cavarero, "Judith Butler and the Belligerent Subject," *Annali d'Italianistic*a 29 (2011): 163.

13. Cavarero, *Inclinations*, 13.

14. Cavarero, "Narrative against Destruction," trans. Elvira Roncalli, *New Literary History* 46, no. 1 (Winter 2015): 10, https://doi.org/10.1353/nlh.2015.0002.

15. Ibid., 11.

16. Ibid., 14.

17. Ibid.

18. Cf. Hannah Arendt, "Total Domination," in *The Portable Hannah Arendt*, ed. Peter Baehr (New York: Penguin, 2003), 135.

19. Sara Rushing, "Judith Butler's Ethical Disposition," *Contemporary Political Theory* 9, no. 3 (2010): 291.

20. See, for example, Butler's "Violence, Mourning, Politics," in *Precarious Life*, 19–49.

21. It should be noted that if the ground of Cavarero's account of humanness—that which makes its articulation urgent—is violence and violation, then what furnishes it are forms of care, sociality, improvisation, and pleasure, drawn equally from the "great works" of literature and from the everyday lived experience of people—especially women—living together.

22. Cavarero, *Relating Narratives: Storytelling and Selfhood*, trans. Paul A. Kottman (London and New York: Routledge, 2000), 13.

23. Both "comprehend" and "apprehend" share a seizing or a grasping in the *prehendō* of the Latin, but the "com" may signify a seizing enacted with others, while the "ap" may signify an outward seizing from one to another. On "the sociality of furtive co-appearance," see my forthcoming "Toward a Fugitive Politics: Arendt, Rancière, Hartman," *Cultural Critique* 110 (Winter 2021).

24. Cavarero, *Relating Narratives*, 89.

25. Cavarero and Elisabetta Bertolino, "Beyond Ontology and Sexual Difference: An Interview with the Italian Feminist Philosopher Adriana Cavarero," *differences: A Journal of Feminist Cultural Studies* 19, no. 1 (2008): 133.

26. Ibid., 137.

27. Ibid., 141–42.

28. Butler, *Precarious Life*, 33.

29. Fiona Jenkins, "Toward a Nonviolent Ethics: Response to Catherine Mills," *differences: A Journal of Feminist and Cultural Studies* 18, no. 2 (2007): 158.

30. Rancière and Panagia, "Dissenting Words," 113–16.

31. See, for example, Danielle Petherbridge, who notes that "Butler's appeal to vulnerability seeks to contest the liberal conception of an autonomous, individualistic subject as the norm for ethics and politics and to replace it with one based on vulnerability and interdependence"; Petherbridge, "What's Critical about Vulnerability? Rethinking Interdependence, Recognition, and Power," *Hypatia: A Journal of Feminist Philosophy* 31, no. 3 (2016): 593.

32. Cavarero, *Horrorism: Naming Contemporary Violence*, trans. William McCuaig (New York: Columbia University Press, 2011), 30; *Inclinations*, 158–62.

33. Butler, *Frames of War*, 5–6.

34. Ibid., 3.

35. Chambers and Carver, *Judith Butler and Political Theory*, 76; Sanna Karhu, "Judith Butler's Critique of Violence and the Legacy of Monique Wittig," *Hypatia: A Journal of Feminist Philosophy* 31, no. 4 (2016).

36. Butler, *Undoing Gender* (Oxford: Routledge, 2004), 4.

37. Rancière and Panagia, "Dissenting Words," 113–16.

# Queer Madonnas

## In Love and Friendship

CLARE WOODFORD

Cavarero's Madonna has the glint of an enigmatic love in her eyes.[1] I do not dispute this but propose that we would do well to hold back from associating this love with inclination,[2] as opposed to rectitude or mothers, any more so than others. Indeed, there are many ways in which we can read inclination, and different ways of reading it will render the subversion differently. So at Cavarero's insistence, let us reposition our gaze,[3] putting our heads on one side for a moment to look at Cavarero's Madonna askance, to see another Madonna in the same image: a counterpoint to Cavarero's Madonna that may provide further resources against patriarchy. Surprisingly, the Madonna I invoke is that of orthodox Catholicism, no innocent when it comes to the patriarchal order of the Catholic Church.[4] But ironically, despite patriarchy's best efforts, we find here a Madonna far stranger than Cavarero's: a "woman" so-called who not only speaks with angels but is pregnant without the obvious presence of a man, passing on no obvious blood ties of patriarchal kinship to her child; she is betrothed, not married; she appears as a disloyal fiancée and disobedient daughter; she is depicted inclined and cradling her baby but at other times upright, awkwardly clutching a wriggling infant or proffering, even brandishing, her baby forward into the world; this baby that, for Christians, was not a man, inasmuch as he came not from man and would never finally die.

This alone is sedition enough: a Madonna of hope, love, *and impropriety* against the propriety of our society's ideal image of motherhood, gender roles, and the identities and distinctions of the world. A queer Madonna against the model mother, against the sacred mother of our patriarchal symbolic. A queer mother who, according to theologians and mystics alike, bore a baby to end the need for any more babies. Recall that in the early church the best life was to reject marriage, kinship groups, and procreation and to live instead in communes, holding property in common, disparaging outdated practices of marriage and kinship. But unlike Bernini's discussion of sex without kinship, this life, problematically for us today, placed the domain of sex (both the act[s] and its categories), although not love, in question. This was a motherhood that nurtured in its womb a love, that refused to distinguish. A love said to know no bounds. Rather than property, blood, and land, we have here an other mother, a mother that ruptures what it is to mother for patriarchy. Cavarero's motherhood is modeled on care between mother and child. It too easily aligns with a patriarchal motherhood of blood and soil aimed at raising obedient workers for the public sphere.[5] As Honig's intervention also implies, this motherhood does not subvert patriarchy. It is constitutive of it.

If we persist in the awkward eccentricity of drawing on the Catholic catechism, an other Other emerges here too in relation to Mary. An other this time that is not a mother, an other to the Madonna to complete the very same "Holy family" image that is often imposed on nonconventional families. Yet if we pause to look carefully, although askance, we see that even in what is often presented as the perfect nuclear family there is more than we may realize. In adding Joseph to the image of the Madonna and child we see even more strongly that the Madonna's child is a child with no male lineage despite having a "stand-in" for a blood father and despite (or perhaps because of?) the insistence in biblical texts on the importance of Joseph's lineage through the House of David, from Adam. Yet the child is not "of" Joseph. There is here a queer patronage of name bestowed without blood tie to break the legacy of Adam: the man who will never die ends the line of the man who was never born.

There is a particular relationality between Mary and Joseph: a surprising trust right from the moment Joseph agrees to travel to Bethlehem with his pregnant betrothed, carrying a child that is not his. A trust and cooperation that remake kinship outside of blood ties. This relationality is problematic with respect to inheritance of property—would Jesus have been able to inherit Joseph's property if known to not be Joseph's blood child? Is it possible that it was only through such a challenge to property, to propriety, that this love (which rejects distinction, order, and demarcation) could be engendered? A love that fails to prioritize family over friend, friend over enemy. Further, we see here a man that seems to oppose the gender stereotypes, too,[6] a man without proven procreative powers of blood and who plays the ignominious supporting role. All we know is that he was a builder (traditionally rendered as a carpenter) usually portrayed as inclined over his tools.

This Queer Madonna with her queer tribe is one of many versions of a familiar tale, and it is hardly a version we would usually call radical. Yet even in her orthodoxy she unsettles. She undermines the assumed necessity of stereotypical gender roles in parenting and severs the necessity between the sexual act and the ability to care (for a child). She queers by indicating that already present, at the heart of a dominant and still influential strand in global culture, stereotypical gender norms are far from given. I do not invoke this Madonna as the best Madonna, the best pattern of intra-human relations, the best idea of (m)otherhood. I use her as a counterpoint to unsettle the inclined Madonna (who, we must not forget, is the correctly feminine Madonna) with a different stereotype that is both totally orthodox and terribly troubling: an upright Madonna. I invoke this so-called queer Madonna to see what she does to inclination— no longer perfect, docile, no longer inclined, no longer obedient to the world of mankind. Too often she is sanitized, tidied up, assumed to be married, veiling Jesus's fundamental but awkward conception, allowing her and Joseph to be neutralized into what from a distance appears as a conventional family structure. This woman that did not engage in sex with a man, who according to the doctrine of the immaculate conception did not herself emerge from what could be considered a normal act of sex between a man and a woman,[7] has been inclined anyway. She is reworked in cultural appropriation as the traditional mother that serves patriarchy, too often allowing us to read her as continuing, rather than rupturing or replacing, the lineage (and inheritance) of Eve. She is seen as a contradiction that requires sanitizing to gloss over the embarrassing story that sets her out on a path as an unmarried young pregnant woman to change the course of history, bringing into the world another form of love that is totally severed from masculine genesis. An enigmatic love that is radical and emancipatory in its refusal to discriminate.

Indeed, this Madonna need not be depicted as inclined. Many statues and paintings show the Madonna standing, on foot, erect. Some of the earliest depictions and many more throughout the ages are more often upright, calm but resolute, such as the sixth-century icon in Saint Catherine's monastery (Fig. 1), upright, although seated, and the icon of the standing Madonna in Rome's Santa Maria Maggiore, thought to date from at least the eleventh century, but possibly much earlier (Salus Populi Romani, Fig. 2). Or the many Madonnas painted by Bellini, some seated but upright (for instance, Fig. 3), displaying a range of distracted expressions:

FIGURE 1. Artist unknown, *Virgin and Child between Saints Theodore and George* (second half of sixth century), encaustic on wood, Saint Catherine's Monastery, Mount Sinai. Source: Erich Lessing Archive.

FIGURE 2. Traditionally attributed to Saint Luke, *Madonna "Salus Populi Romani"* (590 A.D.), encaustic on cedar wood, Santa Maria Maggiore, Rome. Source: Alinari Archives.

FIGURE 3. Giovanni Bellini, *"Alzano" Madonna* (c. 1485), oil on panel, Academa Carrera, Bergamo. Source: Wikimedia Commons.

bored, pensive, detached, preoccupied. Or Raphael's Sistine Madonna (Fig. 4) standing erect, her eyes gentle but fearful, offering the child out as if in the process of handing him to the viewer, perhaps wishing to share her charge? Or maybe just wishing to be rid of the burden, the responsibility that would change her life. These depictions, among others, have either not yet been taught, or seek to reject, the discipline of good art, which says that a good mother always inclines her head in a nod of subservience to her patriarchs. Indeed, when erect, the Madonna is not always right in her relation, is not co-rect, for she is perhaps then, in her erect stance, not deemed feminine enough, is not motherly in the right, docile, way. She proffers her child out, away from herself, into the world, her face not always serene, sometimes fearful, sometimes confrontational. She provokes us to confront the damage that this enigmatic love can do to our ordered world. If there is love or care here it is a *confrontation* of love and care to the world. This Madonna shows that Cavarero is right to emphasize that verticality need not be the only posture that we value but reminds us that there is something of rectitude in care that could be useful for confronting a world of violence and exclusion.

Furthermore, even though inclination could provide a model for care, which type of inclination are we referring to here? As Butler also observes, there are many forms of inclination, and they are not all the same. In rethinking the relation between the female symbolic and inclination let us call to mind Caravaggio's painting "Death of the Virgin" (Fig. 5). This Madonna is fully inclined. So incorrect in her inclination that she caused scandal, spread out under the gaze of the men surrounding her, her pose considered temptingly erotic despite being dead, looking instead as if she has just fallen into a sensuous slumber. Yet how does her inclination, celebrated by some as a subversion of religious dogma, subvert patriarchy? Would this inclined woman, inclined by a male hand, while other men look on, upset patriarchy? Could she even evoke care of others? Is inclined woman not the (erotic) object of patriarchy? The cause of male rectitude? What do we know of the life of the model who posed for Caravaggio? Why did she incline for him? These ruminations make us wonder: which inclination should we use to challenge which rectitude or even whether, in actual fact, female rectitude, erecting dangerous alternative worlds—in a gesture of refusal exemplified by Honig's bacchante—could not more effectively, or at least just as effectively, unsettle masculine rectitude?

There are many narratives of inclination, and Cavarero rightly observes that it is a narrative that is all too familiar to those who live as women, yet she wants to read inclination as inclination in care toward others. What, then, of the inclination toward the floor, the bow of subservience,

FIGURE 4. Raphael, *Sistine Madonna* (1512), oil on canvas, Gemäldegalerie, Alte Meister. Source: Wikimedia Commons.

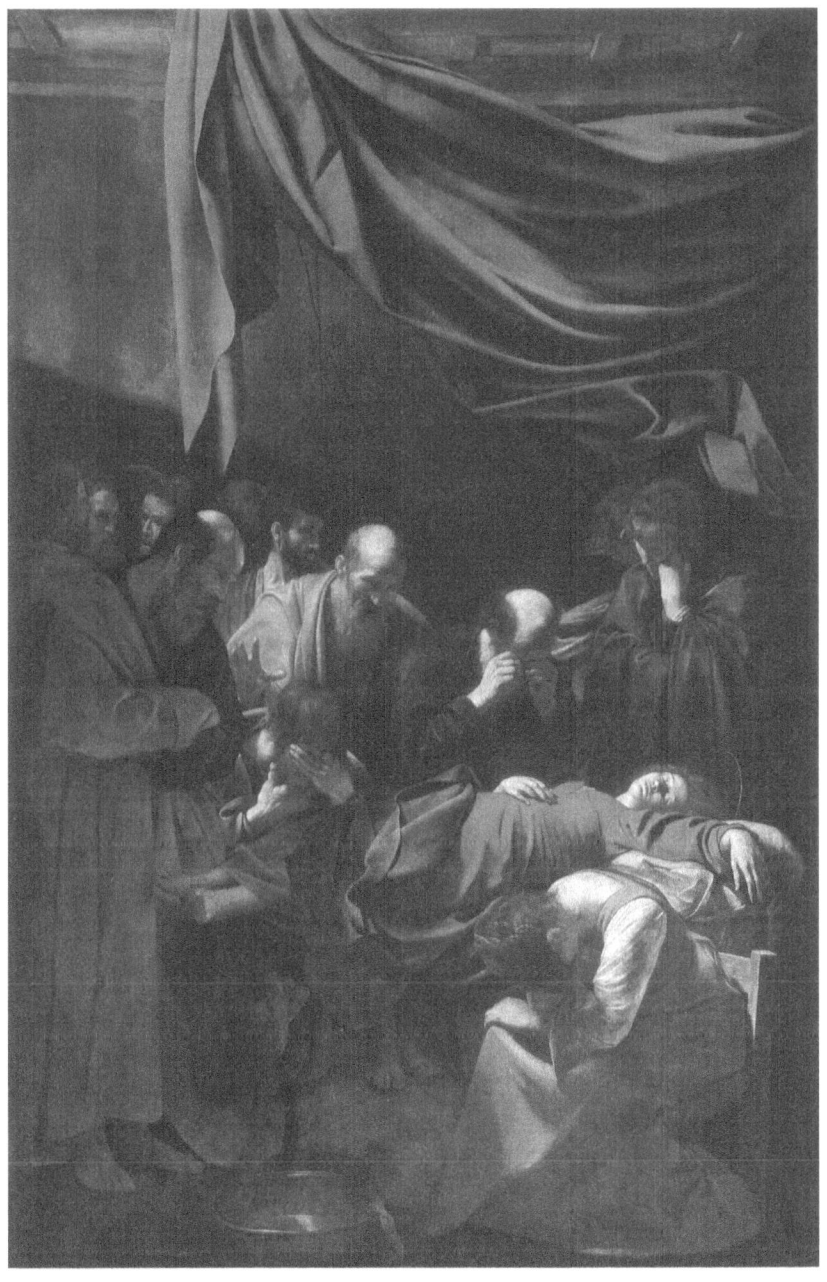

FIGURE 5. Caravaggio, *Death of the Virgin* (1606), oil on canvas, Louvre, Paris. Source: Wikimedia Commons.

the inclined back that cleans and scrubs, the stooped posture and drooped breast, weary of life, bringing life, supporting life. This inclination is not just female. It is often shared with others, shared with the lowly, the poor, the weary, the worn down. So we also have in inclination a resignation, an acceptance, of pain, of backbreaking work; an inclination, whether chosen or forced, to authority. Despite the tranquility of Cavarero's argument, the humor and its very real resonances, I agree with Butler that the order of inclination and rectitude cannot be so easily mapped onto the apparent clear distinction between male and female: inclination inheres a dark side of domination, too.

Cavarero's Madonna, the inclined Madonna straightened out into her inclination, is, as Devenney also observes, too easily the legitimate Madonna, the patriarchal Madonna, the hetero-Madonna, the safe Madonna. The Mother that is The Other—safe, binarized, positioned, and proper. A tool to enable redemption and salvation of men and women, if they can all but incline themselves to serve the current order. Cavarero, of course, wants to mobilize her narrative of the Mother to use it against the symbolic order, but this inclined mother *is* still within the auspices of the patriarchal order—the yin *of* the yang, perhaps the part that was in shadow but always there, always needed.[8] We can cast a spotlight on it, show it for what it is, show patriarchy's dependence on it, but could this not just be an erotic revelation of the hidden that is now exposed—propping up patriarchy further, rather than subverting it? A secure order can allow its foundations to be revealed and stay standing. When there are two dominant positions within an order, prioritizing the other part does not automatically overturn the order, it just rebalances power within it. As long as each part remains recognizable, as long as women remain inclined, caring, not just for their children but for everyone, head bowed, baby on their knee, then they are invited to dine at the top table.

As Honig too leads us to wonder, where in this story is the fierce mother, the defensive aggressor, fighting to protect her children from the threats of the world? Where is the threatened mother, the scared mother, the struggling mother, the mother who feels little love for her children? Is she a bad mother? A failed mother? A wrong mother? Cavarero implies that she too cannot escape inclination. As Forti describes the torturer inclined over his victim, I recall that Medea no doubt inclined over her children in order to kill them.[9] Inclination for Cavarero is just the intertwining of lives that is denied in the erect vertical autonomous self of the philosophical canon. But what then does inclination give us over rectitude? It just becomes another posture from which good or bad can come. Perhaps, unlike rectitude, inclination acknowledges our interconnectedness when doing good or evil, rather than our independence. Yet to appreciate interconnectedness we need not reject rectitude. Huzar's étude emphasizes the insurrectionary quality of Cavarero's inclination, further endorsed by Cavarero's theorization of democracy as surging or rising up (insurrection is from the Latin *insurgere*—to rise up).[10] Thus within the ethics of inclination, we have a rising up—an establishment, assertion, or even erection, of inclination—that, unless it is to become the new proper, as Devenney fears, must instead indicate to us the entwining of inclination around and within rectitude, too, to decenter and undermine its righteousness.

Perhaps we might assist this task if we could discern behind this tangle of mothers, the woman who is not a mother. Othered twice, not just distanced from the thrones of power, is she here denied meaningful existence as one who can care? In this question we start to tease apart the entwining of inclination and maternity in Cavarero's account. Where they combine is in the way that maternity shows us that inclination is always inclination toward the other. But there is also here the potential for a radical reworking of maternity that could be further developed. Cavarero mysteriously comments that Arendt is not only childless but perhaps lacking in love for mothers and children,[11] but why would the inability or refusal to bear children of one's own imply lack of love for children or motherhood in general? It seems the childless mother has no place in this story of Madonnas unless we see the child Jesus not as a baby but symbolic of a practice of love that is meant to reject any particular inclination, a child that, born once, can be carried by all, irrespective of biology.[12]

To critique rectitude and philosophy from the position of the inclined Madonna is problematic in four ways. It is to risk tying women to motherhood, to their wombs, gendering birth even more and ensuring the continuation of a patriarchy where the domestic work will never be disrupted. Second, it is to risk dividing men from birth—their responsibilities, love, partnership, support, duties, and the rethinking of gender roles and relationships supporting birth and care, and also to emphasize the normative nuclear family and thereby distance all nonbiological parents and caregivers from the scene of birth, from care for a newborn, for a child, for care for our future. Third, it is to risk overlooking the way that birth and care are tied too easily through the "ties of eros" to property and inheritance, to blood and soil. Finally, it rejects for no reason the rectitude of the feminine, erect womanhood, which also has its place in the geometrical matrix of meaning and human relations. Cavarero is not ignorant of these risks. She makes an informed and careful decision to run this gauntlet because of the need to revalorize the mother as a political posture *for* peace and *for* the woman against those who wish to keep the mother in her place of servitude. My concern at this point is that her strategy might need something more to give it critical purchase against patriarchy. Otherwise we swing from the paternal to the maternal, leaving patriarchy intact, in place, waiting for us to swing back again. We stay suspended inside the conventional family structure with no obvious way out.

## Eros, Friendship, Domination

So how else might we relate to one another? Cavarero implies that eros might help us here, since it takes us outside of ourselves.[13] But it is strange that for Cavarero eros is always inclined.[14] Eros is not well known for respecting the rules of order—even an inclined order. Eros cannot be constrained, and certainly not to just two dimensions. In *Dedicated to Derrida*,[15] Cavarero suggests that ideas emerge before names and language (of infancy) in which selves can incline toward one another in uniqueness, entwining their voices. But let us recall that in the same way in which bodies entwine when having sex, we never exist simply on one plane. Eros is the unsettling force that will not respect our order, our promises, our property and propriety; vows or contracts, whether of marriage, fidelity, friendship, or commitment; age or time. Eros plays between planes. The geometric ordering of philosophy is too static, too flat. But replacing rectitude with inclination is just a first step toward our need to put these planes in motion.

Despite the promise of Guaraldo's scherzo, I fear that Cavarero's lovers are not so dangerous. Eros may be unsettling, but this need not be radical. Erotic, sensual partners in pleasure and desire, her lovers comprise an asymmetric relation always between the two, between self and Other, who learn each other through narration. But asymmetry is also a requirement for domination. Lacan's famous assertion that "there is no sexual relation"[16] reminds us of eros' dominatory tendencies—it is a power relation, even as it disrespects other power relations. Eros thus unsettles order but remakes it, too. Eros ties not just to blood through reproduction, but to soil—dominion. What then of friendships that are not fixed in asymmetry? Friendships that move in a play between friends? Friendship as a shared endeavor could dissolve distinctions that may or may not cross gender lines, but where they do, could loosen or remake them? Friendship too can temper eros and the drive to domination. The ties of friendship (*filia*) need not necessarily be ties of inclined relationality as we might usually assume, nor would they exclusively be ties of rectitude.

In fact, they may operate through incorrectitude: critical, ambiguous inclination both toward and away from.

The friendships or relationalities that sustain a political community are not of sameness, of consensus to a shared ethic. They are a provocation, or moreover a commitment to continue the provocation. A shared community only inasmuch as it shares nothing other than a shared consent to dissent.[17] This is a commitment without kinship (indeed, Battersby emphasizes the particular difficulties and benefits this can bring), without blood, a *filia* without fraternity (or even sorority?), riven too no doubt, as all human relations, by an eros, but that works against or tempers eros's excesses, too. This filia is not tied to the person or any particular sexual relation but to the open relation to the other that provokes. It is a break with blood (family), with land (no proper place), with time (no initial event).[18] If there is a relationality here it is not one of inclination per se: motherly inclination can too often be fixed in one-directional asymmetry—an inclining down toward the other who is weak, who is vulnerable, who is dependent. The Other who must remain Other so we can remain inclined. The practice of friendship for democracy must be a relationality in motion, upright and inclined, together, entwined, in play, back and forth, between.

Like the image of friendship between Kant and Joseph Green that I take from Christine Battersby's account, this is a kind of parrhesiastic critical friendship. Perhaps a nongendered (where gender is just not so important, rather than neutral) *filia* that acknowledges, yet tempers, its eros. This is not just an upright friend who keeps you on the "straight and narrow" but a *filia* that is not related to you through sex or blood, an equality that is not the same as you, not a part of you: a *filia* that pushes you off the straight and narrow too, that unsettles and challenges you and the certainties you thought you knew. Its geometry, if it has one, is of both inclination and rectitude. It is at first glance a *filia* starred with eros, but this is not all. The most intricate of patterns are woven at multiple inclinations. The vertical and horizontal axes are never enough; they lack depth and space through which we move in the world. Friendships incline toward as they incline away, in refusal as well as accord, upright at times and inclined at others. This is a relationality that is not always a preference, an inclination toward. It can be critical; its caring can, at times no doubt, seem unsympathetic, hence its riskiness.[19] We have seen that inclination alone can be dangerous. It can too often take us back toward that which we know, that which we understand, that which we prefer. Sometimes, as Butler emphasizes too, in dissenting we may have to fight our inclinations in order to break with blood and soil.

Critical friendship that provokes is a friendship that exceeds inclination. It undermines distinctions and places. It works across gender distinctions. It is a working together that undermines the blood and soil of throne and home. A weaving that is a tangling, of voice, of things, of words and names, of writing and meaning; unwieldy complexity in which we try to weave and unweave and end up tangling and untangling. Here perhaps I evoke the sinuous snaking feminine that Cavarero plays with in her opening chapter. Yet these tangles may be less than smooth or seductive. They can be jagged. They can snag and catch, tying together those who would rather be separate. Forcing us to find our way through, dissenting in our joined-ness. Such critical, parrhesiastic friendships can undermine sex and gender differences, they can stand against or undermine property and properties, but while they can challenge, if they are united by the consent to dissent, they can never end.[20]

## Weaving Dissent

The love of the Queer Madonna can be mobilized, along with so many other caricatures, against property and properties, but must also be mobilized against any particular inclination, whether it be for inclination or rectitude. It worries at the heels of Cavarero's call for inclination to become our new fundamental schematism.[21] If we are to be cautious of our own blindness to exclusion we could do well here to invoke Honig's call for passionate ambivalence.[22] A critique of rectitude indicates that it is any and every particular inclination of which we must be wary. Cavarero's project is the first step in the complication of rectitude, complicating and interrupting the linear narrative of the Enlightenment patriarchal project of rectitude with a counternarrative, pushing us away from one but toward another. This initial jolt is a starting point but persistent as the seemingly endless motion of Penelope's needle working back and forth, perhaps Cavarero's project should be taken as one verse of an irreverent ode to never remaining still. To fighting the linear onward march of time with a movement that does not suspend it, but every day reworks and undoes, taking us closer to something else, something different, a working together across borders and boundaries to continually craft different, perhaps less violent, worlds. Her weaving of narrative provokes us to critique the masculine symbolic by invoking care against battle and inclination against rectitude. But the provocative friendship (which is ambivalent inasmuch as it does not force you to choose) and the axiomatic equality of democracy, of *my* understanding of democracy, invokes not care *instead of* struggle (where struggle encompasses all form of disagreement, not just war of all against all), but care *as* struggle, for if we did not care we would not be motivated to struggle in the first place.[23]

As all the contributors here acknowledge, Cavarero's work of postural ethics is exemplary in method as well as content. It irreverently provokes its readers, inspiring us not to simply apply her critique, but to travel with her, retracing her steps through the terrain we thought we knew so well. In our iteration of her journey, we undo and reweave her threads again, inspired by her to never let them lie still. We weave an account that is not a repetition, but that, stepping into her rhythm, captured in her momentum, creates a new tangle not of a new core for community, but another world from the mess of bodies and matter where we dwell today. Moved through our scene by the push of the Queer Madonna's enigmatic love, we dodge and weave around violence's perpetual drive to infinite justice, evading just in time its final blow by ever consenting to dissent, drawing politics back in.

## Notes

1. Adriana Cavarero, *Inclinations: A Critique of Rectitude*, trans. Amanda Minervini and Adam Sitze (Stanford, Calif.: Stanford University Press, 2016), 174.
2. Even in the sense of a model as Cavarero wishes to use it; ibid., 129.
3. Ibid.
4. If anyone would wish to dispute this I refer them to Marina Warner's *Alone of All Her Sex*, which charts the way the official orthodox version of the Madonna's life was pieced together over 2,000 years as the politics of the church necessitated; Warner, *Alone of All her Sex*, 2nd ed. (London: Vintage, 2000).
5. Carole Pateman, *The Sexual Contract* (Stanford, Calif.: Stanford University Press, 1988). See interventions by Honig, Devenney, and Forti on the violence that this inheres.
6. Cf. *Catechism of the Catholic Church*, 2nd ed. (Vatican City: Libreria Editrice Vaticana, 1997), 499–501, and Warner's discussion of the politics of these debates; Warner, "Virgin Birth," in *Alone of All Her Sex*, 34–49.
7. The immaculate conception is often depicted in Christian tradition as a standing embrace between St. Anne and St. Joachim as he returned to the city from a time of fasting and prayer in the desert. St. Anne, then, is another upright woman, here involved in what is meant to symbolize an upright, perhaps less erotic, but also nondominatory relation.
8. See also Alison Stone, "The Ontology of the Maternal: A Response to Adriana Cavarero," *Studies in the Maternal* 2, no. 21 (2010): np.
9. Cavarero, *Inclinations*, 105–6.
10. Cavarero, *Surging Democracy: Notes on Hannah Arend's Political Thought*, (Stanford, Calif.: Stanford University Press, 2021).
11. Ibid., 120.
12. Perhaps this could, in response to Bernini's étude, help decenter the cloying idealization of the child and childhood in our social lives.
13. Ibid., 6–7.

14. "Sexual and emotional inclination towards a person—for brevity's sake we'll call it eros"; Cavarero, *Inclinations*, 3.

15. Cavarero, "Appendix: Dedicated to Derrida," in *For More Than One Voice*, 213–41.

16. Jacques Lacan, *The Seminar of Jacques Lacan: The Other Side of Psychoanalysis*, vol. 17, trans. Russell Grigg (New York: W. W. Norton, 2008).

17. Clare Woodford, "In Defence of Dreaming," in *Cinema, Democracy, Perfectionism: Joshua Foa Dienstag in Dialogue*, ed. Joshua Foa Dienstag (London and New York: Macmillan, 2017).

18. Indeed, Honig suggests that a challenge to blood ties is actually to counter incest, not to raise it as taboo, since incest is anti-democratic. It closes the circle; Honig, "Antigone's Laments, Creon's Grief: Mourning, Membership, and the Politics of Exception," *Political Theory* 37, no. 1 (2009): 5–43.

19. Michel Foucault, "Discourse and Truth: The Problematization of Parrhesia," Six Lectures at University of California, Berkeley, Calif., Oct.–Nov. 1983.

20. For a fuller discussion of this, see Woodford, *Disorienting Democracy* (London: Routledge, 2017), Chapter 3.

21. Cavarero, *Inclinations*, 129.

22. Bonnie Honig, *Democracy and the Foreigner* (Stanford, Calif.: Stanford University Press, 2003).

23. By this I just mean if we did not care in terms of "if we had no interest"—this also incorporates thicker notions of care invoked in the phrase to "care for one another" but also can be opposed more thinly to the idea of not caring, as in having no interest in something.

# Coda

ADRIANA CAVARERO

Given that during my entire intellectual life I have tried to be faithful to the reality of lived experience, I can't help beginning to write the epilogue to this volume by mentioning the three full days of discussions and passionate debates of which the selected essays here collected are a representative but inevitably not an exhaustive part. There were real, unique voices sharing the common and exciting task of *Giving Life to Politics* at the conference in Brighton. As Konstatinos Thomaidis—one of the more than fifty speakers whose contribution is not included in this volume—observed in an interview published in the *Journal of Interdisciplinary Voice Studies*, "I could not help but notice that at the recent conference in Brighton, there was much pleasure taken in voicing. There were recorded voices at the background of the book launch and participating philosophers came together to sing at the conference dinner. There were also three keynotes, with responses offered by all keynote speakers to each other, and a multi-vocal final roundtable. For me, these were crucial interventions of vocality in spaces where voice, albeit delivered (see 'reading a paper'), can find itself circumscribed within rigid frameworks of academic intelligibility."[1] I totally agree with Tomaidis's words, and, since my book *For More Than One Voice*, by addressing the issue of a politics of voices, I have managed to emphasize the role that vocality plays in expressing the core of that special, intense, and transient form of politics that I dare name "surging democracy." Indeed, the effort of giving life to politics does involve the act of voicing—that is, within the dialogical context of the conference I am here referring to, it implies the resonating exchange of a plurality of voices whose embodied materiality constitutes the very core of surging democracy before, behind, and in excess of what is said. Which doesn't mean, of course, that what is said doesn't matter: after all, in Brighton, we were participating in a conference where scholars presented and discussed ideas, trains of thought, speculative positions, narratives, and critical concerns. It rather means, in my view, that what gives life to politics, intended in terms of embodied democracy, is an interacting plurality that displays its ontological and relational status through the material uniqueness of resonating singular voices. Differently told, at stake in this template of democracy is not so much the (pleasurable) exercise of undoing rigid frameworks of academic intelligibility, but rather the radical challenge of defining politics in terms of vocal materiality instead of verbal communication. Obviously, there is an explicit polemical stance in this formula and its claimed radical intention. The politics of voices, in fact, purposely confronts the Aristotelian legacy of the Western tradition that, by identifying the *zoon politikon* with the *zoon logon echon*, maintains that politics quintessentially consists of speech. On the other hand, within the anomalous archetype of the political that I name surging democracy, what primarily matters is not speech but the voices that utter it—that is, plural voices communicating their relational uniqueness.

That I am here calling on an Arendtian vocabulary is clear enough, and it is in keeping with my entire intellectual biography. Yet, as Olivia Guaraldo argues in her contribution to this volume, it is first and foremost the tradition of feminist materiality, which permeates my work since *In Spite of Plato*, to encourage me in stressing the bodily aspects of interactive democracy and assuming them as basic tenets for defining politics. These are, not by chance, the same aspects that Judith Butler would perhaps encapsulate in her insightful concept of performativity and relate to the political form of "assembly." From the *listening* standpoint I am here insisting on, however, what materializes the practice of democracy as such is the sphere of the vocal, which is the vibration of that particular soundscape of interacting pluralities that I don't hesitate to call pluriphony. I know of course that there is a big difference between the phonosphere produced by people assembled on public squares, standing, protesting, and resisting, and that produced by an untroubled group of scholars discussing political and philosophical issues. In other words, I know that there is an exaggeration—a sort of Arendtian attitude for pushing ideas to the extreme—in my assuming an apparently ordinary event like that of the conference in Brighton, if not of scholarly conferences as such, as paradigmatic cases of pluriphonic democracy. Yet, let me insist on this point. I believe that there are circumstances where the intellectual and material enjoyment of plural voices sharing a common space of discussion heralds—or, at least, allows us to savor—the taste of democracy in its germinal status—that is, allows us to experience the joy of politics in its birthing phase. As if the exciting perception of what Hannah Arendt calls "public happiness" were not completely secluded from our experience of scholars, students, theorists, and the like. Indeed, I do believe that the endeavor of giving life to politics demands the effort of politicizing our collective experience, wherever it may take place, by empowering its relational condition and imagining the projection and proliferation of this very condition inasmuch as it is the expression of a vociferous interacting plurality that manifests its happiness of being plural. The living experience of interaction and the work of imagination that multiplies and reactivates the happiness of this interacting are strictly connected, in my view, so strictly intertwined that if I had to summarize such a knot in a formula I would speak of revolutionary utopia.

Something of the "vision of altruism and pacifism" that Judith Butler mentions by commenting on my concept of inclination has undoubtedly to do with this utopian stance. If I am here convoking the term "utopia," it is not because I feel particularly at ease with it and the complex conceptual frames it traditionally refers to but rather because I want the naïf vein of my vision of altruistic "humanism" to surface effortlessly. I learned from feminism and the movement of the sixties the generative power of interaction mobilized by an imaginary of hope. I learn from Arendt the option not to think *against* but rather *for* something, which is the effort to resist the *critique-only* temptation of the philosopher and the daring to imagine even the impossible. I think that our sophisticated critical approach to the so-called Western macro-text, precious as it is for deconstructing and unmasking the violent mark of the phallogocentric tradition, that is, the type of approach my critique of rectitude does bank on, must be accompanied by—if not resolved into—a positive, reparative, imaginative, and creative form of thought. I have in mind what Rita Felsky, within the field of literary studies, calls post-critique.[2] Although it is well demonstrated by Mark Devenney's spirited intervention, rather than in the undoing of critical theory—whatever this label could mean—I am interested in the positive task of redirecting the questions of ontology, politics, and ethics toward a framework of altruism and peace capable of capturing our imagination and mobilizing our actions. Be sharp in exercising the critique but dare to be creative and even "impossibilist," I would say to the new generation of feminist theorists and radical thinkers that my work primarily addresses. Risk even the "impropriety" of being assertive and utopian for the sake of sharing an imaginary of hope, I would claim.

In fact, my effort of contrasting the belligerent masculine model of the vertical "I" by proposing a material ontology of inclined and dependent plural subjectivities goes in this imaginative direction. And it goes without saying that "giving life" to politics convokes the maternal act of generating, giving birth, bringing into being, as well as it convokes the complementary act of vivifying, enlivening, and taking care of. Still, although one could say that politics is fragile and helplessly exposed to violence like a child, politics is not a creature or an object, of course, but rather a human practice or, as Hannah Arendt would say, a shared space for action opened up by an interacting plurality. Actually, as I have often argued in my works, it is interesting to notice how the Arendtian speculative gesture of radically rethinking politics, conceiving it in terms of a public space engendered by an interacting plurality, goes along with her original focus on the category of birth and the human condition of natality. Indeed, and in spite of her neglecting the figure of the mother, by shifting the founding principle of politics from death to birth, she provides a significant schema for reconceptualizing the political and its embodied subjectivities within a framework of peace. My call on the maternal figure, and even on the Christian icon of the Madonna with child, as postural models of inclined and relational subjectivities aims at anchoring this imaginary of peace on both a powerful traditional representation of unbalanced relationships and the vulnerability that the protagonists of this very representation share in a different measure. If it is true that human vulnerability is what we have in common—as if vulnerability were the universal trait of the human that defines our community—it is also true, as Judith Butler has often argued, that this vulnerability is differently distributed in space and time, either from a geopolitical or biographical and existential points of view. Which means, primarily, within my perspective, that the fact that the human as human needs care and the inclined posture of the other—be this other imbedded or not in the stereotypical iconography of the oblative mother—displays an ontological condition of dependence that works as the prerequisite of whatever effort of rethinking politics in terms of relationality. And it means, besides, that when I address the issue of an inclined, structurally relational, and unbalanced geometrical posture, I am staging an imaginary that is completely apart from the geometrical verticalism that characterizes the traditional construction of the subject. After all, such a subject is notoriously belligerent and violent; his pride for standing up, in perfect self-sufficiency and autonomy, is paid in terms of aggression and war. Needless to quote Hobbes, the very champion of this egological and belligerent subjectivity: the vertical subject doesn't care about the vulnerable, he doesn't care at all; at least, he transfers to others the gesture of caring.

Bonnie Honig observes that my call on an imaginary completely apart from geometrical verticalism results in a heterotopian separatism that leaves verticality empowered to do its work. Differently told, by playing on distinction and opposition, heterotopia risks frustrating our need for agonistic engagement with the rectilinear, autonomous, domineering subject. This is why, by claiming and demonstrating that inclination may signal not only care but also refusal, Honig argues that "refusal as inclination can take the agonistic form of engaging directly with powers that be." Although I enthusiastically embrace the idea of making of inclination an important part of refusal's repertoire, I have to admit that, on the speculative plane, agonistic engagement with verticality was not exactly the core strategy on which I constructed my critique of rectitude. My challenge, as I wrote in my book, was rather to "geometrically distill the rhetoric of maternity and superimpose it, like a transparent screen, over the rhetoric of the philosophical subject, in order to highlight the difference between two ontological, ethical and political models."[3] To formulate it curtly, within my speculative strategy, heterotopia serves the generative work of utopia. In light of this, I wouldn't put a particular emphasis on my use of heterotopia as a longing for the "separate and pure," but would rather insist on the instrumentality of a heterotopian technique that aims at facilitating the birth of the imaginary of hope I mentioned earlier. Since my *In Spite of Plato* I believe in the effectiveness of the tactic of accentuating, reconfiguring, and recombining stereotypes in order to exploit their potentiality for different frames of signification. Heterotopy is part of this speculative policy. A policy intentionally adjusted to that exciting and productive exercise—that we largely share!—of "doing things" with the words and the figures that each of us reconceptualizes and proposes to the differentiated but relational lot of her "ideal" readers. Fortunately, this has been the case of my idea of "inclination," whose congenital openness to further meanings is purposely inscribed in the very modality I relied on for staging the inclined posture as a generative module. After all, to put it in plain words, aren't we continuously engaged in "doing things" with the vocabulary of the authors we like or dislike? Isn't Sophocles's Antigone an object of interminable interpretations many of us apparently cannot renounce? Or, if you allow me to be autobiographical, isn't Plato the very torment of my intellectual life inasmuch as Arendt is its enduring consolation? And what about the "algid" Kant I dare put into a heterotopian freezer?

Although she appreciates my concern with Kant's drive for conforming the moral rectitude to a vertical axis, Christine Battersby justly accuses me of neglecting Kant's privilege of friendship and his account of "unsocial sociability" as integral to human civilization. Judith Butler, by her part, manages to portray a more sympathetic Kant to the world of vulnerability and dependence by quoting texts where he concedes the possibility of the undoing of the rectilinear subject. I find it interesting how several comments to my work on *Inclination* ponder on Kant or, at least, discuss with a particular intellectual fervor my reading of Kant.

Let me shortly be autobiographical again in order to avoid engaging the question of the innumerable and multifaceted interpretations that an author like Immanuel Kant, of course, generates. I must confess that, in spite of my fundamental bent for Hannah Arendt, I have always been suspicious of her great admiration for Kant and, most of all, of the political use she makes of the *Third Critique*. Namely, among other things, I deem extremely problematic her attempt of refounding the political category of plurality upon the Kantian concept of imagination intended as capacity to make present in our individual mind different perspectives. Yet, I must admit that, while rereading Kant's texts for architecturing my book on inclination, I couldn't help developing a secret sympathy for him, too. Tellingly, by reporting the tender story of the friendship goblet and by focusing on the even more moving story of the old Kant, almost blind and affected by vertigo, Christine Battersby and Judith Butler inevitably succeeded in arousing in me a further stream of sympathy for the philosopher. As a matter of fact, I am sensible to their suggestions. I still find good motives, however, for resisting these suggestions inasmuch as "my" apparently less sympathetic Kant serves as a precise speculative strategy. At stake, in the architecture of my book on inclination, is the construction of a thesis, or if you want of a schema, whose strategic design not only represses the possible sympathy for the authors I deal with, but, for the sake of effectiveness, dares interpret and exploit their texts with a certain lack of scruples. As Timothy Huzar correctly remarks in his contribution to this volume, I am accustomed to using words and ideas of the Western philosophical lexicon with "bad intentions," situating them in a different context that can overwhelm, recodify, and push them toward unexpected meanings. A no less severe treatment I inflict on authors by selecting, sizing, and abducting some of their ideas in order to make them work in different theatres of signification. I don't know if such an attitude has an insurrectional character, marked by uprising, revolt, and mutiny, as Huzar suggests, but would agree on the fact that, in a way, it has a political poetic of its own. Actually, in order to emphasize the opposition between Kant's vertical axis and my inclined postural ontology, I adopted the aforementioned typical Arendtian strategy of pushing ideas to the extreme. By being a scholar of Arendt, I believe in the usefulness of strong and daring theses, theses that because of their provocative assertiveness aim at functioning as generative plots for further speculative narratives to proliferate.

It seems to me that when Christine Battersby, by contrasting the caricature of Kant as an isolated individual, calls on his privilege of friendship and his account of "unsocial sociability" as integral to human civilization, she is engaging in one of these productive narratives. Particularly interesting, in my opinion, is a specific passage she ponders on. It is the passage where Kant, by claiming that a "human being is a being meant for society," writes that "he feels strongly the need to *reveal* himself to others (even with no ulterior purpose)." On the one hand, this is decidedly an Arendtian theme, one that makes of Kant a very appealing philosopher who thinks of friendship in terms of reciprocal exposure and relational subjectivity. On the other hand, this is all the more interesting insofar as, remarkably enough, Arendt in *The Human Condition*, her main political work focused on relationality, neglects the issue of friendship. In so doing she confirms her notorious anomalous position within the protocols of philosophical tradition. The issue of friendship traverses the entire history of philosophy—from Aristotle to Derrida and beyond—intersecting with multiple speculative registers whose complexity, of course, cannot be adequately investigated and discussed here in few words. Inexcusable, anyhow, remains the fact that I neglected the topic of friendship in my work on inclination—namely that, via Kant or not, I missed the occasion to argue that friendship constitutes an exemplary scene for summoning the concepts of inclination and relationality instead of those of verticality and autonomy. It is worth noting that, in her contribution, Clare Woodford manages to "preventively" object to this very formulation through her concept of critical friendship as a friendship that exceeds inclination. Encouraged by Battersby's arguments on the topic of friendship in Kant, I believe, however, that that of rethinking friendship through the module of relational and inclined subjectivities could be a fruitful enterprise.

It is impossible, in this epilogue, to adequately reflect on Butler's important claim that all bodies from the start require support to stand on their own and that they never outgrow that requirement, an issue that she insightfully relates not only to the experience of the fall inherent to the standing body as such but also to the "vertigo" of the aging Kant concerned with the perilous consequences of walking and philosophizing at the same time. Curiously enough, in Ancient Greece, the Peripatetic school adopted the rule of philosophizing while walking; not to mention Socrates, who can be styled as the archetype of the walking philosopher. Kant, however—and in my opinion symptomatically—in the text on the vertigo quoted by Butler, is referring to the silent and solitary exercise of thinking, not to the relational register of dialogue that was so dear to Peripatetic scholars and Socrates. Solitary is the unsettling experience of the sublime's abyss, described by Kant, too. Thus, I wouldn't exactly affirm, as Butler suggests, that what comes back to haunt Kant's rectilinear position in a rather queer way is the "sphere of dependency and passionate inclination" he tries to externalize and disavow. I would rather observe that the problem of the fall is by him essentially situated within the solitary theatre of the self. Nobody else enters this individualistic sphere of concern when Kant discovers that the emphatic verticality he presumes to embody is not really so straight. This doesn't mean that I cannot follow Butler when she puts the question of "whether the inclining figure shadows forth in the upright figure such that the two are *not* radically distinct, and never fully oppositional." At stake, again and crucially enough, is here my strategy of calling on heterotopy, if not indulging in the construction of oppositional schemas. I must confess, however, that the use and abuse of oppositional constructions I often indulge in are partially due to my suspicious attitude for scenarios drawing on dialectic. At the point that I nurture serious speculative doubts about the "immense power of the negative," I try to avoid the issue of the productivity of ambivalence, ambiguity, and contradiction and feel more at ease, if it is the case, with the play of inversion. Both Butler and I, portrayed as young women in philosophy, have been reluctant Hegelians, and this is a theoretical fatigue that, at least for me, is difficult to forget.

I find intriguing the play of inversion staged by Clare Woodford, who, by repositioning our gaze within the Catholic iconography, allows us to see a queer Madonna, an upright figure acting as counterpoint to the inclined Madonna, caring for the child, whose stereotypical representation I focus on. A queer Madonna against the Sacred mother of our patriarchal symbolic. Crucially it is a Madonna standing, on foot, erect, confronting and resisting a world of violence and exclusion. What matters most, for Woodford, is not only to disentangle the maternal from her traditional place of servitude and docility, but, by destabilizing the distinction between the order of inclination and that of rectitude, to call on relational postures of struggle and dissent. Postures of dissent and refusal are as well summoned by the wonderful narrative of Bonnie Honig plotted on the antagonistic sorority that Antigone and Ismene share. Importantly,

Honig proposes a model of inclinational altruism that relates to a posture of care that is sororal, not maternal. In so doing, beyond reframing the issue of inclination within the imaginary of ancient Greece—a move that my classicist soul absolutely appreciates—she succeeds in both offering sorority as a further scenery for "doing things" with the inclined posture and demonstrating how the reorienting geometrical effects of this posture can work as a productive module in multiple and different contexts. Actually, if I had to imagine a list of these contexts, I would include not only maternity, sorority, and friendship but even a certain declination, toward which many of us converge, of democracy in terms of embodied and plural performance. By reading not only Antigone but also the Bacchae in order to dramatize sorority as agency of inclinational refusal, Honig justly argues that "this is important for democratic theory because the sororal relationship is more egalitarian" than the maternal one. I agree with her and think that the various reflections offered by this volume's contributors on the topic of sorority and friendship, beyond succeeding in problematizing the issue of inclination, open insightful pathways for exploring the relational humus in which radical democracy keeps roots and germinates.

By noticing that, notwithstanding my focus on Leonardo's painting *The Virgin and Child with St. Anne*, I daringly never mention Freud, Honig is so gentle as to claim that "you have to admire it." I did neglect the Freudian reference to the vulture purposely: admirable or not, this is true. Actually, that of my polemical attitude toward psychoanalysis is an old, complicated, and maybe tedious story. In his contribution Lorenzo Bernini, by providing a benevolent narrative of this story, justly remarks that, "pushed by Butler," I once had the chance to admit that psychoanalysis can be considered one of the most interesting theories of the twentieth century. I still think so, of course, and if I persist in avoiding speculative engagements with psychoanalysis it is because, on the one hand, I couldn't dream of competing with Butler, Honig, and other eminent scholars who do a superlative job on the matter already, and, on the other hand, I feel it healthy to stay clear from ideas, like those professed by antisocial theorists mentioned by Bernini, that insist "on the negativity of the sexual drive, understood as the death of subjectivity and as the rupture of all social relationships." Actually, even if I appreciate Bernini's task of connecting the issue of women's generative power to the positions of queer subjects who reflect upon the sterility of their own sexual acts, my desire for an imaginary of hope continues to nestle a strategic rejection of discursive registers focused on negativity and destructivity. Psychoanalysis is a wide, multifaceted, and variously articulated narrative, of course.

When negativity and destructivity are at stake, however, I feel more at ease with the speculative style Simona Forti calls on—in her contribution to this volume and her important book *New Demons: Rethinking Power and Evil Today*[4]—when she reflects on the complex issue of evil. As a matter of fact, it is a question of styles, argumentative approaches, theoretical frameworks, and methods of interpretation. It is a question of choice between different languages. Our embodied plurality of scholars substantiates in plural hermeneutic perspectives. Our pluriphony sings the motifs of different cantos.

Notes

1. Adriana Cavarero, Konstantinos Thomaidis, and Ilaria Pinna, "Towards A Hopeful Plurality of Democracy: An Interview on Vocal Ontology with Adriana Cavarero," *Journal of Interdisciplinary Voice Studies* 3, no. 1 (2018): 81–93, https://doi.org/10.1386/jivs.3.1.81_1.

2. Rita Felsky, *The Limits of Critique* (Chicago: University of Chicago Press, 2015).

3. Cavarero, *Inclinations: A Critique of Rectitude*, trans. Amanda Minervini and Adam Sitze (Stanford, Calif.: Stanford University Press, 2016), 14.

4. Simona Forti, *New Demons: Rethinking Power and Evil Today*, trans. Zakiya Hanafi (Stanford, Calif.: Stanford University Press, 2015).

# Bibliography

Agamben, Giorgio. "The Glorious Body." In *Nudities*, translated by David Kishik and Stefan Pedatella. Stanford, Calif.: Stanford University Press, 2011.
———. *Homo Sacer: Sovereign Power and Bare Life*. Stanford, Calif.: Stanford University Press, 1998.
———. *Remnants of Auschwitz: The Witness and the Archive*. New York: Zone 1999.
Ahmed, Sara. *Willful Subjects*. Durham, N.C.: Duke University Press, 2014.
Apollodorus. *Library*. Translated by Sir James George Frazer. Cambridge, Mass.: Harvard University Press, 1963.
Aquinas, Thomas. *Summa Theologiae* (1265–74).
Arendt, Hannah. *Denktagebuch: 1950 bis 1972*. Edited by Ursula Ludz and Ingeborg Nordmann. Munich: Piper, 2002.
———. *The Human Condition*. Chicago and London: University of Chicago Press, 1998. Originally published in New York: Doubleday, 1959.
———. *On Revolution*. London: Faber & Faber, 2016.
———. *The Origins of Totalitarianism*. London: Penguin, 2017.
———. Some Questions of Moral Philosophy." In *Responsibility and Judgment*, edited by Jerome Kohn. New York: Schocken, 2003.
———. "Total Domination." In *The Portable Hannah Arendt*, edited by Peter Baehr. New York: Penguin, 2003.
Arteel, Inge. "Judith Butler and the Catachretic Human." In *Towards a New Literary Humanism*, edited by Andy Mousley, 77–90. Basingstoke: Palgrave Macmillan, 2011.
Austin, J. L. *How to Do Things with Words*. Cambridge, Mass.: Harvard University Press, 1962.

Battersby, Christine. *The Phenomenal Woman: Feminist Metaphysics and the Patterns of Identity*. Cambridge: Polity Press, 1998.
———. *The Sublime, Terror and Human Difference*. London and New York: Routledge 2007.
Christine Battersby, *The Phenomenal Woman: Feminist Metaphysics and the Patterns of Identity* (Cambridge: Polity Press, 1998),
Benjamin, Walter. "Zur Kantischen Ethik." In *Gesammelte Schriften*. Vol. 6, *Fragmente: Autobiographische Schriften*, edited by Rolf Tiedemann and Hermann Schweppenhäuser, 55. Frankfurt: Suhrkamp, 1974–99. https://archive.org/stream/GesammelteSchriftenBd.6/Benjamin Gs6#page/n51.
Bernini, Lorenzo. *Queer Apocalypses*. Berlin: Springer-Verlag, 2017. English: *Queer Apocalypses: Elements of Antisocial Theory*. Translated by Julia Heim. Basingstoke: Palgrave Macmillan, 2017.
Bernstein, Richard J. *Radical Evil: A Philosophical Interrogation*. Hoboken, N.J.: Blackwell, 2002.
Bersani, Leo. *The Freudian Body: Psychoanalysis and Art*. New York: Columbia University Press, 1986.
———. *Homos*. Cambridge, Mass.: Harvard University Press, 1996.
———. "Is the Rectum a Grave?" In *Is the Rectum a Grave? And Other Essays*. Chicago and London: University of Chicago Press, 2010.
Birulés, Fina, and Judith Butler. "Interview with Judith Butler: 'Gender Is Extramoral." *MR Online*, May 16, 2009. https://mronline.org/2009/05/16/interview-with-judith-butler-gender-is-extramoral/.
Bock, Gisela, and Susan James. "Introduction." In *"Beyond Equality and Difference": Citizenship, Feminist Politics, Female Subjectivity*, edited by Gisela Bock and Susan James, 5. Abingdon: Routledge, 1992.
Bono, Paola, and Sandra Kemp. *Italian Feminist Thought: A Reader*. Oxford: Blackwell, 1991.
Braidotti, Rosi. *Patterns of Dissonance*. New York: Routledge, 1991.
Buchholz, Franz. "Braunsberg im Wandel der Jahrhunderte: Festschrift zum 650jährigen Stadtjubiläum am 23. und 24. Juni 1934, http://www.braunsberg-ostpreussen.de/buchholz-ges.htm.
Butler, Judith. *Antigone's Claim: Kinship Between Life and Death*. Chichester: Columbia University Press, 2000.
———. *Bodies That Matter: On the Discursive Limits of Sex*. London and New York: Routledge, 1993.
———. *The Force of Nonviolence: An Ethico-Political Bind*. Brooklyn: Verso, 2020.
———. *Frames of War: When Is Life Grievable?* London: Verso, 2010.
———. *Gender Trouble: Feminism and the Subversion of Identity*. New York and London: Routledge, 1999. Originally published in 1990.
———. *Giving an Account of Oneself: A Critique of Ethical Violence*. New York: Fordham University Press, 2005.

———. *Notes Toward a Performative Theory of Assembly*. Cambridge, Mass., and London: Harvard University Press, 2005.
———. *Precarious Life: The Powers of Mourning and Violence*. London: Verso, 2006. Originally published in 2004.
———. "Soulèvement." In *Soulèvements*, edited by Georges Didi-Huberman. Paris: Gallimard, 2016.
———. *Undoing Gender*. Oxford: Routledge, 2004.
Butler, Judith, and Adriana Cavarero. "Condizione umana contro 'natura.'" In *Differenza e relazione: L'ontologia dell'umano di Judith Butler e Adriana Cavarero*, edited by Lorenzo Bernini and Olivia Guaraldo. 1st ed. Verona: Ombre corte, 2009. Also *Micromega*, no. 4 (2005): 135–46.
Butler, Samuel. *Hudibras: Poem*. New ed. London: Suttaby, Evance, Fox, and Crosby. 1812. https://catalog.hathitrust.org/Record/005641486.
Calvino, Italo. *If on a Winter's Night a Traveller*. Translated by William Weaver. London: Vintage, 1998.
Campt, Tina Marie. "Black Visuality and the Practice of Refusal." *Women & Performance: A Journal of Feminist Theory* 29, no. 1 (2019): 79–87. https://doi.org/10.1080/0740770X.2019.1573625.
Canetti, Elias. *Crowds and Power*. New York: Viking, 1962.
Carver, Terrell. "Gender and Narrative in Locke's *Two Treatises of Government*." In *Feminist Interpretations of John Locke*, edited by Nancy J. Hirschmann and Kirstie McClure. University Park: Pennsylvania State University Press, 2007.
*Catechism of the Catholic Church*. 2nd ed. Vatican City: Libreria Editrice Vaticana, 1997.
Cavarero, Adriana. "Diotima." In *Italian Feminist Thought: A Reader*, edited by Paola Bono and Sandra Kemp, 181–85. Oxford and Cambridge, Mass.: Blackwell, 1991.
———. *For More Than One Voice: Toward a Philosophy of Vocal Expression*. Translated by Paul A. Kottman. Stanford, Calif.: Stanford University Press, 2005.
———. *Horrorism: Naming Contemporary Violence*. Translated by William McCuaig. New York: Columbia University Press, 2011.
———. "Il pensiero femminista: Un approccio teoretico." In *Le filosofie femministe*, edited by Adriana Cavarero and Franco Restaino, 78–115. Milan: Bruno Mondadori, 1999.
———. *Inclinations: A Critique of Rectitude*. Translated by Amanda Minervini and Adam Sitze. Stanford, Calif.: Stanford University Press, 2016.
———. *In Spite of Plato: A Feminist Rewriting of Ancient Philosophy*. Translated by Serena Anderlini-D'Onofrio and Áine O'Healy. Cambridge: Polity, 1995.
———. "Judith Butler and the Belligerent Subject." *Annali d'Italianistica* 29 (2011): 163–70.
———. "Narrative Against Destruction." Translated by Elvira Roncalli. *New Literary History* 46, no. 1 (2015): 1–16.

———. "Prefazione all'edizione italiana." In Judith Butler, *Corpi che contano: I limiti discorsivi del sesso*, translated by Simona Capelli, vii. Milan: Feltrinelli, 1996.

———. "Rectitude: Reflections on Postural Ontology." *Journal of Speculative Philosophy* 27, no. 3 (2013): 220–35.

———. *Relating Narratives: Storytelling and Selfhood*. Translated by Paul A. Kottman. London and New York: Routledge, 2000.

———. *Rethinking Oedipus: Stealing a Patriarchal Text*. Paper at the U.K. Society of Women and Philosophy Conference, 1996.

———. *Stately Bodies: Literature, Philosophy, and the Question of Gender*. Translated by Robert de Lucca and Deanna Shemek. Ann Arbor: University of Michigan Press, 2002.

———. "Towards a Theory of Sexual Difference." In *The Lonely Mirror: Italian Perspectives on Feminist Theory*, edited by Sandra Kemp and Paola Bono, 189. London: Routledge, 1993.

———. *Surging Democracy: Notes on Hannah Arendt's Political Thought*. Stanford, Calif.: Stanford University Press, 2021.

———. "*Who* Engenders Politics?" In *Italian Feminist Theory and Practice: Equality and Sexual Difference*, edited by Graziella Parati and Rebecca West, 88. London: Associated University Presses, 2002.

Cavarero, Adriana, and Elisabetta Bertolino. "Beyond Ontology and Sexual Difference: An Interview with the Italian Feminist Philosopher Adriana Cavarero." *differences: A Journal of Feminist and Cultural Studies* 19, no. 1 (2008): 128–67. https://doi.org/10.1215/10407391-2007-019.

Cavarero, Adriana, and Angelo Scola. *Thou Shalt Not Kill: A Political and Theological Dialogue*. Translated by Margaret Adams Groesbeck and Adam Sitze. New York: Fordham University Press, 2015.

Cavarero, Adriana, Konstantinos Thomaidis, and Ilaria Pinna. "Towards a Hopeful Plurality of Democracy: An Interview on Vocal Ontology with Adriana Cavarero." *Journal of Interdisciplinary Voice Studies* 3, no. 1 (2018): 81–93. https://doi.org/10.1386/jivs.3.1.81_1.

Chambers, Samuel A., and Terrell Carver. *Judith Butler and Political Theory*. London: Routledge, 2008.

Chandler, Nahum Dimitri. *X—The Problem of the Negro as a Problem for Thought*. New York: Fordham University Press, 2014.

Chianesi, Maria, G. et al. *È già politica*. Milan: Scritti di Rivolta femminile, 1977.

Classical Cat. "Scherzo." https://www.classiccat.net/genres/scherzo.info.php; retrieved Feb. 8, 2019.

Cole, Alyson. "All of Us Are Vulnerable, But Some Are More Vulnerable Than Others: The Political Ambiguity of Vulnerability Studies; An Ambivalent Critique." *Critical Horizons* 17, no. 2 (2016): 260–77. https://doi.org/10.1080/14409917.2016.1153896.

Colebrook, Claire. "Materiality: Sex, Gender and What Lies Beneath." In *The Routledge Companion to Feminist Philosophy*, edited by A. Garry, S. J. Khader, and A. Stone, 194–206. London: Routledge, 2017.

Dean, Jodi. "The Politics of Avoidance: The Limits of Weak Ontology." *Hedgehog Review* 7, no. 2 (2005): 55–65.
de Beauvoir, Simone. *The Second Sex*. Translated by Constance Borde and Sheila Maldvany-Chavallier. New York: Vintage and Random House, 2011.
Delaney, Samuel. "Radicalism Begins in the Body." Interview by Junot Díaz. Boston Review: A Political and Literary Forum, May 10, 2017. http://bostonreview.net/literature-culture/junot-d%C3%Adaz-samuel-r-delany-radicalism-begins-body.
de Lauretis, Teresa, *Freud's Drive: Psychoanalysis, Literature and Film*. Basingstoke: Palgrave Macmillan, 2008.
Deleuze, Gilles, and Félix Guattari. *A Thousand Plateaus: Capitalism and Schizophrenia*. Translated by Brian Massumi. Minneapolis: University of Minnesota Press, 1987.
Deleuze, Gilles, and Félix Guattari, *Kafka: Toward a Minor Literature*. Translated by Dana Polan. Minneapolis: Minnesota University Press, 1986.
Denis, Lara. "From Friendship to Marriage: Revising Kant." *Philosophy and Phenomenological Research* 63, no. 1 (July 2001): 1–28.
Denis, Lara, and Oliver Sensen, eds. *Kant's Lectures on Ethics: A Critical Guide*. Cambridge: Cambridge University Press, 2015.
Derrida, Jacques. *Given Time*. Vol. 1, *Counterfeit Money*. Translated by Peggy Kamuf. Chicago: University of Chicago Press, 1992.
———. "White Mythology: Metaphor in the Text of Philosophy." In *Margins of Philosophy*, translated by Alan Bass, 250–72. Brighton: Harvester, 1982.
Descartes, René. *Discours de la methode*. 1637.
Devenney, Mark. *Towards an Improper Politics*. Edinburgh: Edinburgh University Press, 2020.
Dohoney, Ryan. "An Antidote to Metaphysics: Adriana Cavarero's Vocal Philosophy." *Women and Music: A Journal of Gender and Culture* 15 (2011): 70–85. https://doi.org/10.1353/wam.2011.0002.
Domijianni, Ida. "Un/domesticated Feminism." *Soft Power* 6, no. 2 (2018): 13–26.
Dorra, Henri. "The Guesser Guessed: Gustave Moreau's Oedipus." *Gazette des beaux-arts* 81 (March 1973): 129–40.
Elam, Diane. *Ms. en abime: Feminism and Deconstruction*. London: Routledge, 1994.
Edelman, Lee, *No Future: Queer Theory and the Death Drive*. Durham, N.C., and London: Duke University Press, 2004.
Esposito, Roberto. *Immunitas: The Protection and Negation of Life*. Translated by Z. Hanafi. Cambridge: Polity, 2011.
Feldman, Susan. "Reclaiming Sexual Difference: What Queer Theory Can't Tell Us about Sexuality." *Journal of Bisexuality* 9, no. 3–4 (2009): 259–78.
Felsky, Rita. *The Limits of Critique*. Chicago: University of Chicago Press, 2015.
Feola, Michael. "Norms, Vision and Violence: Judith Butler on the Politics of Legibility." *Contemporary Political Theory* 13, no. 2 (2014): 130–48.

Ferreira da Silva, Denise. "Toward a Black Feminist Poethics: The Quest(ion) of Blackness toward the End of the World." *Black Scholar* 44, no. 2 (Summer 2014).

Forti, Simona. *New Demons: Rethinking Evil and Power Today.* Translated by Zakiya Hanafi. Stanford, Calif.: Stanford University Press, 2015.

Foucault, Michel. "The Confession of the Flesh." In *Power/Knowledge*, edited by Colin Gordon, , 194–95. New York: Harvester Wheatsheaf, 1980.

———. "Discourse and Truth: The Problematization of Parrhesia," 6 Lectures at University of California, Berkeley, Calif., Oct.–Nov. 1983.

Frank, Jill. *Poetic Justice: Rereading Plato's "Republic."* Chicago: University of Chicago Press, 2018.

Freedberg, S. J. "A Recovered Work of Andrea del Sarto with Some Notes on a Leonardesque Connection." *Burlington Magazine* 124, no. 950 (May 1982): 285. Sourced at Wikipedia, https://en.wikipedia.org/wiki/Bacchus_(Leonardo).

Freud, Sigmund. *Three Essays on the Theory of Sexuality.* Translated by Ulrike Kister. New York and London: Verso, 2016.

———. "Why War? An Exchange of Letters Between Freud and Einstein." Accessed August 7, 2019. https://www.transcend.org/tms/wp-content/uploads/2017/06/Why-War-Freud.pdf.

———. "Recollection, Repetition, and Working Through." In *The Complete Psychological Words of Sigmund Freud*, standard ed., 12:147–56. London: Hogarth, 1974.

Frost, Samantha. "The Implications of the New Materialisms for Feminist Epistemology." In *Feminist Epistemology and Philosophy of Science: Power in Knowledge*, edited by H. E. Grasswick, 69–83. Dordrecht: Springer, 2011.

Fuss, Diana. *Essentially Speaking: Feminism, Nature, Difference.* New York and London: Routledge, 1989.

Gallop, Jane. *Reading Lacan.* Ithaca, N.Y.: Cornell University Press, 1985.

Gatta, Giunia. "Suffering and the Making of Politics: Perspectives from Jaspers and Camus." *Contemporary Political Theory* 14, no. 4 (2015): 335–54. https://doi.org/10.1057/cpt.2014.52.

Gehlen, Arnold. *L'uomo: La sua natura e il suo posto nel mondo.* Milan-Udine: Mimesis, 2010.

Gensichen, Hans-Peter. "Wie schwul war Kant?" *Forum für Politik, Gesellschaft und Kultur* 234 (March 2004): 43–47. http://www.forum.lu/pdf/artikel/5189_234_Genischen.pdf.

Goldhill, Simon. *Sophocles and the Language of Tragedy.* Oxford and New York: Oxford University Press, 2012.

Goux, Jean-Joseph. *Oedipus, Philosopher.* Translated by Catherine Porter. Stanford, Calif.: Stanford University Press, 1993.

Granger, Bruce Ingham. *Political Satire in the American Revolution, 1763–1783.* Ithaca, N.Y.: Cornell University Press, 1960.

Guaraldo, Olivia. "Public Happiness: Revisiting an Arendtian Hypothesis." *Philosophy Today* 62, no. 2 (Spring 2018): 397–418. https://doi.org/10.5840/philtoday201866218.
———. "Re-locating Politics in the Age of Globalization." In *The Ashgate Research Companion to the Politics of Democratization in Europe: Concepts and Histories*, edited by Kari Palonen, Tuija Pulkkinen, and José María Rosales, 113. Farnham: Ashgate, 2008.
Hartman, Saidiya. *Wayward Lives, Beautiful Experiments: Intimate Histories of Social Upheaval*. New York: W. W. Norton, 2019.
Heckman, Susan. "Vulnerability and Ontology." *Australian Feminist Studies* 29, no. 82 (2014): 452–64.
Hirschmann, Nancy, J., and Kirstie McClure. "Introduction: Johnny, We Hardly Knew Ye." In *Feminist Interpretations of John Locke*, edited by Nancy J. Hirschmann and Kirstie McClure, 2. University Park: Pennsylvania State University Press, 2007.
*The History of Parliament: The House of Commons, 1790–1820*. Edited by R. G. Thorne. Online edition. Accessed September 25, 2018. https://www.historyofparliamentonline.org/volume/1790-1820/member/staniforth-john.
Hobbes, Thomas. *De cive*. 1642. Cap. VIII.
———. *Leviathan*. London: Penguin, 2012.
Hoffmann, Alfons, ed. *Ein Lebensbild nach Darstellungen der Zeitgenossen Jachmann, Borowski, Wasianski*. Halle an der Saale: Hugo Peter, 1902. https://archive.org/details/immanuelkanteinloohoff.
Honig, Bonnie. *Antigone, Interrupted*. Cambridge: Cambridge University Press, 2013.
———. "Antigone's Laments, Creon's Grief: Mourning, Membership, and the Politics of Exception." *Political Theory* 37, no. 1 (2009): 5–43.
———. "Antigone's Two Laws: Greek Tragedy and the Politics of Humanism." *New Literary History* 41, no. 1 (2010): 1–33.
———. *Democracy and the Foreigner*. Stanford, Calif.: Stanford University Press, 2003.
———. *Emergency Politics: Paradox, Law, Democracy*. Princeton, N.J., and Oxford: Princeton University Press, 2009.
———. *A Feminist Theory of Refusal*. Forthcoming.
———. "Is Man a 'Sabbatical Animal'? Agamben, Rosenzweig, Heschel, Arendt." *Political Theology* 20, no. 1 (2019): 1–23. https://doi.org/10.1080/1462317X.2018.1518766.
———. *Political Theory and the Displacement of Politics*. Ithaca, N.Y.: Cornell University Press, 1993.
———. *Public Things: Democracy in Disrepair*. New York: Fordham University Press, 2017.
———. "Twelve Angry Men: Care for the Agon and the Varieties of Masculine Experience." *Theory & Event* 22, no. 3 (2019): 701–16.

Huzar, Timothy J. "Toward a Fugitive Politics: Arendt, Rancière, Hartman." *Cultural Critique* 112 (Winter 2021): 1–48.
Ingala, Emma. "Catachresis and Mis-Being in Judith Butler and Étienne Balibar: Contemporary Refigurations of the Human as a Face Drawn in the Sand." *Literature & Theology* 32, no. 2 (2018): 142–60.
Irigaray, Luce. *Speculum of the Other Woman*. Translated by Gillian C. Gill. Ithaca, N.Y.: Cornell University Press, 1985.
Jagger, Gill. "Beyond Essentialism and Construction: Subjectivity, Corporeality and Sexual Difference." *Women Review Philosophy: Special Issue of Women's Philosophy Review*, edited by M. Griffiths and M. Whitford (1996): 141.
Jardine, Alison. *Configurations of Women and Modernity*. Ithaca, N.Y.: Cornell University Press, 1985.
Jenkins, Fiona. "Toward a Nonviolent Ethics: Response to Catherine Mills." *differences: A Journal of Feminist and Cultural Studies* 18, no. 2 (2007): 157–79.
Kant, Immanuel. *The Conflict of the Faculties*. Translated by Mary J. Gregor and Robert Anchor. In *Religion and Rational Theology*, edited by Allan W. Wood and George Di Giovanni, 233–327. Cambridge: Cambridge University Press, 2001.
———. *Critique of Judgment*. Translated by J. H. Bernard. London: Macmillan, 1951.
———. *Critique of Practical Reason*. Translated by Werner S. Pluhar. Indianapolis: Hackett, 2002.
———. *Critique of Practical Reason*. In Immanuel Kant, *Practical Philosophy*, Translated and edited by Mary J. Gregor, 133–271. Cambridge: Cambridge University Press, 1996.
———. *Critique of Pure Reason*. Translated and edited by Paul Guyer and Allen W. Wood. Cambridge: Cambridge University Press, 1997.
———. *Critique of Pure Reason*. Translated by Norman Kemp Smith. London: Macmillan, 1929.
———. *Dreams of a Spirit Seer Elucidated by Dreams of Metaphysics*. In *Theoretical Philosophy, 1755–1770*, edited by David Walford and Ralf Meerbote, 301–59. Cambridge: Cambridge University Press, 1992.
———. *Gesammelte Schriften*. Edited by der Deutschen [formerly Königlich Preussischen] Akademie der Wissenschaften. Berlin: Walter de Gruyter Verlag, 1902–.
———. *Idea for a Universal History with a Cosmopolitan Purpose*. In *Political Writings*, translated by H. B. Nisbet, 46. Cambridge: Cambridge University Press, 1970.
———. *Lectures on Anthropology*. Edited by Robert B. Louden and Allen W. Wood. Translated by Robert R. Clewis and G. Felicitas Munzel. Cambridge: Cambridge University Press, 2012.

---. *The Metaphysics of Morals.* Translated and edited by Mary J. Gregor. In *Practical Philosophy*, translated and edited by Mary J. Gregor, 353–603. Cambridge: Cambridge University Press, 1996.

---. "On a Recently Prominent Tone of Superiority in Philosophy." In *Theoretical Philosophy after 1781*, edited by Henry Allison and Peter Heath. Translated by Gary Hatfield and Michael Friedman, 425–46. Cambridge: Cambridge University Press, 2002.

Karhu, Sanna. "Judith Butler's Critique of Violence and the Legacy of Monique Wittig." *Hypatia: A Journal of Feminist Philosophy* 31, no. 4 (2016): 827–43.

King, Martin, Luther. "Letter from Birmingham Jail." Martin Luther King, Jr. Research and Education Institute, Stanford University. https://kinginstitute.stanford.edu/king-papers/documents/letter-birmingham-jail.

Kirby, Vicki, and Judith Butler. "Butler Live." In *Judith Butler: Live Theory*, edited by Vicky Kirby, 144–58. London: Continuum, 2006.

Klein, Melanie. *Envy and Gratitude: A Study of Unconscious Forces.* London: Hogarth, 1957.

Koestenbaum, Wayne. *The Queen Throat: Opera, Homosexuality and the Mistery of Desire.* New York: Poseidon, 1993.

Kramer, Sina. "Judith Butler's "New Humanism": A Thing or Not a Thing, and So What?" *philoSOPHIA* 5, no. 1 (2015): 25–40.

Kuehn, Manfred. *Kant: A Biography.* Cambridge: Cambridge University Press, 2001.

Lacan, Jacques. *The Seminar of Jacques Lacan: The Other Side of Psychoanalysis.* Vol. 17. Translated by Russell Grigg. New York: W. W. Norton, 2008.

Laplanche, Jean. *La révolution copernicienne inachevée (Travaux 1967–1992).* Paris: Aubier, 1992.

---. *Vie et mort en psychanalyse.* Paris: Flammarion, 1970.

Lavin, Marilyn Aronberg. "Giovannino Battista: A Study in Renaissance Religious Symbolism," *Art Bulletin* 37, no. 2 (June 1955): 85–101.

Leonard, Miriam. "Freud and the Biography of Antiquity." In *Creative Lives in Classical Antiquity*, edited by Richard Fletcher and Johanna Hanink. Cambridge: Cambridge University Press, 2016.

Levi, Primo. *The Drowned and the Saved.* In *The Complete Works of Primo Levi*, edited by Ann Goldstein, 3:2405–2575. New York: Liveright, 2015.

---. *If This Is A Man.* In *The Complete Works of Primo Levi*, edited by Ann Goldstein, 1:1–207. New York: Liveright, 2015.

Levinas, Emmanuel. "The Face." In *Ethics and Infinity*, translated by Richard A. Cohen. Pittsburgh: Duquesne University Press.

Lloyd, Moya, ed. *Butler and Ethics.* Edinburgh: Edinburgh University Press, 2015.

Lock, Margareth, and Judith Farquhar. "Introduction." In *Beyond the Body Proper: Reading the Anthropology of Material Life*, edited by Margareth Lock and Judith Farquhar, 10. Durham, N.C.: Duke University Press, 2007.

Locke, John. *The Second Treatise of Government*. Edited by Peter Laslett. Cambridge: Cambridge University Press, 2005.

Lonzi, Carla. *Sputiamo su Hegel: La donna clitoridea e la donna vaginale e altri scritti* [Let's Spit on Hegel: The Clitoridian Woman and the Vaginal Woman and Other Writings]. Milan: Scritti di Rivolta Femminile, 1974. For the English translation of this text, see http://blogue.nt2.uqam.ca/hit/files/2012/12/Lets-Spit-on-Hegel-Carla-Lonzi.pdf. Retrieved Feb. 23, 2019.

Morrison, Toni. *Home*. New York: Alfred A. Knopf, 2012.

Moten, Fred. "Blackness and Nothingness (Mysticism in the Flesh)." *South Atlantic Quarterly* 112, no. 4 (2013): 737–80.

———. "The Subprime and the Beautiful." *African Identities* 11, no. 2 (2013): 237–45.

Moten, Fred, and Stefano Harney. *The Undercommons: Fugitive Planning and Black Study*. Wivenhoe: Minor Compositions, 2013.

Motherby, Marianne. "Kant and the Motherby Family." Translated by Terence Coe. Freunde Kants und Königsbergs, 2020. www.freunde-kants.com/kant-and-the-motherby-family.

Murphy, Ann V. "Corporeal Vulnerability and the New Humanism." *Hypatia: A Journal of Feminist Philosophy* 26, no. 3 (2011): 575–90.

———. *Violence and the Philosophical Imaginary*. Albany: State University of New York Press, 2012.

*Online Etymology Dictionary*. "Join" https://www.etymonline.com/word/join, retrieved Feb. 11, 2019.

Ottino della Chiesa, Angela. *Leonardo Pittore*. Milan: Rizzoli, 1967.

Oyama, Susan. *Evolution's Eye: A System's View of the Biology-Culture Divide*. Durham, N.C.: Duke University Press, 2000.

Panagia, Davide. "'*Partage du Sensible*': The Distribution of the Sensible." In *Jacques Rancière: Key Concepts*, edited by Jean-Philippe Deranty, 97–105. Durham, N.C.: Acumen, 2010.

Pateman, Carole. *The Sexual Contract*. Stanford, Calif.: Stanford University Press, 1988.

Petherbridge, Danielle. "What's Critical about Vulnerability? Rethinking Interdependence, Recognition, and Power." *Hypatia: A Journal of Feminist Philosophy* 31, no. 3 (2016): 589–604.

Plato. "Republic." In *Plato Complete Works*, edited by John M. Cooper, rev. edition by G. M. G. Grube, rev. translation by C. D. C. Reeve. Indianapolis and Cambridge: Hackett, 1997.

Proudhon, Pierre-Joseph. Selections from "Pornocracy, or Women in Modern Times." *Cultural Critique* 100, nos. 44–64 (2018): 47.

Ralph, Laurence. *Renegade Dreams*. Chicago: University of Chicago Press, 2014.

Rancière, Jacques. *Dissensus*. London: Continuum, 2010.
———. "A Few Remarks on the Method of Jacques Rancière." *Parallax* 15, no. 3 (2009): 114–23.
———. "Ten Theses on Politics." Translated by Davide Panagia and Rachel Bowlby. *Theory & Event* 5, no. 3 (2001): no pagination. https://doi.org/10.1353/tae.2001.0028.
Rancière, Jacques, and Davide Panagia. "Dissenting Words: A Conversation with Jacques Rancière." *Diacritics* 30, no. 2 (2000): 113–26.
Richardson, Janice. "'Beyond Equality and Difference: Sexual Difference in the work of Adriana Cavarero." *Feminist Legal Studies* 6, no. 1 (1998): 105–20.
Rushing, Sara. "Judith Butler's Ethical Disposition." *Contemporary Political Theory* 9, no. 3 (2010): 284–303.
Russell, T., and H. Macdonald. "Scherzo." *Grove Music Online*. January 1, 2001. Retrieved Feb. 8, 2019. http://www.oxfordmusiconline.com/grovemusic/view/10.1093/gmo/9781561592630.001.0001/omo-9781561592630-e-0000024827.
Ruti, Mari. "The Posthumanist Quest for the Universal." *Angelaki* 20, no. 4, (2015): 193–210.
Ryther, Catherine. "The Other Argument, The Other Existent: A Complicated Conversational Method." *Otherness: Essays and Studies* 4, no. 1 (2013): 1–23.
Salamon, Gayle. "Passing Period: Gender, Aggression and the Phenomenology of Walking." In *Performance and Phenomenology: Traditions and Transformations*, Routledge Advances in Theatre & Performance Studies, edited by Maaike Bleeker, Jon Foley Sherman, and Eirini Nedelkopoulou. New York: Routledge, 2015.
Scarry, Elaine. *The Body in Pain: The Making and Unmaking of the World*. Oxford: Oxford University Press, 1985.
Schnabel, Isabel, and Hyun Song Shin. "Liquidity and Contagion: The Crisis of 1763." *Journal of the European Economic Association* 2, no. 6 (Dec. 2004): 929–68.
Sedgwick, Eve Kosofsky. "Paranoid Reading and Reparative Reading, or You're So Paranoid, You Probably Think This Essay Is about You." In *Touching Feeling: Affect, Pedagogy, Performativity*, edited by Adam Frank, 123–52. Durham, N.C.: Duke University Press, 2003.
Sofsky, Wolfgang. "The Paradise of Cruelty." In *Violence: Terrorism, Genocide, War*, 15–55. London: Granta, 2004.
Sophocles. *Antigone*. In *The Three Theban Plays*, translated by Robert Fagles and Bernard Knox, 490. New York: Penguin, 1984.
Stone, Alison. "The Ontology of the Maternal: A Response to Adriana Cavarero." *Studies in the Maternal* 2, no. 1 (2010): np.
von Hippel, Theodor Gottlieb. *Der Mann nach der Uhr oder der ordentliche Mann*. Edited by Erich Jenisch. 4th ed. Halle: M. Niemeyer, 1928. http://www.zeno.org/nid/20005071739.

Wain-Hobson, Simon. "To See a World in a Glass Engraving." *Glass Matters: Journal of the Glass Society.* Forthcoming.

Warner, Marina. *Alone of All her Sex.* 2nd ed. London: Vintage, 2000.

Watson, Janell. "Feminism as Agonistic Sorority: An Interview with Bonnie Honig." *Minnesota Review,* New Series, no. 81 (2013): 102–25.

Weberman, David. "Are Freedom and Anti-Humanism Compatible? The Case of Foucault and Butler." *Constellations: An International Journal of Critical & Democratic Theory* 7, no. 2 (2000): 255–71.

White, Stephen K. "As the World Turns: Ontology and Politics in Judith Butler." *Polity* 32, no. 2 (1999): 155–77.

Wilson, Elizabeth. *Neural Geographies: Feminism and the Microstructure of Cognition.* New York: Routledge, 1998.

Woodford, Clare. *Disorienting Democracy.* London: Routledge, 2017.

———. "In Defence of Dreaming." In *Cinema, Democracy, Perfectionism: Joshua Foa Dienstag in Dialogue,* ed. Joshua Foa Dienstag. London and New York: Macmillan, 2017.

Yuan, Yuan. *The Riddling between Oedipus and the Sphinx: Ontology, Hauntology, and Heterologies of the Grotesque.* Lanham, Md.: University Press of America, 2016.

Contributors

CHRISTINE BATTERSBY is Reader Emerita in Philosophy at the University of Warwick, UK, where she is also Associate Fellow of the Centre for Research in Philosophy, Literature, and the Arts. She is a Fellow of the Royal Society of Arts (FRSA). Her research and publications are thoroughly interdisciplinary and include feminist aesthetics; feminist metaphysics; philosophies of embodiment; the sublime and the grotesque; and women, genius, and creativity in philosophy, literature, and the visual arts. Christine's most recent book is *The Sublime, Terror and Human Difference* (Routledge, 2007). Recently published essays focus on Beauvoir and Stream-of-Consciousness Fiction; Nietzsche and Freud on trauma; the modernist authors May Sinclair and H. D. (Hilda Doolittle); Sartre and Deleuze on make-up; the metaphysics and artistic representation of pregnancy; and Existentialism, Feminist Theory, and the Temporalities of Dying. She is currently writing on the influence of Schopenhauer on feminist philosophers and writers.

JUDITH BUTLER is Maxine Elliot Professor in the Department of Comparative Literature and the Program of Critical Theory at the University of California, Berkeley. She has held posts at the Wesleyan University, Johns Hopkins University, and UC Berkeley, as well as Birkbeck College, London, and the European Graduate School. Judith is the author of numerous books and essays, including the books *Subjects of Desire: Hegelian Reflections in Twentieth-Century France* (1987); *Gender Trouble: Feminism and the Subversion of Identity* (1990); *Bodies That Matter: On the Discursive Limits of "Sex"* (1993); *Excitable Speech* (1997); *The Psychic*

*Life of Power: Theories of Subjection* (1997); *Antigone's Claim: Kinship between Life and Death* (2000); *Undoing Gender* (2004); *Precarious Life: Powers of Violence and Mourning* (2004); *Giving an Account of Oneself* (2005); *Frames of War: When Is Life Grievable* (2009); *Parting Ways* (2012); *Notes Toward a Theory of Assembly* (2015); and *The Force of Nonviolence* (2020).

LORENZO BERNINI is Associate Professor in Political Philosophy at the University of Verona, Italy. With Professor Adriana Cavarero, he founded the Research Centre PoliTeSse (Politics and Theories of Sexuality, www.politesse.it), which he now directs. He is also founding member of GIFTS—the Italian network of Gender, Intersex, Feminist, Trans-feminist and Sexuality Studies (https://retegifts.wordpress.com/). His interests range from classical political philosophy (especially Thomas Hobbes) and French thought of the twentieth century (especially Michel Foucault), to psychoanalysis (especially Sigmund Freud), contemporary theories of radical democracy, feminist philosophies, critical race theories, and queer theories. His books include *Queer Apocalypses: Elements of Antisocial Theory* (Palgrave Macmillan, 2017), which was previously published in Italian (Edizioni ETS, 2013) and Spanish (Editorial EGALES, 2015); *Queer Theories: An Introduction; From Mario Mieli to the Antisocial Turn* (Routledge, 2020), previously published in Italian (Mimesis Edizioni, 2017) and Spanish (Editorial EGALES, 2018) and forthcoming in French; and *Il sessuale politico: Freud con Marx, Fanon, Foucault* (Edizioni ETS, 2019).

ADRIANA CAVARERO is an Italian philosopher and an Arendtian scholar. Honorary professor at the University of Verona, she has held numerous visiting appointments at the University of California, Berkeley and Santa Barbara, at the New York University, and Harvard University. Adriana is widely recognized for her writings on ancient philosophy, political theory, feminism, and literature. Her books include *In Spite of Plato: A Feminist Rewriting of Ancient Philosophy* (Polity, 1995); *Relating Narratives: Storytelling And Selfhood* (Routledge 2000); *Stately Bodies: Literature, Philosophy and the Question of Gender* (University of Michigan Press, 2002); *For More Than One Voice: Toward a Philosophy of Vocal Expression* (Stanford University Press, 2005); *Horrorism: Naming Contemporary Violence* (Columbia University Press, 2009); *Inclinations: A Critique of Rectitude* (Stanford University Press, 2016); with Angelo Scola, *Thou Shalt Not Kill: A Political and Theological Dialogue* (Fordham University Press, 2015); and *Surging Democracy* (Stanford University Press, 2021).

MARK DEVENNEY is Professor of Critical Theory at the University of Brighton. He has published widely on the politics of post-Marxism, critical theory, the politics of property, and contemporary politics. His most recent book is *Towards a Politics of the Improper* (Edinburgh University Press, 2020). Mark is Codirector of the Centre for Applied Philosophy, Politics and Ethics at the University of Brighton and coordinates a global network researching populist politics. He coedits the Rowman and Littlefield Polemics series.

SIMONA FORTI is Professor of Political Philosophy at the "Scuola Normale di Studi Superiori," Pisa (Italy) as well as part-time Faculty at the Philosophy Department, The New School for Social Research (New York, NY). She has been Visiting Professor in Philosophy at Columbia University (2017) and "Fulbright Distinguished Chair" Professor at Northwestern University, (2014). Simona is widely recognized in Italy and abroad for her far-reaching studies on Hannah Arendt's thought and the philosophical idea of Totalitarianism. In recent years she has given important contributions to the debate on Biopolitics launched by Michel Foucault, by focusing on Nazi biopolitics of the souls and democratic biopolitics of the bodies. In her last volume, *New Demons: Rethinking Power and Evil Today*, translated into English and published by Stanford University Press in 2015, she deals with contemporary and post-foundational reshaping of the notion of evil.

OLIVIA GUARALDO is Associate Professor in Political Philosophy at the University of Verona, where she also directs the Hannah Arendt Center for Political Studies. Her field of research comprises modern and contemporary political thought. She has worked extensively on the thought of Hannah Arendt (two monographs in 2001 and 2014, an Italian edition of Arendt's essay "Lying in Politics") and contemporary feminist political theory, investigating the theoretical and political relationships between Italian feminist philosophy and Anglo-American gender theory. Olivia has also edited and introduced the Italian translations of Judith Butler's works *Precarious Life* (Rome, 2004, Milan, 2013) and *Undoing Gender* (Rome, 2006, Milan, 2014). Among her other publications is "Public Happiness: Revisiting an Arendtian Hypothesis," *Philosophy Today* 62, no. 2 (2018): 395–416.

BONNIE HONIG is Nancy Duke Lewis Professor in the departments of Modern Culture and Media (MCM) and Political Science at Brown University. She is author of *Political Theory and the Displacement of*

*Politics* (Cornell, 1993); *Democracy and the Foreigner* (Princeton, 2001); *Emergency Politics: Paradox, Law, Democracy* (Princeton, 2009); *Antigone, Interrupted* (Cambridge University Press, 2013); and *Public Things: Democracy in Disrepair* (Fordham University Press, 2017). She has edited or coedited *Feminist Interpretations of Hannah Arendt* (Pennsylvania State University, 1995); *Skepticism, Individuality and Freedom: The Reluctant Liberalism of Richard Flathman* (University of Minnesota Press, 2002); *The Oxford Handbook of Political Thought* (Oxford, 2006); and, most recently, *Politics, Theory, and Film: Critical Encounters with Lars von Trier* (Oxford, 2016). Her newest books are: *A Feminist Theory of Refusal* (Harvard University Press) and *Shell-Shocked: Feminist Criticism after Trump* (Fordham University Press), both out in 2021.

TIMOTHY J. HUZAR is an interdisciplinary scholar whose work explores philosophical issues around politics, violence, narration, and care. He frequently engages the thought of the feminist philosopher Adriana Cavarero, as well as the black studies scholarship of Saidiya Hartman and Fred Moten, and the critical theory of Jacques Rancière and Jean-Luc Nancy, among others. Tim's work has been published in numerous academic journals, most recently in *Paragraph* and *Critical Horizons*, with a forthcoming essay due in *Cultural Critique* 110. He is the coeditor of a special issue of the journal *Body & Society* on Elaine Scarry's seminal 1985 book *The Body in Pain*, and he co-organized the 2017 Brighton conference Giving Life to Politics dedicated to Cavarero's work. Tim is a member of the National Coalition of Independent Scholars and has taught at a number of universities in the southeast of England.

CLARE WOODFORD is Principal Lecturer in Political Philosophy in the Centre for Applied Philosophy, Politics and Ethics (CAPPE), School of Humanities, University of Brighton; Director of the CAPPE Critical Theory research group strand; and coeditor of Rowman and Littlefield's Polemics series. She is the author of essays, chapters, and blogs on politics and democratic theory, with a focus on affect, identity, performance, extremism, gender, and ethics. Her book *Disorienting Democracy: Politics of Emancipation* (Routledge, 2017) juxtaposed Rancière's thought with that of Butler, Cavell, Menke, and Derrida to draw out the practical implications for emancipatory politics.

# Index

Agamben, Giorgio, 32, 65–66, 84, 140, 142, 143, 145, 149, 150
agonism, 14, 17, 25, 63, 64, 67, 72, 73, 74, 81, 83, 148, 152
Ahmed, Sara, 67, 84
Antigone, 63, 67, 69–75, 81–82, 84–87, 129, 181, 184–85
Arendt, Hannah, 1, 4, 5, 6, 11, 12, 16, 18, 24, 30, 31, 32, 39, 41–42, 45, 50, 55, 57, 59, 62, 66, 84, 93, 111, 115, 118, 119, 122, 123, 134, 136, 139, 140, 142, 143, 145, 149, 159, 160, 171, 178–80, 181, 182, 183
Austin, John, 16, 63, 83

Bellini, Giovanni, 8, 163, 166
Benjamin, Walter, 110, 118
Bersani, Leo, 125–26, 129, 130
Bock, Gisela, 12, 15, 30, 31
Butler, Judith, 2, 3, 8, 9, 14, 15–17, 20–23, 24–25, 26, 27, 28, 30, 32, 45, 65, 81, 82, 84, 85, 87, 95, 110, 112, 118, 119, 123–24, 125, 127, 128, 129, 142, 143, 149, 151–53, 155, 156–58, 159, 160, 167, 170, 173, 178, 179, 180, 182, 183–84, 185

Calvino, Italo, 23, 33–34, 40, 44
care, 5, 9, 10, 14, 16, 17, 19–30, 41, 46–48, 50–51, 56, 64–66, 72–73, 75, 76, 78, 83, 86, 87, 88, 112, 120, 122, 124, 126–27, 142, 159, 162, 163, 167, 171, 174–75, 176, 180–81, 185
Caravaggio, 8, 167, 169

Carver, Terrell, 99, 105, 158, 160
Cocteau, Jean, 67

Delaney, Samuel, 63
Deleuze, Gilles, 65, 83, 84, 86
democracy, 135, 171, 173, 174, 175, 176, 177–78, 185, 186
dependence, 9, 27, 70, 85, 110–11, 115, 117, 122, 134, 142, 180, 182
Derrida, Jacques, 16, 36, 44, 84, 88, 172, 176, 183
drive, 27, 57–58, 60, 104, 125–27, 129, 140, 141, 172, 185

Edelman, Lee, 125–26, 129, 130
Einstein, Albert, 60, 62
eros, 28, 40, 41, 94, 100, 102–4, 126, 171, 172–73, 176
erotic, 26, 33, 40, 41, 72, 93, 103, 167, 170, 172, 175; eroticism, 126
ethics, 7–11, 17, 19–29, 37–39, 41–42, 46, 48–49, 56–61, 63–66, 69, 81–82, 83, 85, 87, 102, 109–10, 115, 117–18, 120, 121–23, 131–40, 142, 151–54, 157–58, 171, 173, 175, 179, 181
evil, 26, 133, 141–46, 148–49, 171, 186

Farquhar, Judith, 95, 104
feminism, 8, 10–17, 30, 31, 82, 93–98, 102, 121, 123, 179
Freud, Sigmund, 8, 14, 25, 27, 57–60, 76, 87, 88, 124–125, 127, 129, 130, 140, 141, 185
*Freunde Kants und Königsbergs*, 112–14

friendship, 4, 8, 25–28, 109–20, 172–74, 182–83, 185
Foucault, Michel, 38, 135–36, 148
Fuss, Diana, 14, 31

gender, 2, 5, 12, 15–17, 23, 30, 47, 65, 83, 84, 93–96, 99–100, 103, 123–24, 125, 157, 161–63, 171–74
Green, Joseph, 26, 112, 114, 119, 173
Guattari, Felix, 65, 83, 84

Hartman, Saidiya, 81, 88, 160
Heidegger, Martin, 36
heterotopia, 17, 25, 63–64, 66, 68–69, 76, 78, 81–82, 152, 181
Hobbes, Thomas, 57, 121–22, 132, 134, 137–38, 146, 180
Honig, Bonnie, 3, 8, 9, 14, 16–17, 21–32, 117, 120, 134, 152, 162, 167, 170, 174, 176, 181, 184–85
hope, 4, 5, 20, 22, 23, 26, 29, 151, 153, 161, 179, 181, 185
horrorism, 1, 20, 82, 122, 123, 126, 141–49
humanism, 21, 28, 134, 135, 140, 151–59, 179

inclination, 7–11, 14, 17, 22–30, 33–44, 46, 49–51, 55–58, 61, 63–82, 102, 109–11, 117–18, 122–27, 131–38, 161, 163, 167–74, 179, 181–85
inoperativity, 65–67, 84
Irigaray, Luce, 11, 12, 14, 96, 102–3

James, Susan, 12, 15
Jesus, 9, 65–66, 74–75, 87, 139, 162–63, 171

Kant, Immanuel, 8, 23–27, 29, 35, 37–40, 42, 50–55, 57, 64–65, 84, 109–18, 121, 125, 127, 132–33, 135, 173, 181–84
King, Martin Luther, Jr., 60
Klein, Melanie, 60, 88, 138

Lacan, Jacques, 44, 47, 124, 125, 129, 139, 141, 172
Leonardo da Vinci, 8–10, 25, 28, 29, 42–43, 64, 67, 73–81, 87, 88, 185
Levi, Primo, 26, 142, 144–49
Levinas, Emmanuel, 22, 24, 48–49, 57, 59, 60, 75, 85, 87, 88, 122, 138, 142, 143
Lock, Margaret, 95
Locke, John, 26, 93–95, 98–105, 121, 133, 135
Lonzi, Carla, 26, 93–95, 97–98, 102–4

Madonna, 8–10, 17, 28, 64, 66–67, 73–74, 76, 78, 87, 161–63, 165–71, 174–75, 184
Mary, 9, 28, 66, 74, 76, 84, 87, 139, 162
maternity, 9–11, 25, 27–29, 64, 66–67, 74, 76, 84, 87, 88, 110, 123, 133, 171, 181, 185
metaphysics, 2, 11, 18–20, 36, 155
morality, 10, 25, 39, 55, 56, 115, 122
Morrison, Toni, 81
Moten, Fred, 81, 152
Motherby family, 112–14, 119
Mouffe, Chantal, 135

narration, 19, 71, 103, 153–55, 172
natality, 11, 41, 59, 66, 70, 122, 131, 136, 139, 143, 144, 180
nonviolence, 8–9, 17, 21–22, 25–29, 49, 55, 59, 81, 123, 151, 157

ontology, 7, 22–23, 26–28, 42, 44, 48, 51, 57–58, 64, 83, 109–10, 124, 127, 131–40, 142, 144, 151–58, 179–80, 183

pacifism, 57, 60, 66, 67, 69, 72, 179
Plato, 17, 23, 35–40, 42, 64, 84, 86, 102, 111, 121, 135, 178, 181
pluriphony, 2, 5, 8, 178, 186
politics, 1, 3, 5, 7, 10, 12, 15, 17–19, 21–22, 25, 28, 38, 49, 57, 59–60, 63–64, 66, 78, 81, 87, 97, 98, 102, 109, 110, 112, 121–22, 131–39, 151–53, 156–58, 175, 177–80

queer, 50–52, 84, 112, 123–27, 161–63, 174–75, 184, 185

Raphael, 8, 167, 168
Rancière, Jacques, 28, 65, 87, 151
rectitude, 14, 26, 27–28, 34, 37–44, 49, 51–52, 55, 56, 64–65, 67–70, 81–82, 83, 84, 85, 131–34, 161, 167, 170–75, 179, 181, 182, 184
refusal, 14–16, 22, 25, 63–67, 73, 78, 82, 152, 158, 167, 173, 181, 184
relationality, 7, 9, 11, 16, 17, 25–28, 44, 50, 57, 59, 70–71, 103, 110–11, 117–18, 131, 133–34, 137, 139, 143, 153, 156, 162, 172–73, 180, 183
*Republic, The*, 35, 36, 64
Richards, Janice, 10, 14

Sedgwick, Eve Kosofsky, 52, 72
sexual difference, 5, 11–17, 34, 94, 98, 102, 103, 121, 123, 159
sexuality, 16, 39, 52, 94, 103, 125, 126
Söderbäck, Fanny, 13

sorority, 8, 17, 25, 27, 63, 67, 72–74, 117, 173, 184–85
Stillman, Marie, 74, 75

theft, 17, 29, 121; stealing, 11, 24; stolen, 19
torture, 143, 145, 170

uniqueness, 1, 12, 14, 18–20, 24, 48, 93, 100–4, 143, 155, 178

vocality, 1, 19, 177
vulnerability, 11, 16, 20–22, 26–28, 42, 44, 58–59, 64, 109, 117–18, 123, 126, 127, 134, 136–39, 142, 151–53, 156–58, 180

Woolf, Virginia, 49
wound, 20, 26, 75–76, 78, 123, 142, 153, 156, 158

www.ingramcontent.com/pod-product-compliance
Lightning Source LLC
Chambersburg PA
CBHW030441300426
44112CB00009B/1110